S0-AZR-315

Seventeen remarkable lives. All uniquely gifted. All world-changers. All shaped by the grace of God. In *Eternity through the Rearview Mirror*, Annette Hubbell uses creative first-person narrative to bring these characters to life in a way never seen before. This is a fascinating, informative, and entertaining book.

DR. MARK L. STRAUSS
Vice-Chair, The NIV Committee on Bible Translation
and University Professor of New Testament,
Bethel Seminary, San Diego, California

Annette Hubbell has shown that thoughtful, comprehensive, and instructive history need not be dull. Her blend of lively storytelling and thorough research brings to life a diverse cast of extraordinary figures who, through their testimonies of steadfast courage in the face of society's obstacles, remind us that History often lies at the intersection of the personal and the structural.

DAVID MILLER, PhD
Department of History, University of San Diego
Co-Editor, The Journal of San Diego History

Behind every great storyteller is a great story. Annette Hubbell displays both elements in this masterful work. I hear each unique voice as Annette brings to life these remarkable seventeen world changers. The stories—from Galileo to Johnny Cash—are told with the drama of theater and the intimacy of conversation with a good friend. Annette combines the meticulous research of a scholar with the devotion of a Christian.

MARILYN MCPHIE
President, Storytellers of San Diego and
Pacific Region Director, National Storytelling Network
storynet.org, storytellersofsandiego.org

ETERNITY
THROUGH THE
REARVIEW
MIRROR

ETERNITY
THROUGH THE
REARVIEW
MIRROR

How Simple Faith Changes Everything—
Seventeen Extraordinary Lives

ANNETTE HUBBELL

credo
house publishers

Eternity through the Rearview Mirror
Copyright © 2019 by Annette Hubbell
All rights reserved.

Published in the United States by Credo House Publishers,
a division of Credo Communications, LLC, Grand Rapids, Michigan
credohousepublishers.com

All Scripture quotations, unless otherwise indicated, are from The Holy Bible,
New International Version®, NIV® Copyright © 1973, 1978, 1984, 2011
by Biblica, Inc.® Used by permission. All rights reserved worldwide.

ISBN 978-1-625861-26-9

Cover and interior design by Klaas Wolterstorff
Editing by Donna Huisjen

Every effort has been made to ensure accuracy of names, characters, places, events, and incidents. Recorded words of each subject are shown in italics. (Quotation marks enclose the words of others.) In a few cases the quotations have changed tense to preserve the integrity of the story.

For a complete list of permissions granted, see page 187.

Printed in the United States of America

First Edition

What we want is not more little books about Christianity,

but more little books by Christians on other subjects—

with their Christianity latent.[1]

C. S. LEWIS

Wise words from Mr. Lewis. And that's what this is, a little book in which Christianity is not *the* story, but there, in the background, *for* the story, quietly humming. Seventeen individuals allowed their Christianity to empower them to live a life unimagined. All it took was a little faith, and everything changed.

This book is dedicated to you, dear reader,

the one who wants to be, or already is, the eighteenth.

CONTENTS

CONTENTS

INTRODUCTION

If you read history you will find that the Christians who did most for the present world were precisely those who thought most of the next. . . . Aim at Heaven and you will get earth "thrown in": aim at earth and you will get neither.[1]

C. S. LEWIS

In these pages you'll see eternity as these seventeen people saw it. They knew, or came to know, God's presence. Galileo saw the face of God in the universe itself. Ten Boom and Zamperini saw it in the power of forgiveness. For Bach and Cash it was in the sounds of music. For others it was in the faces of those they served, those they cared for. For Newton it was in redemption. *Amazing grace, how sweet the sound that saved a wretch like me.*

Insights from hindsight have 20/20 brilliance—one can clearly see God's involvement. For these seventeen Christians, God used their simple faith and trust in him to turn their lives into something extraordinary. Their journeys attest, in a deeply resonant manner, to what is possible—to what can be—with a recognition of God's ever present, ever powerful, all knowing, and all loving presence in one's life.

Where do you see the face of God? In my own life, I sometimes feel a bit like C. S. Lewis when he said, *If I find in myself a desire which no experience in this world can satisfy, the most probable explanation is that I was made for another world.*[2] I think God might have done that on purpose so that I can feel a small measure of his love, for he loves me—and you—more than we can possibly imagine.

You might wonder why I picked these seventeen. Originally I started with a list of forty, finding them by surfing endlessly (it seemed) on the internet, asking around, reading, and praying for guidance. I looked for people who were famous, or once famous—individuals with a compelling story who believed that their faith carried them through. I didn't include emissaries like Billy Graham, Mother Teresa, or Martin Luther King Jr. Neither will you find stories of people who are still alive, for God is not yet finished with them. I can't really tell you why these seventeen ended up here, other than the guidance I prayed for led me to them. If you want an earthly answer, I worked until I had enough to fill a book!

There are, however, really eighteen stories here. Check out Chapter Eighteen. It has your name on it.

> "He has made everything beautiful in its time. He has also set eternity in the human heart; yet no one can fathom what God has done from beginning to end."
>
> Ecclesiastes 3:11

Note: These essays are told in first-person narrative from a heavenly vantage point. The characters' recorded words, to distinguish them from mine, are in italics. Each essay is introduced by a brief description followed by links to learn more. I tag each story with Scriptures that reflect the individual's journey.

It was quite a task to address the essence of these people while keeping each essay at about four thousand words. I felt a little like POGO the Possum in that I was surrounded by insurmountable opportunities! I wanted to keep the narratives short but interesting enough to invite reflection and a curiosity to learn more. I want you to see the hand of God in the lives of these world-changers. To keep the stories from getting bogged down in detail, I used a lot of endnotes; they are important, and I hope you find them an interesting addition. I'd love to hear your thoughts. Maybe you'd like to add your favorite world-changer.

— 1 —

Galileo Galilei

1564–1642

Galileo transitioned the prevailing scientific worldview from one based on philosophical thought to one based on evident, measurable, fact. A red-headed, fiery Italian whose presence filled the room, his intellect and pride contributed to trying times within the church. *I do not feel obliged to believe that the same God who has endowed us with sense, reason, and intellect has intended us to forgo their use.*[1]

I saw what others couldn't. Branded a revolutionary by some, I often felt compelled to enlighten others whose understanding was restricted by established, traditional thought. *Ipse dixit!*—"He said so himself"—referring to Aristotle as the "ultimate" authority—ended many an academic discussion.[2] My sarcasm, often misconstrued as arrogance, wasn't appreciated, either. (I'd heard the word *bombastic* thrown at me, but what did they know?) I can't complain. Not even over a life punctuated by physical ailments, often confining my activity. My eyesight failed me in old age, too; need I say how distressing that was? My vision, however, never faltered. The brilliance of the heavens continuously filled my soul with wonder. I felt at home amidst the stars, grateful that God permitted me to wander through them, so to speak, with an unquenchable yearning to unlock the mysteries of the heavens.

I was born with a well-ordered mind and a keen intellect that drove my desire for observant clarity, accuracy, precision, consistency, sound evidence, and reasoned results, no matter the subject. I thanked God for that. Across the ages venerated scientists, each esteemed in their particular field, acknowledged my work (the detail of which I need not examine here)[3] by recognizing me as the Father of Modern Science. I excelled in philosophy, mathematics, astronomy, physics, and writing and could play the lute with sweet proficiency.

I never sought to discredit God or his Holy Word through the pursuit of science. I observed the planets but was not starry-eyed; I knew to worship the God who had made them.

Born in Pisa, Italy, in 1564, I was the first of six children. We were a noble family, though not wealthy by any means; Father was from a line of wool merchants. When he realized my inquisitive proclivities, he sent me off to the Vallombresa Abbey, where the monks had a reputation for stimulating the intellect, especially in the sciences and arts. I thrived in that isolated environment; indeed, I decided I would become one of them. Father had other ideas, however, and at fifteen I found myself back home. In 1581—I was seventeen—he enrolled me in medical school.

Wearisome! That's the most charitable thing I could say about it. The schoolwork held no challenge for me, and the professors viewed my lack of interest as disrespect. They said I liked to argue merely for the sake of the argument, citing my frequent recitation of Horace as evidence:

> Perhaps they think it's a weakness
> To yield to your juniors,
> To admit when you're old
> That what you learned, while beardless,
> Was a waste.[4]

I looked at things differently—some might say I never grew out of that childhood inquisitiveness—always asking *what*, *why*, and *how*.[5] In 1583, for example, I was attending Mass in the cathedral at Pisa. Lulled by the professing of the liturgy and gifts, I turned my attention to the movement of a lamp hanging from the ceiling. The slight draft of air caused it to swing, but its swing was constant, even though the angles changed. Why? What would that mean for anything that depended upon time intervals? Objects like metronomes and mechanical clocks—how could I improve them? The practical applications were not far from my thoughts.

Unable to conceive of medicine as a lifelong pursuit, I left the university, determined to master mathematics on my own. Even though my decision would entail a sacrifice for Father—a doctor in the family would have brought recognition and wealth—he allowed it; as a composer, musical theorist, and lutenist, he understood my attraction to mathematical patterns and formulae. It didn't hurt, either, that leaving school would allow me to work as a tutor and contribute monetary support to the family.

I found my calling in mathematics. Determined to elevate the stature of the mathematician—and to make a name for myself—I set out to find employment. In 1589, after many failures to secure gainful work, I secured a three-year appointment as a mathematics professor at the University of Pisa—without the benefit of any degree, I would note. I was twenty-five, and my salary was barely enough to live on. I was always preoccupied, it seemed, with the desire to be generously compensated for my work.

Nor did I fit in. It wouldn't be an exaggeration to say that I knew more about mathematics than almost anyone else—especially my fellow professors. Their ideas were dated—they still wore togas, for heaven's sake, which I refused to do. My contempt was noted.

I had some time on my hands and began to investigate further the swing of a pendulum, setting up an experiment using two pendulums, one with a long sweep and the other a short one. No matter the length of the swing, the elapsed time was the same; the proof was in the comparison to my own heartbeat. I was happy to see the professors use my observations to devise a pulsilogium—a pendulum clock used to mark a patient's heartbeat.

In 1592 I moved to Padua, one hundred twenty-five miles northeast of Pisa, where I taught at the university for eighteen years. While there, I met the charismatic Marina Gamba, and she bore my three children. We never married or lived together and after four years ended our relationship. Wedding Marina was out of the question for me; there were social and financial constraints. Financially I had not the means—paying off my sister's dowry as I was duty bound to do. More prohibitive, Marina was not of noble birth.

My daughters, Virginia and Livia, became nuns—often the only reward for a woman's illegitimacy. I could not make them heirs—that would have required a suitable dowry, which I could not provide. Since male children required no such accompaniment to the altar, I was able to make Vincenzo my legal heir. He gained notoriety as a lutenist and composer.

I was a cheerful man and a gracious host, I thought. I did have a fiery temper, but it was also short lived. Was I any different from any other redheaded Italian? I could be witty, humorous, and light-hearted—entertaining guests with my vast knowledge of prose and poetry. I loved a good glass of wine, too, and later in life I had vineyards to cultivate.

I was a pioneer in experimentation. Observation, measurement, and open-mindedness were essential in determining facts. Promoting observation over dogma, however, gained me even more enemies. My experiments and writings were unconventional, and I became paranoid of any criticism, returning differing opinions with a swift and forceful volley. At times I was certainly argumentative and mocking, but *in questions of science, the authority of a thousand is not worth the humble reasoning of a single individual.*[6]

In pursuit of the unknown, I believe, fundamentally, that one must first learn its language. The rich harmonies of the lute, the sweet complexity of the wine's bouquet, the perfection of the telescope's optics—none of these can be understood without first savoring their language. *The universe stands continually open to our gaze, and it is best understood through its language of mathematics—through triangles, circles, and geometrical figures.*[7]

For a time my research centered on the nature of motion. I was critical of Aristotle's ways of doing things because his principles were not based on controlled, quantitative experiments. But new and controversial ideologies often give rise to myths and legends. For example, my climb to the top of Pisa's Leaning Tower—to disprove Aristotle's theory that objects of a different mass fall at different rates of speed—was a legend. Highly inefficient! To test that hypothesis I stayed on the ground and used ramps—inclined planes—allowing me to reliably observe the descents.[8] One must experiment relentlessly.

Around 1609 I turned my attention to astronomy. About that time

I also became fascinated with a Dutch toy—a spyglass. Could it be improved? I set about to do just that and was able to increase its magnification, enlarging a subject a thousandfold![9] *I do not doubt that in the course of time further observations will improve this new science. But this need not diminish the glory of the first observer.*[10] Someone suggested I call this magnification tube a telescope, and so I did. *To apply oneself to great inventions, starting from the smallest beginnings, is no task for ordinary minds. To divine that wonderful arts lie hidden behind trivial and childish things is a conception of superhuman talents.*[11]

As an important aside, I foresaw that this invention would be of great value militarily and thought the Doge of Venice, Donato, should know about it. In my letter to him, I described it and told him *this telescope has the advantage of discovering the ships of the enemy two hours before they can be seen with the natural vision and to distinguish the number and quality of the ships and to judge their strength and be ready to chase them, fight them, or to flee from them.*[12] That certainly caught his attention!

The Church followed the traditional astral and philosophical schema, envisioning the heavens as pure, smooth, perfectly circular, and unchanging, but with this telescope I could discern valleys, mountains, and jagged spots on the moon and blemishes in the sun (some countered that I was merely seeing swarms of small planets passing close in front of the sun). I discovered the moons of Jupiter(!) and moved through the Milky Way, marveling at the thousands of stars now shining brilliantly. *I rendered infinite thanks to God for being so kind as to make me alone the first observer of marvels kept hidden in obscurity for all previous centuries.*[13] (Later I detected the phases of Venus—did that mean that Venus, a planet like Earth, orbited the sun? How could that be if the sun orbited the earth?)

I outlined my telescopic discoveries in *The Sidereal (Starry) Messenger* (1610). The work became so revered that I became the most famous scientist in all of Italy. Indeed, all of Europe knew of me—my wealth and future were confirmed. I petitioned the court in Florence and was rewarded with a new position. On July 10, 1610, Cosimo II de'Medici granted me the title of Philosopher and Chief Mathematician to the grand duke of Tuscany. I had become affluent.

In 1615, in a letter to my friend and benefactor the Grand Duchess Christina, I supposed that the earth could revolve around the sun and still

7

not violate Church doctrine. One must take into consideration, I pointed out, what the biblical writers knew and what they did not. They called out, for example, the sun, the moon, and the morning star—knowing of no others. Scripture referring to natural phenomena should be understood within its literary context anyway, I ventured. The "setting" of the sun, for example, is just imagery.

I failed, however, to persuade Church officials that I was not attacking its dogma.[14] Perhaps in my zeal I came across as overly confident in suggesting that I, a layman, should purport to interpret Scripture. Some years later Father Grassi[15] wrote jealously of me, "But he has ruined himself by being so much in love with his own genius, and by having no respect for others. One should not wonder that everybody conspires to damn him."[16]

I continued to study the heavens, taking copious notes, drawing, and gazing endlessly at the moon, Venus, and other celestial bodies—all the while pondering their movement. I had earlier suspected the ebb and flow of the tides to be a result of a moving earth,[17] and now I was even more certain that the movement of the sun, moon, and planets around an immobile earth—Ptolemy's geocentric theory—was incorrect. Copernicus's heliocentric theory—the sun as the center of the universe—was more plausible.

It's true, I did not have conclusive evidence to prove Copernicus's sun-centered theory, and the Church, which had had enough of this controversy, ruled in 1616 that the sun-centered Copernican theory was physically false and contrary to Scripture.[18] I was warned by Bellarmine not to publish anything that could be interpreted as supporting or defending Copernicanism, and I complied, believing that my duty as a scientist required harmony with the destiny of my soul.

In 1623 Pope Gregory XV died, and my friend Cardinal Barberini became Pope Urban VIII. My newly published book *The Assayer*[19] was dedicated to him, and it became a favorite of his. He would have it read to him at bedtime, delighting in its observations, wit, and sarcasm. More than a treatise on the nature and orbits of comets, it was an exposition of the scientific method in which I asserted that all things of nature, including comets, should be read with mathematical tools rather than scholastic philosophy. *Ipse dixit* was not a valid argument.

With Barberini as Pope, I felt confident enough to revive my heliocentric-favored writings. In 1632 I published *The Dialogue Concerning the Two*

Chief World Systems, in which I examined the scientific and philosophical arguments for and against Copernicanism. I knew enough not to venture into the theological arena, because I maintained *that the intention of the Holy Spirit is to teach us how one goes to heaven, and not how heaven goes.*[20] The Bible was about faith and morals, not about scientific phenomena. Besides, I was still under the 1616 warning—the one that was issued to me in private—not to defend the earth's motion. How could I disobey that order?

In the *Dialogue* I advanced my argument—hypothetical, of course—among its three characters. There was Sagredo, a noblemen willing to listen to both sides; Salviati, a reasonable person representing my views; and Simplicio, a person who believed in the traditional views of the earth's immobility.

Simplicio, named after the Greek philosopher Simplicius, was a fitting name since it represented old, traditional views. My enemies, however, were quick to suggest that this Simplicio character represented the Church—by inference the Pope himself—and, further, was an insult because the Italian word for *simpleton*—or its root, *stupid*—is the very word *Simplicio*.[21]

I was told that the Pope was outraged, yet I find that hard to believe. Surely my friend and benefactor must have realized that I would infer no such thing. My intended target, in fact, for the Simplicio character was the Aristotelian academic Lodovico delle Colombe. He was part of the Pigeon League, the communal name I gave to those scientists and philosophers—simpletons—whose views differed from my own.

My detractors alleged that I had presented Salviati's argument—my point of view—as a real possibility rather than merely as a hypothesis. I had not. I did acknowledge that the Church mistakenly *thought* I had contradicted Holy Scripture and fifteen hundred years of scientific study—but I was saying there was no contradiction at all.[22]

No longer a harmless eccentric in their view, I was deemed a heretic.[23] Summoned to Rome in early 1633, I was to stand trial before the Inquisition, the judicial arm of the Catholic Church. Yes, I did receive admonition, but any violations were unintentional. The *Dialogue* did not defend that the earth moved, but rather "suggested that the favorable arguments were inconclusive and so did not violate Bellarmine's warning."[24]

The trial continued for four months. Would I be convicted of heresy, burned at the stake like Bruno?[25] Or would my fame—and age—protect me? These questions I anxiously pondered while awaiting the outcome. On June 22, 1633, I learned my fate: I was found guilty of "vehement suspicion of heresy."[26] I was ordered to retract everything in the *Dialogue*; swear allegiance to everything held, preached, and taught by the Church; and curse my errors. I signed the statement thus:

> I, Galileo Galilei, *abjure, curse, detest the aforesaid errors and heresies and generally every other error, heresy and sect whatsoever contrary to the Holy Church.*[27]

I was not tortured—though this was threatened—but I was condemned to prison for as long as the court saw fit. *Dialogue* became prohibited reading by anyone.[28] I was also required to recite, once a week for three years, the Seven Penitential Psalms.[29]

Because of my advancing age and poor health, I was allowed to live out the sentence under house arrest in my villa outside Florence. Isolation, limited access to outside medical assistance, and being forced to publicly reject my own work—these were heavy consequences. Even at that, however, God in his mercy gave me grace undeserved. I used those last nine years of my life to review and finish a previous work. The publication of *Two New Sciences* revolutionized the physics of motion. Some consider it my finest work. Having begun it so much earlier and all but forgotten it, would I have completed this work had I not been forced into isolation? I do not know. Was it my work or my prideful demeanor that ultimately brought me to trial and conviction? Looking back through the lens of eternity, I see the obvious answer.

After the trial, God's grace also allowed me a deepened relationship with my daughter, Sister Maria Celeste (Virginia).[30] We had always written letters to each other; I even encouraged her opinions on my work. I enjoyed our visits—we even made jam together! She stood by me throughout the ordeal of the trial, and our relationship flourished. *She was a woman of exquisite mind, singular goodness, and most tenderly attached to me.*[31] Maria's death at thirty-three, just ten months after the trial, grieved me inconsolably. *I felt immense sadness and melancholy . . . and continually heard my beloved daughter calling to me.*[32]

I became blind five years before my death in 1642—likely because of cataracts.[33] At seventy-seven I died and was quietly buried in an unmarked grave. Ninety-five years later my body was moved to consecrated ground in Florence's Santa Croce Basilica, opposite that of Michelangelo's tomb, but not before parts of me had been taken as relics: a vertebra, a tooth, and three of my fingers. You can see the fingers I used to adjust my telescope at the Galileo Museum in Florence. If you visit me at Santa Croce, note that the inscription doesn't reveal that the bones of my beloved daughter, Suor Maria Celeste, are entombed with me.

I marvel, even more now, at the majesty of the universe. To quote Moses: "And God saw that it was good."[34] And yes, it is good.

◆ ◆

"And when you look up to the sky and see the sun, the moon and the stars—all the heavenly array—do not be enticed into bowing down to them and worshiping things the LORD your God has apportioned to all the nations under heaven."

Deuteronomy 4:19

"And we know that in all things God works for the good of those who love him, who have been called according to his purpose."

Romans 8:28

"Godly sorrow brings repentance that leads to salvation and leaves no regret, but worldly sorrow brings death."

2 Corinthians 7:10

► Have a look at the original telescope made by Galileo: https://catalogue .museogalileo.it/object/GalileosTelescope_no1.html.

► Have a look at Galileo's fingers and tooth in this video from the Galileo Museum: https://catalogue.museogalileo.it/room/RoomVII.html.

► In 2002 Nova produced a movie, *Galileo's Battle for the Heavens*, about Galileo from Dava Sobel's bestseller *Galileo's Daughter*. You can find it on YouTube.

— 2 —

Johann Sebastian Bach

1685–1750

Orphaned as a boy, *Sebastian* grew up with a musical pedigree. Although he was gifted, he worked as hard as though he were not. Driving him in his pursuit of excellence was his desire to glorify God. *The aim and final end of all music should be none other than the glory of God and the refreshment of the soul. If heed is not paid to this, it is not true music but a diabolical bawling and twanging.*[1]

No greater gift hath God wrought to any composer than the ability to create music. For me, it was as though the notes, caressed by angelic voices, flowed through my pen and assigned themselves to each other in a harmonious manner exquisite to the ear, allowing the soul a glimpse of heaven's glory.

Music has always been my passion—creating,[2] directing, singing, and playing. As a boy,[3] I loved to sing *a capella* in the boys' chorale, for I had an "exquisitely beautiful soprano voice,"[4] and for a time I could sing soprano and alto tones simultaneously! Really![5] An exceptional dexterity and keen ear increased my ability and agility to improvise complicated masterpieces on the organ as no other living soul could—except perhaps Handel.[6] (I was disheartened at never having personally known Handel, even though

I attempted to meet him several times—always just missing him.) Playing twenty notes concurrently was not difficult either. At times, though, I did have to employ the use of a stick held between my teeth to strike that additional note. Someone observed that my accomplishments "effect what not twenty Arions [swift horses] could achieve."[7] Such welcome flattery, however, did not pay the bills. There were many family members—I fathered twenty children through the years—and an adequate income was a necessity. Sometimes there were acceptable barters, such as beer. Next to money, however, I would have been happiest with coffee. A coffee aficionado I was, to the point that I even wrote a comic work about it: *The Coffee Cantata*.[8]

> *Ah! How sweet coffee tastes*
> *More delicious than a thousand kisses*
> *Milder than muscatel wine.*
> *Coffee, I have to have coffee,*
> *And, if someone wants to pamper me,*
> *Ah, then bring me coffee as a gift!*

Generations of gifted musicians groomed my abilities: great-grandfather, grandfather, father, brothers, uncles, cousins, nephews, second cousins, and four sons were musicians[9]; indeed, our family name had become synonymous with the word *musician*. Every year our extended family would gather at a central place, our sole purpose being musical amusement. From pious chorales to naughty songs, we had great fun. With our extemporary harmony we would sing the same songs over and over, using different words, garnering hearty laughter in all who heard.

A rigorous course of study allowed me to readily grasp theory, and I began composing in my teens.[10] Orphaned at nine, my much older brother Christoph (who studied under Pachelbel) brought our other brother and me to live with him, and I thrived under his talent and kindness, strict though he was. I thought him the "the profound composer."[11] He had to be strict, for I was by no means good or endearing.[12] In part to keep me busy and in part to make sure I learned, he required me to copy score upon score of music.

Because Christoph was the organist at the Ohrdruf church, I was allowed to watch the building of the new organ, which I did with a delighted and steadfast eye, climbing in and around and through, studying every aspect of its construction. My singing voice earned for me a chorale scholarship at St. Michaelis in Lüneburg (1700–1702), and there I received instruction in French, Italian, Greek, Latin, history, geography, genealogy, heraldry, German poetry, mathematics, physics, linguistics, theology, physics, and classical literature. Often I would walk to Hamburg, which wasn't far away—about thirty miles—to hear the master organist Reinken playing on North Germany's most famous and beautiful organ at St. Catharine's Church. It had fifty-eight stops on four manuals and pedal.[13] On one particular occasion, I stayed longer than "the state of my purse" would allow. Just as I was passing an inn, with all the wonderful smells wafting out, hungrily wondering where my next meal would come from, I was quite happy to see a pair of herring heads thrown out the window and onto the rubbish pile. My mouth watered as I set upon them to dine. Another surprise! A Danish ducat[14] was hidden in each head, and I was able to supplement my dinner with meat. Whether it was a prankster or a kind-hearted soul, I was thankful to the person who hid them there for me to find, for surely he was watching out the window as I traveled by.[15]

After graduating from St. Michaelis, I no longer had access to free room, board, or any monetary support, which meant that a university education was not to be mine. I nevertheless took a path of intensive self-instruction, which afforded me an ability to be a good teacher—usually not a skill realized by composers. I think it was the stumbling and persevering on my own that allowed me a perspective useful to my students. I wrote many preludes and exercises for beginners. Eventually I became a court musician in Weimar to Duke Johann Ernst in 1703.

Curious about anything and everything and desirous to master any academic and musical scholarship, I would study other musicians' work, envelop myself in the technological advances and technology of organ building, and go to great lengths to hear musicians play. As I said, I often would walk from Lüneburg to Hamburg, and I once took a three-to-four-month pilgrimage, trekking two hundred fifty miles from Arnstadt to Lübeck (ten days each way) to drink in the different styles and types of composition—*to comprehend one thing and another*.[16] Perhaps that is why my compositions, though ornate, extravagant, and heavy, as Germanic music tended to be, could also capture the beauty of a French dance or the gracefulness of an Italian song.

I always lived in central Germany, but I was compelled to move many times, either to pursue opportunity or to flee unfavorable circumstances. In 1707 I married Maria Barbara Bach (my second cousin), and we had seven children. My position as organist and concertmaster in various courts, societies, and universities afforded me considerable autonomy to pursue my favorite work—composing and performing.[17]

My early pieces, like the *Toccata in D minor* written in my twenties, are bold and unrestrained. Eight years later the ear could detect maturity and grace in *Jesu, Joy of Man's Desiring*. Listen to the complexity and daring combinations of *The Brandenburg Concertos*, presented to the Margrave of Brandenburg when I was thirty-six. Throughout my life I had a desire to improve my repertoire (I revised my own work), to use the newest instruments, to learn from the finest artists, and to write music such as the world had never heard before. But the composition and playing of music had a higher calling: *to make a well-sounding harmony to the honor of God and the permissible delectation of the soul.*[18]

I could be overbearing. As I saw it, though, others, and especially my employers, caused most of the problems. It was at Weimar that I found trouble—or, rather, it found me. In 1717 I asked to be released from the Duke of Weimar's employ to take a coveted position offered to me in Köthen. So sure was I of being released from the duke's service that I accepted an advance in salary and moving expense money from my new employer. I sought the duke's release, but it was in vain—the duke would not give me an answer. In utter frustration I exploded in anger at his unwillingness to resolve the issue. He retaliated by throwing me in jail for almost four weeks.[19] This was the lowest point in my professional life.

It was in 1720 that my new employer, Leopold, Duke of Köthen, required me to accompany him to a spa at Carlsbad to provide entertainment for the summer festival, While I was there, my wife, Maria Barbara—who had been in good health when I left—suddenly died! Returning home with only the thought of seeing her and the children, I was quite overwhelmed to learn the news at my front door. It had been a bleak period; three of my children had died before their fifth birthdays, and now my dear wife, my inspiration and encourager, was gone too.

Eighteen months later, in 1721, I married Anna Magdalena Wilcke at home; it was a grand affair with lots of fine Rhine wine.[20] Together we had thirteen children. Of my twenty children,[21] twelve lived beyond infancy. My beloved Anna Magdalena was a gifted soprano, and though she was sixteen years younger than me, we had a very happy marriage. Sought after for her voice, she continued to sing professionally. Our shared love of music contributed to our bliss—she worked as a copyist, transcribing my music, and I dedicated many compositions to her. Although seven of our thirteen children died at a young age, our other children (including the ones from my first marriage) were musically inclined, and our house became a musical center; we spent many an evening playing and singing together.

In 1723 the Leipzig council found itself in need of a cantor[22] for its five main churches in the city. Only after two musicians turned down the position did they turn their attention to me, for in their opinion I lacked superior qualifications. Notwithstanding my bruised ego, *it pleased God that I should be called hither to be Director Musices and Cantor at the St. Thomas School*,[23] and I accepted the position. It was April 1723, and I served there until my death—for twenty-seven years. While cantor I composed and presented voluminous works, including two hundred ninety-five church cantatas, five masses, the Passions, *Magnificat*, the thirty *Goldberg Variations*, the *Well-Tempered Clavier* (Book Two), and the *Brandenburg Concertos*. My last work, *The Art of the Fugue*, in which I had desired to incorporate all I had mastered about that complex form,[24] was never finished.

The anguish of having to deal with self-centered officials was lifelong. *The authorities are strange people, with little devotion to music, so that I had to endure almost constant vexation, envy, and persecution.*[25] I felt somewhat like the apostle Paul, who did not suffer fools gladly.[26]

Personal glory was not important; I was God's servant, and I created music to glorify him. I frequently annotated my manuscripts with the initials J. J. ("Help me, Jesus") and S. D. G ("*Soli Deo gloria*—Glory to God Alone").[27] I liked to use musical and numerical symbolism to reference biblical themes, such as the Trinity.[28] (Because I loved puzzles, I would sometimes insert references to my own name, using code to spell out *J S B A C H*). *In devotional music, God is always at hand with his gracious presence.*[29] It was said that I could stir the soul, but I knew I was just the instrument.

I did have friends who said I was hospitable and generous, good-natured, somewhat modest, an indulgent father, and a loyal citizen. And I had a sense of humor, though not subtle, and believed in offering my support wherever I could, often deferring to others. If ever the music were slighted, however, my demeanor would quickly become obstinate; the organist Görner, whom I thought arrogant and unskilled, would attest to that. Frustrated at his lack of effort, I yanked the wig off my head and threw it at him, yelling "You should have been a cobbler."[30]

I also recall the incident in Arnstadt when I became very irritated at Geyersbach,[31] one of my choir students, and in anger called him a Zippel-Fagotist! It wasn't a nice name, but then neither was his voice, which I couldn't discern from the braying of the neighbor's nanny goat. Geyersbach took it as an insult and persuaded six of his friends, all with clubs in their hands, to join him and lie in wait for me a few nights later. He ordered me to apologize, *for the last time.* For his sake, he should have picked another night, as I happened to be wearing my full dress uniform (I was returning from the sovereign court). Part of that uniform was my epee (a blunt-edged dueling sword), and fortunately none of them realized my expertise in the art of fencing! I unleashed my epee and made a big step forward, pointing directly to the chest of this Geyersbach, the leader of those hooligans. (Can't you just picture the scene?) That caused them to rethink his plan, and they retreated, assaulting me only with bad names.

Of course I complained to the town council. But because Geyersbach's family was part of the "honorable society" of Arnstadt, I was the one admonished to live in peace with my students. I responded with a leave of absence.

And then there was that time when the superintendent criticized my organ solos for being too long, and I fell to the other extreme and ended far earlier than I should have.[32] The silence was deliciously awkward. (I did not take criticism gently—or gallantly.)

To anyone who ponders what it would take to attain the same degree of perfection that I achieved, I would tell you that *it's easy to play any musical instrument: all you have to do is touch the right key at the right time and the instrument will play itself.*[33] While I do have a sense of humor, it really *is the soul of the Diligent who shall be made rich.*[34] Some say I was a genius, but I would argue that genius is in the detail. From my perspective, one should practice at any endeavor until excellence is achieved. Indeed, *one can do anything if only one really wishes to, and if one industriously strives to convert natural abilities, by untiring zeal, into finished skills.*[35] Unfortunately, I couldn't say that about a single piano tuner. Because I could not find one person who could properly assess the vibrational interaction among the notes to correctly align the tensions of the strings, I had to teach myself the craft of tuning so that I could always have a well-tempered clavier.

Life had its disappointments. Of course, my children who did not survive were a constant source of sorrow. With regard to work, my technical skill at playing the organ was appreciated far more than were my compositions—a constant source of consternation. So little did some think of my music that after I died my written music was used to wrap fish and garbage, and many compositions have been lost. I knew that Jesus, who had said that no prophet is ever welcomed in his hometown,[36] would have understood my disheartenment.

More important to me than music, however, was my faith; I thought myself a theologian with a keyboard. I loved to read the Bible—my three volumes of the 1681 edition of Martin Luther's translation[37] I especially revered. Although Luther and I were separated in time by 200 years, I felt a kinship with him as we had both attended the same school, sang in the same church, and were both part of the Currendem, a musical choir that sang in the streets of Eisenach to collect money for the teachers and students.[38]

Scripture was my inspiration—the Gospels especially—and some even hailed me as the Fifth Evangelist after Matthew, Mark, Luke, and John.[39] I set Scripture and hymns to music, turning time and again back to Luther's work. I immersed myself in the Bible for the treasure it was, writing in the margins, inserting missing words, and correcting errors. I loved to underline passages—especially in places that spoke to me of *God-pleasing music.*[40]

Until 1749 I enjoyed good health, but then my eyesight began to fail. I was advised of an excellent surgeon who could fix my condition. I could have still worked, but I wanted to get the surgery done and over with. I had two operations in March and April of 1750—both seemingly ill performed, because I was never again the same. My eyesight was restored for ten days before I died, but only for a few hours. The surgery brought about an infection that likely caused my death by a stroke.[41] It was July 28, 1750, and I was sixty-five.

In those last months, spent in a darkened room, I wrote my final chorale, creating music for these hymnal words:

I herewith step before Thy throne,
O God, and humbly beg thee:
Turn not Thy gracious countenance
From me, a poor sinner

Confer on me a blessed end,
On the last day awaken me,
Lord, that I may see you eternally;
Amen, amen, hear me.

This was sung at my burial—a hasty one in an unmarked grave in the churchyard (near the foundation) of St. John's Church. In 1894 my bones were reburied inside the church. When the church was damaged by the bombs of World War II, I was once again moved to St. Thomas Church in Leipzig.[42]

Some three hundred years later, my music has found favor across all genres[43]—even those called rock and heavy metal. Asteroids in the heavens and a crater on Mercury bear my name, and my music is roaming through outer space on the Voyager Spacecraft.[44] Corrie ten Boom once said she had a fantasy that heaven makes beautiful Bach music and that Bach himself is directing the angels' choir.[45] The American composer Aaron Copland said, "If one were asked to name one musician who came closest to composing without human flaw, I suppose general consensus would choose Johann Sebastian Bach."[46] An honor, surely, these words, but all glory belongs to God. I always knew I was just the instrument.

I play the notes as they are written, but it is God who makes the music.[47] I've heard others say, too, that when the angels praise God they play my music.[48] I can tell you, with some boldness: it's true!

◆　◆

"All of them were under the direction of their father. They played music for the LORD's temple. They served at the house of God by playing cymbals, lyres and harps. . . . All of them were trained and skilled in playing music for the LORD."

1 Chronicles 25:6, 7 NIrV

"Shout for joy to the LORD, all the earth, burst into jubilant song with music."

Psalm 98:4

"But do not forget this one thing, dear friends: With the Lord a day is like a thousand years, and a thousand years are like a day."

2 Peter 3:8

- ▸ For all things Bach, here is a great resource: https://www.bachonbach .com/ (Scroll down to the 33 Werke in 333 Sekunden video for an abridgment of 33 works in six minutes. Apologies to Bach, of course.) Or you can listen to it here: https://www.johann-sebastian-bach-for -children.com/johann-sebastian-bach-music-in-333-seconds/.
- ▸ A good horror movie isn't worth its salt without this one: *Toccata and Fugue in d Minor by J. S. Bach*, https://youtu.be/ho9rZjlsyYY.

— 3 —

John Newton

1725-1807

We know him as the writer of the soul-stirring hymn "Amazing Grace," but as a young man he was a slave trader, naval deserter, and poster child for all things obnoxious and offensive. *When God is about to perform any great work, He generally permits some great opposition to it.*[1] God changed him, and he spent fifty years as an author, beloved pastor, and founder of a global ministry pledged to spread the gospel. You may be surprised at why he wrote those treasured lyrics—it's probably not what you think.

Amazing Grace! (how sweet the sound)
That sav'd a wretch like me![2]

The cherished words to this hymn are affixed with my name, but it is only God's mercy and grace that made it thus. Who am I, God, that you would bless me, for I was an infidel—*a rebel blinded by the god of this world.*[3]

My mother certainly never envisioned such a career path for me. (Would any mother curse her child so?) She had hopes that I would become a preacher. Memorizing the catechism, Bible verses, and hymns came easily, even when I was just five years old. I also preferred singing with Mother rather than playing outside—I don't remember thinking that odd. I do recall being really happy—until Mother died. I was six[4] and inconsolable. Under father's dispassionate care, I was shuffled between boarding school and his merchant ship.

In 1744 I was press ganged[5] into the British Royal Navy. Nineteen years old, I should have known better than to walk the streets when war with France was afoot. Forcefully set upon and dragged aboard the *HMS Harwich*, I found the work to be strenuous, difficult, and often rewarded with the boson's cane. At least I had a father with some influence who saw fit to intervene. I would've rather he saw to my release; instead, I had to settle for a promotion to midshipmen with the promise of a rise to lieutenant. Was I grateful for a second chance? Hardly. Treating with scorn my once-fellow sailors, I became arrogant and headstrong. To my superiors I was disobedient and angry at being on board in the first place. God turned his back on me—or so I thought—and I reciprocated in kind.

I was especially angry because Navy service kept me away from my true love. I had fallen in love with Polly Catlett the moment I saw her. Polly was only thirteen when we met and I seventeen, yet I was convinced of our future together. Because of my station in life, however, I could not reveal my ardor—and would not until I had means to support her.

Ships orders meant a five-year sailing to the East Indies. That would have meant five years away from Polly—simply out of the question. I did what any young fool desperately in love would have done—I walked away without leave. Deserted. Unfortunately, I didn't get very far before they found me, *entangled* me in irons, and marched me back to the ship. Death could have been my sentence, but it wasn't. Instead I endured a public flogging, administered with greater severity at the urging of shipmates who now detested me; the cat o' nine tails tore open my back.

Despair consumed me. Enraged at the captain—and at myself—I became obsessed with murder. Whose life would I take, the captain's or mine?

Thro' many dangers, toils and snares,
I have already come.

I did neither, instead being transferred to the Sierra Leone-bound *Pegasus*. Not at all desirous of mending my ways, I continued the attitude. *I was exceedingly vile. I not only sinned with a high hand myself but made it my study to tempt and seduce others upon every occasion: nay, I eagerly sought occasion sometimes to my own hazard and hurt.*[6]

My bad behavior—especially my cringe-worthy profanity—was abhorrent. So vile—and yet I couldn't stop—that my life would have been in jeopardy had I stayed on board. I learned of high profits being made in the slave trade—a ticket to a means of wealth worthy of approaching Polly. With good riddance I was released from service and signed up with Mr. Clow, a rich slave trader.

An egregious mistake! I thought I was to be a partner; instead, I became a slave myself. Worked to the bone, starved and kept in chains, my condition was such that even slaves awaiting transport felt sorry for me and gave me what food they could spare. It was my twenty-first birthday, and I wondered whether I'd ever live to see my twenty-second. One solitary possession saved my sanity: a mathematical book—*Euclid's Elements*. Enslaved for months in Sierra Leone, it was my only diversion. Father again came to the rescue. Word had reached him of my circumstance, and he had organized a search.

I can look back on those years and see Divine Providence at work, even in the midst of my turmoil and bad behavior. I had many narrow escapes that would have, but for God's intervention, ended my life. I paid no attention at the time.

Rescued, I was now aboard the *Greyhound*, a ship in search of gold, ivory, and beeswax. I had kept *Euclid*, and except for the study of it had no other business to attend to. *My life, when awake, was a course of most horrid impiety and profaneness. Not content with common oaths and imprecations, I daily invented new ones, so that I was often seriously reproved by the captain, who was a very passionate man.*[7] Captain Swanwick often said that with me he had a Jonah[8] on board—all the ship's troubles, invited by my presence.

Out of boredom, I picked up another book found in the ship's library, *The Imitation of Christ* by Thomas à Kempis. *I read it with indifference as if it was entirely a romance.*[9] Something, however, made me shut the book before its finish. Was it fear? What if these things à Kempis spoke of should be true?[10]

But God who called me here below,
Will be forever mine.

I went to bed that night in my usual security and indifference, but was awakened from a sound sleep by the force of a violent sea that broke on us. Much of it came down below and filled the cabin where I lay with water. This alarm was followed by a cry from the deck that the ship was going down.[11] Crawling up on deck, I could barely see—Were we already submerged? Giant waves crashed over us—throwing everything around as though it all weighed nothing. The sea tore away sails and timbers, and we bailed all night long with pumps, buckets, and pails. Filling the holes with clothing and bedding was poor remedy, but it was all we could do. Were it not for the beeswax in the hold making the ship somewhat buoyant, we most assuredly would have sunk. Exhausted after a long night of pumping as fast as we could, I took over the wheel, steering the *Greyhound* for eleven straight hours, lashing myself fast with ropes lest I be swept overboard—each wave crashing nearly over my head. *What mercy can there be for me?*[12] Was there hope for a wretch like me? At that moment, I became astonished that I had given any thought to hope or mercy, something that I had not cared about since I was a boy.

'Tis grace hath brought me safe thus far,
And grace will lead me home.

His secret guidance, leading us by a way which we knew not, till his time of love came.[13] That was a day never to be forgotten—March 10, 1748[14]—prompting a yearly ritual of remembering and prayerful gratitude that I never missed, for on that day the Lord indeed delivered me from deep waters. I had for so long stood in direct confrontation with God, but I heard him in the fury of the sea.

'Twas grace that taught my heart to fear,
And grace my fears relieved;
How precious did that grace appear,
The hour I first believed!

I changed my ways, I changed my behavior. I went to church and kept a clean mouth. God is strong, but I was weak. Despite good intentions, though, I had many relapses.

Still in the slave business, I would make, all told, four trips to Africa, buying and selling slaves. As first mate on the slave ship *Brownlow*, I lost sight of God again, falling back into the old ways. *The enemy prepared a train of temptations, and I became his easy prey.*[15]

I was out on one of the islands when the Lord, determined to save me, intervened with a violent fever, one *which broke the fatal chain and once more brought me to myself. . . . Weak, and almost delirious . . . I made no more resolutions but cast myself before the Lord to do with me as He should please. . . . The burden was removed from my conscience, and not only my peace but my health was restored. I cannot say it was instantaneous, but I began to recover from that hour. And from that time, I trust, I have been delivered from the power and dominion of sin.*[16]

> *I once was lost, but now am found;*
> *Was blind, but now I see.*

I had for the most part peace of conscience, and my strongest desires were for the things of God.[17] I never again fell back into those sinful ways.

In 1750 I became captain of my own slave ship, the *Duke of Argyle*. Now I had good prospects for the future and could propose marriage to Polly, the only woman I'd ever love. We married that year, on February 12. I was twenty-five.

It must be considered that English society, the churches—and everyone else, for that matter (except perhaps the slave)—saw no conflict between the slave trade and being a good person, and neither did I. *I think I would have quitted it sooner, had I considered it to be unlawful and wrong. But I never had a scruple upon this head at the time, nor was such a thought once suggested to me, by any friend. What I did, I did ignorantly; considering it as the line of life which Divine Providence had allotted me, and having no concern, in point of conscience, but to treat the Slaves, while under my care, with as much humanity as a regard to my own safety would admit.*[18]

Four years of slave trafficking, however, made me realize its demons, and I prayed for God to give me a more humane calling. Evil had had enough of me, and I of it.

Divine Providence intervened once again and answered my prayer. Not through a remedy of my choosing, however, for I fell to an illness so severe that being at sea was no longer possible. It was 1754, I was twenty-nine, and I resigned my commission, done with sea life.

> *The Lord has promised good to me,*
> *His word my hope secures;*
> *He will my shield and portion be,*
> *As long as life endures.*

For almost nine years I worked as a tide surveyor, but always there was the question of how I would serve God. I knew that I wanted to serve him as a preacher. To prepare myself for ordination, I spent three hours each day reading the Bible and immersed myself in the study of Hebrew and Greek to better understand the original. (I had already taught myself Latin on the ship.) I attended many weekly sermons and wrote my own essays and messages. I attempted to be consistent in prayer, meditation, and study. *By an act of humiliation, fasting seems very proper to be sometimes joined to our solemn prayers and* confessions . . . However it is a duty of which I have long lived in habitual neglect. It is a weakness in my *faith . . . and I ought the more diligently and frequently to endeavor a strict mastery over my appetites.*[19]

The question surrounding me was apprehension: Could I even be an ordained minister? Yes, I had received a call from God, *a real desire to promote the glory of God and the salvation of souls.*[20] My first sermons, however—standing there in front of everyone—were of little merit, so disastrous that they might have been enough to stay my heart from ministry. But the day did come, and I was ordained into the Church of England on April 29, 1764.

It seems my mother's prayers were answered after all.

Sponsored by the wealthy philanthropist John Thornton, I settled in as curate of Olney, a vicarage north of London. Polly and I were there for sixteen years, and Olney, even though one of the poorest towns in all of England, became a place of hospitality for all, Anglicans and Nonconformists alike. Fortuitously, my skill behind the pulpit improved, enough so that we had to add a gallery to accommodate the crowds. My patron, however, thought I should move to London to take the position of rector at St. Mary Woolnoth, and so at the end of 1779 we did.[21]

Polly was the love of my life, my closest friend, and we shared every confidence. Through our forty years of marriage we held the bonds of romance. I wrote volumes of love letters to her. *I prefer the little vicarage of Olney with you in it to the palaces of kings without you,* I wrote.[22]

But the end of earthly existence comes to us all. Polly and I knew when her time had come. It had been a long illness. *I took my post by her bedside, and watched her nearly three hours, with a candle in my hand, till I saw her breathe her last, on December 15, 1790, a little before ten in the evening.*[23]

My world shattered. How often I had told of being strong, declaring that the power of divine grace would carry one through grief. But now the grief was mine. Could I be like Job, steadfast in my worthiness to heaven, or would I be more like Job's friend, Eliphaz, who erroneously believed suffering was inflicted only because of secret sin? I prayed for deliverance and found *I had not prayed in vain. From the time that I so remarkably felt myself willing to be helped, my heart trusted in Him, and I was helped indeed.*[24] I was able to return to my duties—and even gave her eulogy. Polly's love was part of God's amazing grace to me.

> *Yes, when this flesh and heart shall fail*
> *And mortal life shall cease;*
> *I shall possess, within the veil,*
> *A life of joy and peace.*

Over the decades at Olney, William Cowper, one of England's most renowned poets, and I wrote hymns regularly for the local congregation. These were published as *Olney Hymns,* and one of my hymns, hymn 41, "Faith's Review and Expectation," came to be known by its opening line: "Amazing Grace." (When it was put to the tune of New Britain, an American folk melody, twenty-two years after my death, it became a worldwide favorite.)

Hymn 41 was written expressly to accompany my New Year's Day 1773 sermon. I thought I should have *a proper subject for our meditations on the entrance of a new* year[25] and chose 1 Chronicles 17:16–17.[26] In this Scripture, King David reflects on his life and asks God: "Who am I, LORD God, . . . that you have brought me this far?" I encouraged my congregants to look back on how God had led them in the past, sustained them in the present, and held for them a promised wonderful future.

I was at St. Mary Woolnoth's for twenty-eight years, until my death in 1807. I lived for eighty-two years and penned the words for my own epitaph at St. Mary Woolnoth's:[27]

> *Once an infidel and libertine, a servant of slaves in Africa was by the rich mercy of our Lord and Saviour Jesus Christ restored, pardoned and appointed to preach the Gospel which he had long laboured to destroy.*

Lest you think my story done, there is an important footnote.
I had known the Wilberforce family for years and was delighted when young William Wilberforce was elected to the House of Commons—a member of Parliament (MP) in 1780. At twenty-one, he was just out of Cambridge! Alas, William, quite full of himself, did not yet take himself seriously—Were not partying and gambling part of the social requirement? Indeed, his melodious voice could easily be heard in the taverns. But he too had his destiny with the Lord and turned to loftier things. Perhaps, he puzzled, politics should be quit in favor of the ministry. It fell to me to convince him that his newly found values were needed more in Parliament than on the pulpit. We became close, and ours was a relationship that changed the course of history.

Wilberforce and I took on the slavers. I worked to support his decades of formidable efforts at fighting slavery, and I wrote a piece to help him cajole his fellow MPs: *Thoughts upon the African Slave Trade.*[28] In it I described the uttermost horrors of the slave trade and my own role in it. Because of Wilberforce's work, the British Empire abolished the transatlantic slave trade on March 25, 1807.[29] I lived to see it.[30] *I hope it will always be a subject of humiliating reflection to me, that I was, once, an active instrument, in a business at which my heart now shudders.*[31]

> *The earth shall soon dissolve like snow,*
> *The sun forbear to shine;*

30

But God, who called me here below,
Will be forever mine.

The words of "Amazing Grace" have met their appointed task. Sung by millions each year, they bring solace, assuring that our great God carries their burden. It is my continual prayer that those words will bring hope to those who feel lost and alone, realizing that there is an almighty God who loves them and is ready to bestow upon each his amazing, wonderful, glorious grace.

◆　◆

"You shall remember that you were a slave in the land of Egypt, and the LORD your God redeemed you."

Deuteronomy 15:15 NKJV

"Then King David went in and sat before the LORD; and he said: "Who am I, O LORD God? And what is my house, that You have brought me this far?"

1 Chronicles 17:16 NKJV

"Blessed be the God and Father of our Lord Jesus Christ, the Father of mercies and God of all comfort, who comforts us in all our tribulation, that we may be able to comfort those who are in any trouble, with the comfort with which we ourselves are comforted by God"

2 Corinthians 1:3–4 NKJV

"Faith's Review and Expectations"—Retitled "Amazing Grace"
1 Chronicles 17:16–17 (KJV)
John Newton, Olney Hymns, 1779, Book 1, Hymn 41

Amazing grace! (how sweet the sound)
That saved a wretch like me!
I once was lost, but now am found,
Was blind, but now I see.

The Lord has promised good to me,
His word my hope secures;
He will my shield and portion be,
As long as life endures.

'Twas grace that taught my heart to fear,
And grace my fears relieved;
How precious did that grace appear,
The hour I first believed!

Yes, when this flesh and heart shall fail
And mortal life shall cease;
I shall possess, within the veil,
A life of joy and peace.

Through many dangers, toils and snares,
I have already come;
'Tis grace has brought me safe thus far,
And grace will lead me home.

The earth shall soon dissolve like snow,
The sun forbear to shine;
But God, who called me here below,
Will be forever mine.

- ► Listen to "Amazing Grace." Pick your favorite rendition on YouTube.
- ► The "John Newton Project" is a great resource for all things John Newton: https://www.johnnewton.org/.
- ► For a comprehensive look at the history and culture of slavery and abolition in the British Empire, click here for Brycchan Carey's website: http://www.brycchancarey.com/index.htm.
- ► Pastor Todd Murray wrote an excellent analysis of Newton's writings

in a devotional, *Beyond Amazing Grace*. He also produced a CD of some of Newton's lesser known hymns set to his own (Todd's) compositions. You can download the recordings here: https://soundcloud.com/ gibcmusic/sets/beyond-amazing-grace.

— 4 —

Elizabeth Fry

1780–1845

Betsy's obstinate behavior as a young girl matured into a strong-willed streak that would not be deterred when it came to righting wrongs. And she wasn't afraid to speak her mind—to anyone. Look what she said to the king of France: *"When you build a prison, you had better build with the thought ever in your mind that you and your children may occupy the cells."*[1]

Saturday August 27, 1796. *Dear Diary,* as I have confided everything to you since I was eight, you know Mother expects of me a consummate maturity in all things. *It is your reasonable duty, Elizabeth,* she says, *to improve your faculties—to be well spoken in English, French, and Latin, and to be versed in the simple beauties of mathematics . . . ancient and modern history, geography and chronology . . . to which may be added a knowledge of the most approved branches of natural history* [2] Oh, I do have trouble studying and do not like it much, but for dear Mother's sake I shall persevere.

Friday, January 20, 1797. *Diary Dearest,* I just love when Mother calls me her *dove-like Betsy.* Is there anyone who doesn't treasure our dear mother? I so want to be like her—full of goodness.

Sunday, September 3, 1797. *If I am bid to do a thing, my spirit revolts; if I am asked to do a thing, I am willing.*[3] Today we attend Meeting. I go because I am bid; therefore, I shall pay no attention whatsoever.

Sunday, January 7, 1798. *Dear Diary*, you will agree that I have matured beyond that indifferent, recalcitrant attitude of twelvemonth past—thankfully. Those dark, opinionated attitudes, gone! Well, mostly gone. I no longer fear the night, either. It seems adulthood, *Dear Diary*, has carried me out of myself, allowing a sensitivity to others to emerge. I would venture that those immature and childish traits laid the groundwork for bolder counterparts: tenacity, courage, compassion, and unswerving loyalty. Unfortunately, *Dear Diary*, I can never seem to shake the rise and fall of a depression—as if a shroud rose and fell upon my bosom. So many trials of faith, too! *My mind is so inclined to skepticism and enthusiasm that if I argue and doubt I shall be a total sceptic [sic].*[4]

Sunday morn, February 4. *Dear Diary*, why do some Quaker people dress so plainly? There is so little enthusiasm among them! Thank goodness my parents believe life not to be so severely lived. I shall go to Meeting as bid this day, but *I shall be wearing purple boots with scarlet laces!*[5] And in my maturity, perhaps I shall attend with a more willing spirit. Then again, perhaps not.

Sunday eve. Would it be unseemly, *Dear Diary*, to say that my life this day has been forever changed? Minister William Savery came from the New World to address our Meeting of Friends at Norwich. Despite myself, I couldn't help but listen. He spoke of a loving life and of the obligation to help others, especially those in poverty. To my surprise—no one knew why, least of all me—I wept the journey home. *Oh, I wish the state of enthusiasm I am now in may last, for today I have felt that there is a God! . . . Minister Savery and I had much serious conversation; in short, what he said, and what I felt, was like a refreshing shower falling upon earth that had been dried for ages.*[6] I think I am done with folly, and gladly so!

Minister Savery has been a houseguest, and he matter-of-factly prophesied of my being led into important work for God! As you know, *Dear Diary*, I am already in pursuit of teaching children to read, collecting clothes for the poor, and ensuring that the local children are vaccinated.[7] Those visits to the sick and poor in the London slums have *opened my eyes to the condition of the poorest classes of the day.*[8] Diary Dearest, is there something else in the offing?

Thursday, March 1, 1798. *Dear Diary*, family is noticing the change in me. I continue to accompany them to London, but the shopping, theaters, and dinners I once loved are now so mundane and empty, not worthy of pursuit at all. *I now think them all so artificial.*[9] (I would rather be visiting Cousin Priscilla in Coalbrookdale. She is as I want to be: no fancy clothes, a plain dress, devoid of accouterment, with white linen cap as her preference.) The evening brought a most odd occurrence, though. Elderly Deborah Darby looked straight at me and said, *"A light to the blind; speech to the dumb; and feet to the lame."* Can it be? She seems as if she thought I was to be a minister of Christ. Can I ever be one? If I am obedient, I believe, I shall.[10]

Tuesday, May 8th, 1798. *I want to set myself in good order for much time is lost and many evils committed by not having some regular plan of conduct. Now I have rules; my favorite is Rule 3: Never say an ill thing of a person, and when I can say a good thing, not only speak charitably, but feel so.*[11]

Tuesday, August 19, 1800. *Dear Diary*, wedding day today! By nightfall, I shall be Mrs. Joseph Fry! As I have pondered greatly of his friendship, my hesitancy in accepting his proposal has been resolved. He has sufficiently demonstrated support of my philanthropic endeavors, and the match seems right. As a wealthy tea dealer, he can support my work, and he is, like me, a devout Quaker. But really, *it is droll how much fonder I am of Joseph sleeping than waking, for I dream very lovingly of him of a night.*[12]

I always found time to write in my diaries. The entries above are typical of the ones I wrote in my forty-four diaries, tracing the path of my work—my life. If you do read them, you would find me a nervous girl—sickly and dyslexic. Throughout my life I suffered from a terrible cough, and postpartum depression afflicted me long after the birth of each of my eleven children. Toothaches plagued me endlessly, but the remedy was often worse: leeches applied to the gums.

My childhood home, Earlham Hall, a pleasant family home of red brick, was about two miles from the city of Norwich. Mother, Catherine Bell, was a member of the Barclay banking family and a devout Quaker. Father, John Gurney, an owner of a wool-stapling and spinning factory and partner in Gurney's Bank, could well afford as many boots and dresses as I had desired. Father was known for his reliability, honesty, and fair dealings. Mother died soon after one of my brothers did—there were twelve of us remaining—when I was myself twelve. It fell to me and my older sister,

Catharine, as the two oldest girls, to become the mother, of sorts, to our ten siblings. I was devastated by Mother's early death, but her pursuits of helping the poor and educating girls stayed in my heart, shaping my character. I was most distressed by Father's death, as well. But, wanting so much to please him, I had stayed away from the "thees," the "thous," and certain other giveaway behaviors belying my evolving faith. With dear Father's death, I no longer was so confined. However one defined me, however my behavior exhibited, my constitution was definitely not that of an eighteenth-century English woman.

Joseph and I moved to St. Mildred's Court in London, and our family increased rapidly there to five sons and six daughters. I always resolved to do good works while still being responsive to husband, children, and daily duties. Because my husband was rich enough to employ servants, I was able to continue my involvement in charitable causes. Despite a desire to serve a bigger purpose, however, the demands of motherhood kept me busy for the next decade; I felt life slipping away to but little use.

My vision, however, did not slip away. By 1811 I was a Quaker minister myself and took up the work once again. The pivotal year of my life, however, was 1813. Looking back, it was the smallest thing that changed the entire course of my life. I simply accepted an invitation from Friend Stephen Grellet to one day visit the women inside the Newgate prison. The turnkey there tried to prevent me from entering: "You should not go in alone, ma'am," he warned. "They'll tear off your things and scratch and claw you. And first of all they'll snatch your watch."[13] Nevertheless, I went in (I left my watch outside), transfixed at what was before me: three hundred women with their children—*tried and untried, misdemeanants and felons*[14]—packed into two wards and two cells, the stench unbearable even in the freezing cold.[15] There were no beds, no blankets, and an open sewer ran through! Filth and disease flourished, as you might imagine. Half naked, they were; whatever clothes these poor women had on were not identifiable as such, being merely rags. I shall never forget the sight of two of them stripping a dead infant of his bunting so that another might have it. *I think if you saw how small a piece of bread they are each allowed a day you would be very sorry.*[16] More food than that was yours only if someone from the outside remembered you. I could only say that *the filth, the closeness of the rooms, the furious manner and expressions of the women to-*

38

wards each other, and the abandoned wickedness, which everything bespoke are really indescribable.[17]

I might very well have run, but I did not. Could not. I stayed and spent time with them, returning again and again, bringing food and clothing and sometimes staying through the night. I showed them kindness—altogether unfamiliar to them—and they responded tenfold. As much time as I spent with them, though, I still had a home to go to, one with manicured lawns, lovely furniture and artwork; I remember asking myself, Would I have had the strength of those women otherwise?

Strict and harsh punishment—far exceeding the crimes (real or alleged)—was the only goal of prisons—rehabilitation nary a thought. The punishment bore no relation to the severity of a crime, either. Spreading false rumors (barratry), imitating a gypsy (vagabonding), throwing firecrackers, stealing an heiress, stealing food, or passing a small forged banknote were some of the two hundred offenses that would claim your neck in a hanging. And unless you could afford to pay "easement," you were manacled in leg irons! Most awaited transport to the prisons in Australia and the colonies.[18] Conditions were horrific, and anyone, it seemed, who entered innocent of mind left—if indeed they ever left—deprived and debauched.

In 1817 I persuaded ten friends to form with me the "Ladies' Association for the Reformation of the Female Prisoners in Newgate" devoted to the pursuit of humanity and justice at Newgate. We taught them of hygiene, civilized manners (their manners being ferocious), and how to sew and knit so they could embark upon a livable trade when released. We worked with the government to improve their manner of living and, with the women, pressed the message of the Scriptures. Our care and concern motivated these women to improve their own lot. With a show of hands these women voluntarily agreed to discontinue their drinking, cursing, and card playing. We persuaded the officials to allow chaplain visits and urged the warden to urge the guards to keep their hands to themselves— especially in the night. A strong, abiding faith was often our only ally in the struggle against seemingly insurmountable odds; years of hard work; and, at times, seemingly little progress.

We did not do this work alone, however. In 1871 I helped to establish a nationwide "British Ladies' Society for Promoting the Reformation of

Female Prisoners" to aid and encourage small groups of women to provide aid and instruction to female prisoners. These societies also donated sewing supplies such as fabric, thread, needles, pins, and scissors to assist in the learning of a trade.

As for me, I became a mark of criticism from society, newspapers, and even some family members. Prison reform was solely a man's purview, and my work was perceived as an exhibition of nothing less than unflattering egotism—not to mention, they clucked, a neglect of family and a disrespect to husband. I was resolute, however, and refused to be stopped by petty gossip. *No person will deny the importance attached to the character and conduct of a woman in all her domestic and social relations. . . . But it is dangerous error to suppose that the duties of females end here. During the last ten years much attention has been successfully bestowed by women on the female inmates of our prisons. But a similar care is evidently needed for our hospitals, our lunatic asylums and our workhouses. Were ladies to make a practice of regularly visiting them, a most important check would be obtained on a variety of abuses, which are far too apt to creep into the management of these establishments.*[19]

Both Queen Charlotte and the young Queen Victoria[20] became interested in my work, and each granted me a personal audience to impart news of prison evils. I was also able to persuade certain royal gentry to set foot inside them. Mayors and sheriffs from across the country observed our progress, and my brother and I were able to inspect eleven other prisons, exerting enough influence to vastly improve inmate living and working conditions. In 1818 I became the first women to present evidence to Parliament. I told them how women slept thirty to a room in Newgate, *each with a space of about six feet by two to herself; old and young hardened offenders with those who had committed only a minor offence or their first crime; the lowest of women with respectable married women and maid-servants.*[21] I returned many times to the House of Commons to strongly recommend that women, not men, should look after women prisoners; expounded on the value of useful employment for women and their children; and promoted prisoner classification (so that hardened criminals would not be confined with others), religious instruction, and a sufficient diet, clean water, and daylight in the cells. The Parliamentarians did not, however, subscribe to all my views, one being that *capital punishment was evil and produced evil results.*[22] There was some success, however, in changing laws to vastly reduce the number of crimes eligible for the death penalty.

As I said, many prisoners were sent to Australia and the colonies, and our ladies inspected every convict ship carrying female prisoners bound for New South Wales and established schools on board for their children. We provided each prisoner with a bag of useful items they could call their own. I traveled to Scotland, Ireland, and often to the continent, promoting reform.

Prison reform was not my only focus. The poor needed help, and so the Brighton Provident and District Society was established to "encourage industry and frugality among the poor, by visits at their own habitations—the relief of real distress, whether arising from sickness or other causes—and the prevention of mendacity and imposture."[23] Especially successful, and replicated across the country, was a program to encourage poor families to make small deposits into a savings bank for especially hard times.

And as I also said, help was needed as well in hospitals, asylums, and workhouses. In 1824 I happened to be on the coast in Brighton, recovering from ill health—the cough that continually plagued me. While there I became aware of the plight of the men serving in the Coast Guard. Not only was their work dangerous (thwarting smugglers made them very unpopular among those who benefitted), but they and their families suffered from semi-banishment, for their outposts were dreary, isolated, and lonely places. I could be of help here, I thought, and began to organize a plan to supply libraries to the various stations. Some ten years later, five hundred libraries were in place, serving some 21,000 men, women, and children. I also could not fail to lend my hand in fighting homelessness and slavery.

In 1812 a loan scandal enveloped my husband's tea business, forcing bankruptcy, and we lost almost everything. Brother Joseph took over the affairs of the bank, sorting out the debts, and I was able to continue my work. It was the largess of my siblings, and our faith, that carried us through.

In 1840 I helped establish The Institution of Nursing Sisters[24] so that the poor could be attended in their houses with the same kindness and care bestowed upon the wealthy. We sent "Fry Nurses" first into the homes of those who could afford to pay; then, once the institution was established and funded, we sent nurses everywhere. I continued to urge parents to vaccinate their children against smallpox—no small feat, as many opposed the vaccine based on the many political, religious, sanitary, and scientific objections.[25] I also persuaded the authorities to stop allowing visits from those who frequented asylums only to gawk at the insane.

Sunday October 12, 1845. *Oh! My dear Lord, help and keep thy servant.*[26] With those final words I bid an earthly farewell. I was lauded as the *Angel of the Prisons*, and a thousand people attended the burial of my earthly remains.[27] Flags flew at half-mast, a custom ordinarily reserved for the ruling monarch. Surely an honor, but the glory belonged to God. Perhaps they were acknowledging my presence at the royal court, at the throne of our Lord God Almighty. Should you desire it, there is a place reserved just for you as well.

◆ ◆

"The LORD hears the needy and does not despise his captive people."

Psalm 69:33

"'For I was hungry and you gave me something to eat, I was thirsty and you gave me something to drink, I was a stranger and you invited me in, I needed clothes and you clothed me, I was sick and you looked after me, I was in prison and you came to visit me.'"

Matthew 25:35–36

"About midnight Paul and Silas were praying and singing hymns to God, and the other prisoners were listening to them."

Acts 16:25

- ▶ Newgate Prison was notorious. Built in 1188, rebuilt several times, and finally demolished in 1904, it was a "vision of Hell on earth." https://londoninsight.wordpress.com/2011/02/01/newgate-prison -old-bailey-london/
- ▶ There are organizations worldwide dedicated to helping women in trouble. Here's a link to a Canadian association dedicated to working with and for at risk women and youth, The Elizabeth Fry Society: http://efrypeelhalton.ca/.

— 5 —

Sojourner Truth

1797–1883

Sojourner, though uneducated, was articulate and profound. How does that happen? She was also fearless—and given her history, there was nothing she couldn't survive. *I carry no weapon; the Lord will preserve me without weapons. I feel safe in the midst of my enemies, for the truth is powerful and will prevail.*[1]

The world will always have causes worth fighting for. For me there was no lack of personal wrongs to right, either. I should know—I had my share of both. I was born Isabella Baumfree in a Dutch house in New York. Born a slave.[2] Sold and resold, finally to the Dumonts, I was theirs for sixteen years.

The first thirty years of my life[3] were marked by verbal and physical beatings, especially from the Master and Missus Dumont. It didn't matter that I was most of six feet tall, arms muscular from work, and a back that showed a strong will, for a slave did not return a fight—or a talk. Physical, mental, and sexual abuse were doled out regularly by the two of them. The master was the kinder of the two.

Before the Dumonts bought me, my second owner, John Neeley, helped me to learn English. I thank him for that. Bought from a Dutch-speaking family, I couldn't figure a lick of what he was telling me to do. Were it not for his beatings—motivating me to decipher his commands—I might never have learned it![4]

I was fair-minded, honest, and had a stick-with-it sense about me. That came from Mau Mau—Mama. I much loved her. Mau Mau fiercely believed in God. *"My children, there is a God, who hears and sees you,"* she told me and my dozen brothers and sisters. *"He lives in the sky . . . and when you are beaten, or cruelly treated, or fall into any trouble, you must ask help of him, and he will always hear and help you."*[5] The stubborn, prideful part about me I'll own. The stubborn part's what kept me alive. As for the prideful part, I'd as soon go hungry or let my children go hungry as take a morsel of food from Master's shelves without asking him first.

In my day the whole country believed white people to be better than others. What drove the country to separate itself into the North and the South—a combination of differing opinions on slavery, money, and politics—had not yet been birthed. By 1799 the state of New York decided people should not own other people and set up a freedom date of July 4, 1827. Master Dumont and I, however, bargained a freedom date one year earlier than the law laid down. He broke his promise—claiming an injury of mine caused me to produce less than I said I would. He obviously changed his mind about releasing me, for that was surely an excuse. Injury or not, I worked harder than anyone else did.

What was it about that broken promise—after everything else I had endured—that made me say "enough!"? Even so, I kept my side of the bargain and stayed around long enough to spin his wool—about 100 pounds— which, along with my other chores, took about six months. I needed to get away, all right, but didn't know how. *I told God I was afraid to go in the night, and in the day everybody would see me. Then the thought came to me that I could leave just before the day dawned, and get out of the neighborhood where I was known before the people were much astir. Yes, that's a good thought! Thank you, God, for that thought.*[6]

So be it. Tattered clothes, no shoes on my feet, I took with me baby Sophia and some food—my own food—wrapped in a kerchief. I should have left Sophia with my other three,[7] for none of them belonged to me, but she was little and needed me. *I did not run off, for I thought that wicked, but*

I walked off, believing that to be all right.[8] I walked and walked and walked until I came to the very house God had put in my mind to see. (I often got visions.) The house belonged to Mr. and Mrs. Wagenen, a Quaker couple. They thought slavery wicked and nicely paid twenty dollars for me and five dollars for Sophia, keeping us safe for a year until New York's freedom date arrived. I remember thanking Mr. Wagenen, calling him Master—to which he stopped me short: *"There is but one master; and he who is your master is my master."*[9]

While at the Wagenens's, I heard that a Solomon Gedney had re-sold my son Peter across state lines—from New York to Alabama. As the New York freedom date drew nigh, many slaveholders, seeing their last chance to profit from their "investment," would sell their soon-to-be-freed slaves to Southerners who had no freedom dates to fuss with. Not only was that illegal, but it meant Peter would never be free. No! *I would find this man who had thus dared, in the face of all law, human and divine, to sell my child out of the State; and if possible, to bring him to account for the deed.*[10]

I first went to my former mistress Dumont for help. "Ugh!" she said. "A fine fuss to make about a little n-r." I then turned to Gedney's mother. "Dear me," was her more refined reply. "What a disturbance to make about your child!"[11] "Lord, I need a helper," I prayed, "for I am not to do this on my own." Some kindly people advised me to walk into the nearby court-house and find some men who called themselves a grand jury. I did just that, and made my case. Right then and there one of those fine men wrote out a writ summoning Gedney to court, instructing me to deliver the writ to the constable at New Paltz, which I did. That made me, I reckon, the first black woman to sue a white man. A lawyer took pity on me and took my case. Five dollars was his price, which I didn't have. I went out and raised it—even gave him another $15, figuring that with it he'd work that much harder. It was 1828, and when the pleading was at an end the judge declared that Peter was to be delivered into my hands, and that he was "to have no other master but his mother."[12]

While Mau Mau had taught me that God is big, she had also put me of a mind that God was as close as I'd let him be, and that when she wasn't around I was to talk to him. Maybe that's why I spoke aloud to him. I spoke aloud to Mau Mau, didn't I? For some reason I thought it had to be *loud*, too—maybe to get his attention. (I eventually grew out of that.) I took to talking to him in times of trouble—fully expecting him to answer.

When things were going good, though, he wasn't much in my thoughts, and it was easy to take part in worldly pleasures. I'd even considered going back to Dumont for a while, for sometimes there was drinking and dancing and smoking under his roof. Yes, Dumont had beat me, but only (I thought at the time) when I needed it. He had taken to visiting me at the Wagenens, and I did care for him. So I thought I'd give it a go. But just as I was stepping up into his carriage to go back with him, God stopped me—almost in midair, it seemed. *God revealed himself, with all the suddenness of a flash of lightning, showing me, in the twinkling of an eye that he was all over, and there was no place where He was not. Oh, God, I did not know you were so big.*[13]

With my new sight I feared to stand before God; I was far too vile to talk directly to him. I prayed for someone else to speak to God on my behalf, and most directly a vision formed—of someone, a friend—standing between God and me, and I felt as refreshed as if some neighborly friend with an umbrella had stopped by to shade me from the scorching sun. The vision took shape—it was someone of holiness, beaming with love. *Who are you? I know you, and I don't know you.* "Who are you?" I repeated over and over, until I got an answer: "It is Jesus."[14]

Jesus? I'd heard of him but thought he was just someone important, like General Lafayette. But he had to be much more, for otherwise how could he know me? He must have loved me a great deal if he would stand there between us—God and me—reflecting my sins away so that I could stand before him. God, my God, no longer terrified me, and I was filled with love for everybody—even for the white folk.

I moved to New York City around 1829 and worked as a housekeeper to support my children. I did my first speaking out there but spent most of my spare time working among the outcasts. But New York grew wild. In 1843 it was a sin-filled city, and I needed to leave. I understood the need to walk away from that life, and I thought to mark the occasion I would ask for a new name. "What's it to be?" I asked God. "Sojourner," he said, "for you will be traveling." *Afterward I told the Lord I wanted another name, 'cause everybody else had two names; and the Lord gave me Truth, because I was to declare the truth to the people.*[15]

I learned to dress proper and became a traveling preacher. I spoke fiercely against slavery—never knowing beforehand what I'd say—never had to, for I depended on the Holy Spirit to put the right words in my mouth. Since I couldn't read, I'd do a fair bit of memorizing so I could better understand what the Holy Spirit was trying to say. I had children read the Bible to me 'cause adults would always add their own thoughts, and all I wanted was the Word.

I traveled all around, making my way up to Florence, Massachusetts,[16] where people loved each other regardless of their color! In my travels I tended to those in need, held prayer meetings, and led others in song, for I had a rich and powerful voice (still do). Some said I had a tongue of fire and that my preaching "was so miraculous that even learned and respectable people ran after me."[17]

In 1850 I saw how the abolitionist Frederick Douglass increased his income by writing his autobiography, so I decided to do the same thing. (Olive Gilbert and William Lloyd Garrison fixed a lot of my words.) The book did well enough that in three years I owned my land and home in Florence outright. The Ohio *Anti-Slavery Bugle* sometimes supported my travels, too, allowing me to join the antislavery circuit.

My speeches, though, were often interrupted by hecklers who insisted—perhaps because of my looks and deep voice—that I was really a man in disguise. I was at a meeting in Indiana, as I recall, when I'd had enough of that—it was time for that rumor to die. And so right there up on that stage, in front of everybody, I disrobed my bosom! I most certainly did. "*Not to my shame but to yours*," I told the crowd. Shaking my finger at them, I told them that *I suckled many a white babe to the exclusion of my own offspring.*[18]

It felt natural to fall into righting things for women. As I saw it, *if colored men got their rights, and not colored women theirs, you see the colored men will be masters over the women, and it will be just as bad as it was before.*[19] I once had a mob of young men boo and hiss at me from the crowd over that. "*You may hiss as much as you please*," I told them, "*but women will get their rights anyway. You can't stop us, neither.*"[20]

As I said, I never thought about the words I'd use. Sometimes I'd show up just to see what I'd say! I was particularly partial to the words that came out of my mouth at that women's convention out in Akron back in 1851:

"May I say a few words? I want to say a few words about this matter. I am a woman's rights.

"I have as much muscle as any man, and can do as much work as any man. I have plowed and reaped and husked and chopped and mowed, and can any man do more than that? I have heard much about the sexes being equal; I can carry as much as any man, and can eat as much too, if I can get it. I am as strong as any man that is now.

"As for intellect, all I can say is, if women have a pint and man a quart—why can't she have her little pint full? You men need not be afraid to give us our rights for fear we will take too much, for we can't take more than our pint'll hold. The poor men seem to be all in confusion, and don't know what to do. Why children, if you have woman's rights, give it to her and you will feel better. You will have your own rights, and they won't be so much trouble.

"I can't read, but I can hear. I have heard the Bible and have learned that Eve caused man to sin. Well if woman upset the world, do give her a chance to set it right side up again. . . . Jesus never spurned woman from him. . . . When Lazarus died, Mary and Martha came to him with faith and love and besought him to raise their brother. And Jesus wept—and Lazarus came forth. And how came Jesus into the world? Through God who created him and woman who bore him. Man, where is your part? But the women are coming up, blessed be God, and a few of the men are coming up with them. But man is in a tight place, the poor slave is on him, woman is coming on him, and he is surely between a hawk and a buzzard."[21]

The Civil War meant another fight to fight. I spoke out against the war, recruited slave refugees to fight for the Union, and raised money for their food and clothing. I worked for the federal government between 1864 and 1870, teaching freed-people about moral living; cleanliness; and how to sew, knit, and cook.

I did have a bit of infamy in 1863 when Harriet Beecher Stowe wrote about me in the *Atlantic Monthly* magazine.[22] She called me the Libyan Sibyl[23]—whatever that means. The article was so full of wrongs, though, that I had to publish a correction. For one thing, she quoted me as saying *honey* to everyone, and I can tell you *I never made use of the word honey.*[24]

Ordinarily, captured runaway slaves had to be returned to their own-ers, but the war meant that slaves could be claimed as contraband—spoils of war—and kept in the North. This *contraband*, now belonging to the government, meant that housing—refugee camps—sprang up, and all this free living made my people less self-reliant. Since they had never experienced an opportunity to make their own way, useful industry would have to take its time. For heaven's sake, poor people don't want to stay poor!

And then a plan began to form in my mind. If the government could give millions of acres to Indian tribes and railroad companies, why not do the same thing out west, in Kansas, for freed-people so they could "work and earn their own living"?[25] I went on the road, persuading folk to take up the idea, collecting signatures for a petition to President Grant. Grant never did cotton to it, and nothing ever came of it.

I was getting too old to fight any more and returned once more to Battle Creek, Michigan, where I had been living since 1857. Before I knew it, it was 1883, and about all I was good for, given my failing health, was to continue urging others to support the resettlement project.

I could see the end of my life coming. I was weak, very weak; about all I could do was sing:

> *It was early in the morning—it was early in the morning,*
> *Just at the break of day,*
> *When he rose—when he rose—when he rose,*
> *And went to Heaven on a cloud.*[26]

I lived long enough to learn that my former master, Dumont, had seen the error of his ways. *Oh! how sweet to my mind was this confession! And what a confession for a master to make to a slave! A slaveholding master turned to a brother! Poor old man, may the Lord bless him, and all slave-holders partake of his spirit!*[27]

I died on November 26, 1883.[28] Many newspapers said I was one hundred eight. I might've looked it, but I wasn't; I was only eighty-six. I'd been a slave, a freedom fighter, and a tender to others. I fought my battles, but I was never alone. Thank God, I was never alone.

◆　◆

"'The LORD and King has taught me what to say. He has taught me how to help those who are tired. He wakes me up every morning. He makes me want to listen like a good student.'"

Isaiah 50:4 NIrV

"'Come to me, all you who are weary and burdened, and I will give you rest. Take my yoke upon you and learn from me, for I am gentle and humble in heart, and you will find rest for your souls. For my yoke is easy and my burden is light.'"

Matthew 11:28–30

"There is neither Jew nor Gentile, neither slave nor free, nor is there male and female, for you are all one in Christ Jesus."

Galatians 3:28

- ▶ Visit the website of Sojourner Truth's Memorial in Florence, Massachusetts: http://sojournertruthmemorial.org/.
- ▶ Listen here to the 1851 historically correct transcription of Truth's "Ain't I a Woman" speech: https://www.thesojournertruthproject.com/.

Abraham Lincoln

1809-1865

Abraham Lincoln was the sixteenth president of the United States. Self-educated, he came to lead the country at its most vulnerable time, the Civil War. He was truly a great man for all the ages. *Perhaps I might be an instrument in God's hands of accomplishing a great work and I certainly was not unwilling to be.*[1]

In a country that four score and seven years earlier had dedicated itself to the proposition that all men are created equal, we had found ourselves engaged in a great civil war to test that very declaration. It was a somber November day in Gettysburg in 1863, and I came to help dedicate the final resting place of those who had died so that the nation might live as conceived.

It was fitting, I suppose, that my physical malaise reflected the spiritual melancholy of those gathered. (They told me later it was smallpox.) I did not dwell on the question, as there were more pressing matters at hand. Even though I thought my words would not long be remembered, I knew the world would never forget what these brave men had fought and died for, and I had to give my full attention to encouraging our nation to believe that we possessed the strength to endure.

It fell to me to inspire and direct this great task that remained for us, the living, and I called upon our nation to *resolve that these dead shall not have died in vain; that the nation shall have a new birth of freedom, and that government of the people, by the people, for the people, shall not perish from the earth.*[2]

I was born in 1809 in the Kentucky wilderness. My father, Thomas, was an honest man (I even gave my youngest son, "Tad," his name), but we never understood each other. Although my mother was illiterate, she was very smart, and insisted I learn my letters; I think the kindness and patience of her gentle soul stayed with me all my years. When Mother died—I was nine—my heart broke in two.

Father remarried the widow Sarah Bush. Along with her three children, she made our house a home; I think I can say she was my best friend. Desperately poor, I remember *when my toes stuck out through my broken shoes in the winter, when my arms were out at the elbows, when I shivered with the cold.*[3] My father hired me out, and I became proficient in house raisings, fieldwork, plowing, and logrolling. An axe was put in my hands when I was eight, and there it stayed, rewarding me with an uncanny lifelong strength. I could outwrestle anyone, too. I loved animals—especially horses and dogs—especially my horse, Old Bob. (Someone once asked my wife, Mary, whether I had any hobbies. "Cats" was her reply.)[4] I loved to tell stories, jokes, and rhymes with a wide, laughing grin. I read everything I could get my hands on and really enjoyed reading Shakespeare and writing poetry. My Bible, *Pilgrim's Progress, Aesop's Fables,* and borrowed volumes of Blackstone's Law showed great wear, as did the science journals and newspapers I was able to lay my hands on. I won spelling bees and wrote letters for the neighbors. (In every spare moment I read—Father thought me lazy for it). I copied pages of law and grammar—repeatedly— until I had the rules firmly in place.

Sorrow comes to us all, it's true, *but to the young it comes with bitterest agony, because it takes them unawares.*[5] Mother's death, which had come a few weeks after my beloved aunt's and uncle's,[6] darkened my spirit with an overpowering sorrow. I must have been predestined to it—this heartbreak—for in me melancholy made itself a home, burrowing into my soul, never to let go. The deaths of my sister Sarah, my sweet love Ann Rutledge—for whom *I could not even bare [sic] the idea of its raining on her*

Grave,[7] and my sons Eddy and Willie, each in their own time, would throw me into a profound state of sadness. Each goodbye brought me closer to a heart unable to beat at the strain of it, and I wanted nothing to do with a God who would allow such adversity.

Then there was Mary. Our off-and-on again courtship was so stormy that friends once put me on suicide watch—calling my wasted physique and sorrow truly deplorable. *I am now the most miserable man living,* I lamented to my law partner. *If what I feel were equally distributed to the whole human family, there would not be one cheerful face on the earth.*[8] Mary and I worked through it, though, and married in 1842, despite her sister's objections to my impoverished state and low political prospects. (Mary, quite sophisticated, was from a wealthy Kentucky family.) We were perfect for each other, there being much more to our relationship than my depression and annoying enthusiasm or her moods. Our mutual passions—especially politics—kept our ties strong. We both adored and indulged—perhaps too much—our four sons, Robert, Eddy, Willie, and Tad.

I did bring the law practice to our marriage. Self-taught, I had never attended more than a few months of formal school. Motivated by an unquenchable ambition, I would study late into the night until the Illinois Supreme Court granted me a license to practice law. I was thorough and candid in my court dealings, gaining a reputation for being honest, fair, and logical. As a member of the Whig Party, I served eight years in the Illinois legislature and one term, 1847 to 1849, as a United States Congressman before returning to private life as a Springfield lawyer.

Every man is said to have his peculiar ambition[9]; mine was politics. In 1858 I returned to it and ran for the U. S. Senate as a member of the new Republican Party. It was a contentious race, and I lost to Democrat Stephen Douglas. My advisors thought I should have campaigned only on the belief that slavery should not be expanded, but my conscience dictated more—that *he whose wisdom surpasses that of all philosophers has declared that a house divided against itself cannot stand.*[10] Others would reflect later that while those words may have cost me that election, ultimately they won me the presidency.

By tradition, the presidential nomination could not be sought by the person wanting it—and thus I had to rely on others for it. (Oh! How times have changed!) Tending to clients in Springfield while the 1860 Republican

Convention in Chicago was in session, I kept a close watch on the proceedings. The first ballot failed to secure a majority candidate. The second did no better. Standing around the telegraph in the newspaper office, my friends and I could barely tolerate the suspense. The third nomination: victory! *"Gentlemen,"* I grinned, *"you had better come up and shake my hand while you can—honors elevate some men."*[11]

It was also considered beneath the dignity of a presidential candidate to campaign. I honored that tradition, as did most of my opponents.[12] Only the Democratic candidate, Steven Douglas, broke rank and campaigned across the country. It was a bitter and ugly campaign. Candidate John Bell's supporters rang bells to disrupt my rallies. "Look at his face! Would you elect a gorilla?" detractors jeered. Others insisted that I would enforce a policy of marriage between the races and that within ten years all of the whites would be slaves owned by Negroes.

November 6, 1860. I awaited the returns at home. It was a sleepless night, *for I then felt, as I never had before, the responsibility that might be upon me.*[13]

Three months later, just fifty-one years old and full of hope and trepidation, I boarded a train to Washington and the presidency. The townspeople of Springfield, gathering to say goodbye on that cold and overcast day, saw a man so filled with emotion that he could not command a steady voice. Springfield was my home, and I wondered how, or whether, I would return. *I hope you, my friends, will all pray that I may receive that Divine assistance without which I cannot succeed, but with which success is certain. I bid you an affectionate farewell.*[14]

On my way to Washington, I made sure to meet little Grace Bedell during one of my stops. She had written me a letter while I was a candidate. In it she told me that her family would vote for me only if I would grow whiskers because, as she said, "You would look a great deal better for your face is so thin." I took her advice, and when I saw her I sat with her on the edge of the platform. *"Look at my whiskers, I have been growing them for you,"* I said to her, and gave her a big kiss.[15]

The South exploded in anger at the election results. By January, seven Southern states announced a new Confederate States of America. Its vice president, Alexander Stephens, declared that "the new government . . . rested upon the great truth that the Negro is not equal to the white man."[16]

That idea was as absurd as slavery was wrong, and I *could not remember when I did not so think and feel.*[17] But I also knew that the Union had to have been—must have been—preserved at any cost. *"I have no purpose, directly or indirectly,"* I told the people in my first inaugural address, *"to interfere with the institution of slavery in the States where it exists. I believe I have no lawful right to do so, and I have no inclination to do so. In your hands, my dissatisfied fellow-countrymen, and not in mine, is the momentous issue of civil war. The Government will not assail you. You can have no conflict without being yourselves the aggressors. You have no oath registered in heaven to destroy the Government, while I shall have the most solemn one to preserve, protect, and defend it."*[18]

Both parties deprecated war, but . . . the war came.[19] A country of thirty-three million sent four million of its own into battle, and some six hundred twenty thousand died,[20] never again to see their mortal home. This was a wretchedness I could not stop. *Doesn't it strike you as queer that I, who couldn't cut the head off of a chicken, and who was sick at the sight of blood, should be cast into the middle of a great war, with blood flowing all about me?*[21]

All of us naively assumed that the conflict would be a short-term affair. Both sides were too civilized, too certain of being right (each knowing the other side would fall quickly), and the South's culture of honor—which couldn't admit the possibility of defeat—was greatly underestimated.

It soon became apparent that the country could never exist as a single entity, part free and part not. Legalities supporting the validity of slavery had to be broken; I knew that it was within my war powers to dictate emancipation to the opponent. Even though an emancipation proclamation would not end slavery outright, I could declare an end to slavery to states in open rebellion. Not only would I be able to free some who were enslaved, but that move would also deprive the enemy of labor and add former slaves—men—to Union ranks. I began moving in that direction, but I needed a victory on the battlefront. Without it there would have been little chance to enforce my declaration within the Confederate States.

It came with Antietam! Slim victory that it was, Antietam offered the needed conquest. In September 1862, I issued a preliminary Emancipation Proclamation as an executive order: *"On the first day of January in the year of our Lord, one thousand eight hundred and sixty-three, all persons held as slaves within any state, or designated part of a state, the people whereof shall then be in rebellion against the United States shall be then, thenceforward, and forever free.*"[22] This action didn't free all slaves,[23] but it was all my executive powers allowed at the time. In 1864, after my re-election I was able, using all my powers of authority, negotiation, and persuasion, to effect the passage of the thirteenth amendment[24] to abolish slavery—the "original, disturbing cause of the rebellion."[25] *I never in my life,* I wrote, *felt more certain that I was doing right than I do in signing this paper. If my name ever goes into history it will be for this act, and my whole soul is in it.*[26]

I'm getting ahead of myself. That war was so severe that only God could have dictated its outcome. I came to think that he permitted *it for some wise purpose of his own, mysterious and unknown to us.*[27] I tried to express these thoughts in my second inaugural address on March 4, 1865: whatever the case, the *judgments of the Lord are true and righteous altogether.*[28]

Perhaps it was fitting that I would become the war's last casualty.

I think I might have succumbed under the crushing weight of my duties had I not maintained my sense of humor. No one loved a punch line or tall tale more than me. I used humor to put people at ease or to diffuse political combatants. Self-deprecating humor diverted attention from my wizened visage and high-pitched voice, too. If height could be considered a redeeming quality, then I was victorious, for I was tall—tall enough to reach the ground![29]

April 4, 1865, and the end was in sight. The Navy controlled the ocean, its blockade strangling the South. Confederate general Lee advised Confederate president Jefferson Davis to flee its capitol. Ah, stately Richmond, did it survive?[30] Much to the chagrin of my bodyguards, I had to have a look. Tad came with me and we landed our boat without ceremony, for I was coming as a peacemaker, not a conqueror. I was first recognized by some Negro workmen. "Bless the Lord—there is the great Messiah," one of them yelled as crowds gathered, some falling to their knees. "*Don't kneel to me,*" I told them. "*That is not right. You must kneel to God only, and thank him for the liberty you will hereafter enjoy.*"[31]

Admittedly, though with great reluctance back in 1861, I had signed the Confiscation Act, and many demanded I uphold its provision to confiscate the property of any and all rebels. I just couldn't do it—peace was my focus, and I was determined to reunite the country. Neither did I want to capture or punish their leaders. Much to the vexation of those bent on revenge, I issued a proclamation for amnesty and reconstruction in December 1863 that offered full pardon, restoring rights to all property, except as to slaves, conditioned upon an oath inviolate to support and defend the Constitution of the United States.

In so doing I sought to echo Jesus' exhortations to love our enemies. *"With malice toward none,"* I asserted in my last address to the nation, *"with charity for all, with firmness in the right as God gives us to see the right, let us strive on to finish the work we are in, to bind up the nation's wounds, to care for him who shall have borne the battle and for his widow and his orphan, to do all which may achieve and cherish a just and lasting peace among ourselves and with all nations."*[32]

Life is a journey filled with self-contemplation, is it not? In my twenties I lived in the deeply religious community of New Salem, and there I considered myself the town's atheist. I parodied the Bible and even denied my disbelief if to do so benefited my position. As one ages, if one cannot meet circumstance with a degree of betterment, I reasoned, then life must be for naught. *In my poor maimed and withered way, I bear with me as I go on a seeking spirit of desire for a faith that was with him of the olden time, who in his need, as I in mine, exclaimed: Help thou my unbelief.*[33]

If I had a greenback for every earnest word wrangled over my views of God, I'd be a neighbor of King Solomon and all his treasures. Scholars argue endlessly: Did I believe in God—or not? Did I believe in predestination—or not? Did my children's deaths move me to conclude that the Supreme Authority was also a God of solace and profound love—or not?

In some small measure, the evolution of my faith paralleled the growth of our nation as it strived to grow out of its immaturities and settle its differences. Even those who knew me well could not keep up with my evolving faith.[34] But it was a journey, my friends, and *through all, I groped my way until I found a stronger and higher grasp of thought, one that reached beyond this life with a clearness and satisfaction I had never known before. The Scriptures unfolded before me with a deeper and more logical appeal through these new experiences than anything else I could find to turn to, or ever before had found in them.*[35]

Everyone knew where I would be on that evening of April 14, 1865. That afternoon, however, it was only Mary and me, alone, on a carriage ride, and we were in grand moods. The war was over, my inauguration last month, and the Thirteenth Amendment, forever abolishing slavery, would soon be ratified by enough states—I just knew it. Lee had surrendered at the McLean House in the village of Appomattox on April 9. Even Mary commented upon my spirits. "Dear husband, you almost startle me by your great cheerfulness,"[36] she laughingly observed.

We were late to the play. The press of business had detained me, and Mary was not feeling well; we even considered not going, but I otherwise would have labored at home and disappointed a full house of sixteen hundred theatergoers, eagerly anticipating the president's arrival. It was Good Friday, and my mind was on restoration, renewal, and rest. John Wilkes Booth, however, full of hatred and full of himself, had murder on his mind.

It was 8:30 in the evening when our carriage brought us to Ford's Theater to see *Our American Cousin*. The night air swirled about us, gently drifting into a misty fog as though to shield us in a protective shroud. Noting our entrance, the conductor interrupted the performance with his baton, calling for the orchestra to play "Hail to the Chief." The crowd stood, applauding politely. The play resumed, but Mary and I found more interest in each other, continuing our flirtations of the afternoon's carriage ride. Close to each other, Mary's hand on mine, I whispered of the coming days. *"We will not return immediately to Springfield after the war,"* I told her. *"We will go abroad among strangers where I can rest. We will visit the Holy Land."* Another moment went by. I bent forward, whispering these words to my beloved Mary: *"We will visit the Holy Land and see those places hallowed by the footsteps of the Savior. ... There is no place I so much desire to see as Jerusalem."*[37]

The bullet pierced my skull.

About nine hours later, at 7:22 a.m. on April 15, 1865, I was pronounced dead—mortally wounded from the assassin's bullet.[38] Secretary of War Stanton, known as "Mars" to his friends, hadn't wanted me to go to the theater; too many death threats, he had said. It was forthwith left to him to utter the fateful words: "Now, he belongs to the ages."

Mars, it seems, was a perceptive man in warning me not to go. I should know; *he's called me a d-d fool more than once, and I certainly must be one, for he is nearly always right.*[39]

◆ ◆

"God is our refuge and strength, an ever-present help in trouble."

Psalm 46:1

"The fear of the LORD is the beginning of wisdom, and knowledge of the Holy One is understanding."

Proverbs 9:10

"Jesus knew their thoughts and said to them, 'Every kingdom divided against itself will be ruined, and every city or household divided against itself will not stand.'"

Matthew 12:25

► For a well-balanced discussion of Lincoln's faith, read *Lincoln's Battle with God* by Steven Mansfield, Thomas Nelson Publishers, 2012.
► The Abraham Lincoln Presidential Library and Museum is an essential resource for understanding his personal life, legal career, political development, and presidency. Visit it in Springfield, Illinois. https://www2.illinois.gov/alplm/library/aboutus/visit/Pages/default.aspx
► You can find a daily chronology of Lincoln's life, among other resources about him, at the Abraham Lincoln Association: http://www.abrahamlincolnassociation.org/. Click on the "Collected Works" button to access The Collected Works of Abraham Lincoln. There you will find his correspondence, speeches, and other writings, edited by Roy P. Basler, or click here: https://quod.lib.umich.edu/l/lincoln/.

— 7 —

Harriet Beecher Stowe

1811–1896

Harriet was a preacher's kid and a sister to seven preachers. She was passionate, dedicated, and totally absorbed in everything she did: teaching, motherhood, writing, fighting slavery, and building and furnishing her mansion, Oakholm. Harriet loved being an author. Of her famous novel, however, she was explicit: *I did not write it. God wrote it. I merely did his dictation.*[1]

I was born in 1811, in Litchfield, Connecticut, part of a very large family. Father encouraged all of his children—including us girls—to think for ourselves. Quite unlike society, antiquated in its ways, which dictated that a girl need only the refinement of social graces and domestic virtues to fulfill her future duties as wife, mother, and housekeeper. Teaching at the lower levels was an acceptable option, though I thought that choice a rose with many thorns. Girls, it was thought, could never ever compete with boys and remain healthy, for that would have required diverting the blood supply to the brain, thereby starving the reproductive system.[2]

There were nine of us children in the Beecher family—that is, until there were thirteen.[3] Mother had been ill for a time before she died, and though I was just five, I still remember our cries and sobs during her last days. She told us that God could do more for us then she had done, and that we must trust him.[4] Our oldest sister, Catharine, became like a mother to us; she was the one I leaned on.

A year after Mother's death, father married Widow Harriet Porter, and the four additional children made our household even noisier and more boisterous than before.[5] Adding to the commotion were our boarders—mostly law students from the nearby school.[6] Dinnertime was always lively with their analytical discourse, and I paid attention, learning the value of critical thinking. With so many people around, from so many parts of the country, I had no shortage of story ideas, perfect for the writer I aspired to be.

Father was a fire-and-brimstone preacher, known for rallying against social ills such as drunkenness and dueling.[7] All of us found it difficult to see him as a loving father; however, I do think Father was proud of us and much enjoyed hearing others compliment us. One of his friends, Theodore Parker, observed that he was the "father of more brains than any other man in America." My siblings became educators, authors, ministers, and theologians.[8] Catharine championed equal education for women, and Isabella established the National Women's Suffrage Association (NWSA). All seven of my brothers became prominent ministers in their communities[9]; brother Henry Ward was *the* famous preacher of the day, primarily I think, because his sermons were spellbinding and humorous. A staunch abolitionist, he held fictitious slave auctions, using the money raised to purchase an enslaved person's freedom. He also furnished abolitionists with rifles—or, as they came to be called, Beecher's Bibles.

Catharine also founded the Hartford Female Seminary for teenage girls. A student there myself, I was well schooled in philosophy, Latin, Greek, French, Italian, mathematics, geography, history, the sciences, and literature—especially poetry. I discovered a natural talent for drawing and painting, too. I won my first writing contest when I was seven, and oh, how pleased Father was! I think his pleasure may well have been the catalyst for my wanting to become a writer. When away at school, and having myself made the declaration of faith at age thirteen, I wrote long letters back home about God and religion. Upon graduation, I stayed at Catharine's school, teaching and keeping the books for a while—at only sixteen.

Teaching became my life—that's all I did, and I loved it. Writing was my only outlet, and it became a passion and a compulsion.

In 1832 Father picked us all up and moved us to the American wild West—Cincinnati—where souls were restless and waiting to be won.[10] I was twenty-one, and Cincinnati was my home for the next eighteen years.

Father's purpose in moving coincided with a desire of mine to broaden my own horizons; I was determined to make a living as a writer, to say something worthwhile—and to be generously compensated for it! Since women were not allowed to utter a single word publicly, vote, or hold office, any influence I might extend would have to come from the pen. With that I risked becoming a society rebel—unfeminine and eccentric. My first venture was a textbook, *Primary Geography for Children*, published in 1833. It sold 100,000 copies, and I earned $187 from it. I couldn't have earned nearly that much in a year of teaching.[11]

Back in those days, one made one's own entertainment, and many a night my friends and I would read our favorite contemporary literature together and then finish the evening with dancing and sandwiches. We called ourselves the Semi-Colin Club.[12] The sweet couple Eliza and Professor Calvin Stowe were part of our literary circle. Eliza and I became fast friends.

Now you may think the name of our little Semi-Colon Club had its origins in our literary interests. But one of us—I can't remember who—remarked that the Spanish word for Columbus is *Colon*, and what a pleasure it must have been for Colon to have discovered a new continent. Our pleasurable discoveries should certainly be entitled some portion of that same sense of exhilaration, and so Semi-Colons we became![13]

In 1834 Eliza died suddenly—of cholera. Forlorn as I was, dear Calvin was even more so. He became a frequent dinner guest at the Beecher house once we realized the invitation would ensure that he would remember to eat. My sympathies for Calvin soon ripened into love, and we announced our engagement on Thanksgiving Day, 1835. I loved that he was a scholar of some renown,[14] and I loved that he needed me. "I have a sort of feeling," he wrote to me, "of inseparableness," as though my blood somehow circulated through your veins, and if you were to be torn from me I should bleed to death."[15] We were married quietly, at home, on January 6, 1836.

I don't know how it escaped me, but for many years I wasn't mindful of slavery as a living institution. *I had avoided all reading upon or allusion to the subject of slavery, considering it as too painful to be inquired into, and one which advancing light and civilization would certainly live down.*[16] . . . *Scenes of blood and cruelty are shocking to our ear and heart. What man has nerve to do, man has not nerve to hear.*[17] Living in Cincinnati, however, I no longer could ignore what was happening right across the Ohio River in the slave state of Kentucky. *No one can have the system of slavery brought before him without an irrepressible desire to do something, and what was there to be done?*[18]

Perhaps I can offer an excuse, feeble though it may be: motherhood. It became my sole preoccupation for the next fourteen years or so. Beginning with twins (the second twin was quite the surprise!), we had seven children.[19] In the early years we couldn't afford any help, and I had to do everything myself. Calvin was *rich in Greek & Hebrew, Latin & Arabic, & alas! rich in nothing else.*[20] Though our children never lacked for love and attention, sometimes the house wasn't cleaned, or supper may have been late. I was a working woman, after all—always at home, of course. I wrote for *Western Monthly Magazine; Godey's Lady's Book* (which paid $15.00 per page); the *New York Evangelist*; and later, the *Atlantic Monthly*. I honed my writing skills with scores of articles about domestic matters and small town life. *I determined not to be a mere domestic slave. . . . I meant to have money enough to have my house kept in the best manner and yet to have time for reflection and that preparation for the education of my children which every mother needs.*[21] As I told a friend, *if you see my name coming out everywhere, you may be sure of one thing—that I do it for the pay.*[22]

In 1845 I contracted a serious case of cholera and was not expected to live. I survived, of course, but it took a good year for me to recover. With that, God and family became my only concern; I insulated myself from the outside world. Texas finally became a state? Did the country acquire vast territories of land extending all the way to the Pacific Ocean? I think I heard of a frenzy out in California—gold or some such thing—but these things were of only a passing notice. What I couldn't keep at bay, however, were the moral horrors of slavery. They began to invade my thoughts and my writing.

My focus on the family was clear, but my thoughts of God became clouded, my heart troubled. Had I accepted my faith with that declaration made so long ago only because that was what Father had wanted?[23] It was brother George's sudden death, though, that threw me into a helplessness from which I was powerless to extricate myself. I yearned for something much more than I had as yet experienced, and it was only through utter despair that I realized my "deep, immortal longing" could only be filled with the grace of God. *My all changed—whereas once my heart ran with a strong current to the world, it now runs with a current the other way. . . . The will of Christ seems to me the steady pulse of my being.* What I thought I found at the tender age of thirteen verily burst forth, baptizing me with his spirit. *I am calm, but full.*[24]

In the summer of 1849, cholera again struck. Henry, our oldest, recovered. Charley, our youngest, not yet two, did not.[25] Oh Charlie, my sweet Charlie! Oh, how his "golden hair caught the sun."[26] He was, by his living and dying so young, my most special one. I remember thinking *I could never be consoled for it.* Never. Eventually I came to see that perhaps . . . perhaps *this crushing on my own heart might enable me to work out some great good to others.*[27] Look about you now, Harriet! What do you see? Look at the desperate plight of the enslaved mother, sobbing as her baby—babies!—are torn from her bosom, never to be seen again. I became, such as that suffering enabled me to, one of them.

In 1850 Congress passed the Fugitive Slave Act, forcing everyone to participate in the capture and return of runaway slaves. Any white man could seize any Negro, declare him to be a fugitive, and swear to his ownership in court! The "slave" did not have a right to speak, and the "guilty" would be remanded to slavery. Ten dollars was paid to the hearing commissioner for every such guilty pronouncement, five dollars for each declaration of freedom. This was legalized kidnapping! People who heretofore could turn a blind eye were suddenly brought straight into the atrocity. The country spiraled into turmoil and discord. *"Some unions are better broken than kept,"*[28] I exclaimed.

I had to do something—write something—but what could I do? Thoughts of freedom weighed upon me night and day: *I felt that the time had come when even a woman or a child who could speak a word for freedom and humanity was bound to speak.*[29]

I prayed. Fearful of acting, fearful of not acting, I was even more fearful of reaching the limits of God's patience with all of us. *A day of grace is yet held out to us. Both North and South have been guilty before God; and the Christian church had a heavy account to answer.*[30]

It was 1851, and the answer, for me, came with great clarity and suddenness. We had settled into a rented home in Brunswick, Maine—Calvin had accepted a position at Bowdoin College there. I was in the college chapel one morning, praying, when the cross before me seemed to transform itself—a vision—into that of a bleeding and dying slave being flogged to death.[31] Startled, I seized upon it! At home I started writing and couldn't stop. I wrote of all my past encounters, and when I ran out of paper wrote on the brown paper in which the groceries had been delivered. I read everything I could get my hands on about slavery.[32] I wrote to Catharine: *Oh, what wrongdoings have been done!*[33] To Henry: *Would to God I could do something even the humblest in this cause. I have actually & really found tears dropping on my pillow when I have thought of the wrongs and sorrows of those oppressed ones.*[34]

Calvin and I became part of the Underground Railroad and harbored fugitive slaves, all the while listening to their stories. I became friends with former slaves like Frederick Douglass. I needed to know not just what had happened *to* them but what had happened *inside* them. They became characters in a story: Eliza, Dinah, Eva, Henry, and Topsy. I poured my grief over baby Charlie's death into it. *I looked all the facts over with despairing eyes.*[35]

Has there ever been a child like little Eva?
Yes, but their names are always on grave-stones.[36]

The slave in my vision became Tom in my novel.[37] Originally, the story appeared in serial form in the *National Era Weekly Magazine*. A twenty-four week venture, that's all, I thought, but people clamored for more. Forty-five weeks of it—on April 1, 1852, the final chapter ran. The story was published as *Uncle Tom's Cabin* in book form the next month, and no one—including me—was prepared for the country's reaction. Three thousand copies sold the first day, ten thousand in four days, and seventeen printing presses ran around the clock to meet the first year's demand of three hundred five thousand copies. (All without benefit of your social media, I might add.) It sold millions and became the second best-selling book, behind the Bible, of the entire nineteenth century! Translated into forty languages,[38] it buried Europe's patronizing attitude that we American women had no literary talent. In the first four months *Uncle Tom's Cabin* earned more money for us than Calvin could have made teaching in an entire decade! (My first royalty check, $10,300, went toward the remodel of our home, an old stone workshop, in Andover. We moved there because of Calvin's new job as a professor of Sacred Literature at Andover Theological Seminary.)[39]

Uncle Tom's Cabin awakened the nation's consciousness and energized the antislavery movement. Indeed, when I met President Lincoln he shook my hand with a smile and a wink: "So you're the little woman who wrote that book that started this big war!"[40] *But I could not control the story. I the author of Uncle Tom's Cabin? No indeed, The Lord Himself wrote it, and I was but the humblest of instruments in his hand. To Him alone should be given all the praise.*[41]

Because slavery had been outlawed in England for decades, the British people were more than sympathetic to the cause and bought 1,500,000 copies in the first year. I visited England, Ireland, and Scotland in 1853, specifically to receive a petition signed by 562,448 women who opposed slavery, and was greeted by cheering crowds wherever I went. In addition to the signatures, twenty thousand dollars was raised and given to me to fight slavery.[42] The Duchess of Sutherland presented me with a gold bracelet in the shape of a slave's shackle. One of the links was inscribed with the date of Britain's abolition of slavery, "Aug.t 1, 1838." I told her that, God willing, I would someday add a similar inscription for America.[43] (I later did.)

War was inevitable; Lincoln's election made it so. My brothers and I took a stand, our concern the fate of the Southern slave. The younger Beechers did their part—half-brother James enlisted within twenty-four hours of the attack on Fort Sumter. Of the band of Beecher cousins who joined, son Frederick would meet the enemy five times and be severely injured at Gettysburg.[44] On a trip to see Frederick at Fort Runyan in Maryland in 1862—it was Thanksgiving—I met with President Lincoln and was encouraged by our discussions. He said it well: "If slavery is not wrong, then nothing is wrong."[45]

In 1863 Calvin retired, and we moved to Hartford, where I built Oakholm[46]—it helped to think about something other than the Civil War. I oversaw its building, from the digging of trenches to the opening of the street. Most of the money I made from the novel went into building my "gorgeous Italianate mansion."[47] By 1870, however, the upkeep had become too much, and we moved to another home in Hartford, next door to that of Mark Twain, who proved to be a staunch supporter.[48]

I had many enlightening experiences throughout my eighty-five years[49]; I was blessed with a wonderful family and published thirty books, but whatever part I played in slavery's undoing far surpassed anything else I did. I could never have envisioned what God had in mind for me to do, it was enough that I trusted in him, just as Mother had instructed.

◆ ◆

"'Have I not commanded you? Be strong and courageous. Do not be afraid; do not be discouraged, for the LORD your God will be with you wherever you go.'"

Joshua 1:9

"We were also chosen to belong to him. God decided to choose us long ago in keeping with his plan. He works out everything to fit his plan and purpose. We were the first to put our hope in Christ. We were chosen to bring praise to his glory."

Ephesians 1:11–12 NIrV

"As the body without the spirit is dead, so faith without deeds is dead."

James 2:26

▶ Read *Uncle Tom's Cabin* online at: http://xroads.virginia.edu/~hyper/ STOWE/stowe.html.

- ► Visit the Harriet Beecher Stowe Center in Hartford, Connecticut: https://www.harrietbeecherstowecenter.org/.
- ► Visit the Harriet Beecher Stowe House in Cincinnati, Ohio: http://stowehousecincy.org/index.html.
- ► Visit the Harriet Beecher Stowe House in Brunswick, Maine; it was here that she wrote *Uncle Tom's Cabin*: https://www.bowdoin.edu/stowe-house/.

— 8 —

Harriet Tubman

1822–1913

Harriet's story will teach you at least one thing: never, ever judge a book by its cover. Genuinely grateful in all circumstances, she never let her sufferings shape her. And what circumstances they were: an escaped slave, she spent the rest of her life rescuing others, taking them to freedom. What took Harriet to freedom? It was her faith. Nothing more. Nothing less.

On my underground I never ran my train off the track and I never lost a passenger.[1]

The blood of my African ancestors coursed through my veins. Only two generations away, my people were known for their deep spiritual and physical ties with the earth. I felt that connection, too. "I will protect you, Harriet," the earth seemed to whisper as she told me her secrets. From the women of Ghana I inherited traits of strength, leadership, and a fierce desire to protect my family.

Moses. That's what they called me. A stranger hearing that would surely cock his head in surprise, for I myself had been a slave, small and plain; you'd never pay me no mind. I couldn't read or write. Hardly a force to be reckoned with.

The fifth of nine children, I was born Araminta (Minty) Ross on the Thompson plantation[2] in Dorchester County, Maryland, probably about the winter of 1822. I don't rightly know the day or month—no one kept birth dates on horses, cattle, or slaves. I changed my name to Harriet in 1844 when I married freedman John Tubman.

Slavery is the next thing to hell.[3] No one could say I had an easy life. I'm not complaining, mind you—just setting the record. It was strange, though, that the slave owners who treated us so cruelly would never think of keeping anyone from church—including those of their human goods. I grew up attending churches and camp meetings, and I knew a great deal of the Bible by heart.

For twenty years I was treated meanly and poorly fed. I was only five when master first hired me out as a nursemaid, and part of my keep was to rock a sickly baby. Try as I might to keep from nodding off in the night hush, I'd surely do so. The baby would start a crying, and the missus would thrash me, every time. She kept a whip under her pillow.

I was six when I first ran away—I stole a lump of sugar and knew enough that a whipping would surely be mine. I hid in a pigsty for four days until hunger drove me back home for food—and a beating. At seven I was hired out to James Cook, who sent me out at daybreak to work the muskrat traps in the cold waters of the nearby marshes. Another time—I was about thirteen—I found myself in the line of fire between an overseer and a slave. The slave was escaping, and the angry overseer tried to take him down with a two-pound weight. His aim wasn't so good—it hit me with full force—opened my skull and nearly killed me. They laid me down in a room for two days and just left me there. Not a soul came to see if I was dead or alive. On the third day I was forced into the fields, and *there I worked with the blood and sweat running down my face until I couldn't see.*[4] Master Brodess, realizing I couldn't work in the fields for a time, tried to sell me, but at that point I was disabled and sick, the skin stretched over my bones—who would buy damaged goods?

It was a big long time before I could return to the fields. Blinding headaches, seizures, and blackouts plagued me the rest of my days. Many times a day I'd fall deep asleep—nothing or nobody could wake me. In my own time I'd open my eyes and pick up the talk right where I'd left off. And then came the vivid dreams and strange visions, many of which I used to avoid capture. *I'd dream of flying over fields and towns, and rivers and mountains, looking down upon them like a bird.*[5] My daddy could do that, too. He could also predict the weather. I had powerful visions where God would speak to me, lead me, warn me. I came to depend on those visions.

Our owners never knew we slaves had ways of talking to each other, and what's more, they'd be right fired up to know it was they that allowed it. Always separating us from our families or hiring us out to others meant we had to find ways to spread any news without seeming to. As a loaned slave, I often worked side-by-side with free black men, and we learned quiet ways to talk—a look, a hand gesture, a song. I became shrewd and discerning, a master of disguise. Secret movements became second nature.

In spite of my beatings, I became strong. On the plantations and farms I did the work of men: driving oxen, chopping and hauling wood, and plowing. Master allowed me to hire my own self out; of course I'd pay him a yearly fee for it. I bought a pair of oxen and plowed fields, hauled timber, and saved my money. The Lord was preparing me for bigger things.

In 1849 there was talk of putting me and my siblings up on the auction block to pay some of Brodess's debts. Brodess was not fit to own a dog, but I didn't want to be taken from the family, so I prayed every night for him to change his mind—as bad as things were, they could have been worse. When he didn't change his mind I changed my prayer: *Oh Lord, if you ain't never going to change that man's heart, kill him, Lord, and take him out of the way.*[6] A week later he died![7] I never again prayed like that.

With his death it was all but certain that some of us would be sold. On September 17, 1849, I and my brothers Ben and Henry ran away. A reward was offered, posted everywhere:

THREE HUNDRED DOLLARS REWARD

RAN AWAY from the subscriber on Monday the 17th, three negroes, named as follows: HARRY, aged about 19 years, . . . BEN aged about 25 years; . . . MINTY, aged about 27 years, is of a chestnut color, fine looking, and about 5 feet high. One hundred dollars reward will be given for each . . .

Eliza Ann Brodess

Near Bucktown, Dorchester county, MD

October 3d, 1849[8]

My brothers, scared to death of the punishment that would come with capture, soon ran back home. I knew enough to track the North Star to get to the first shelter. Traveling along the eastern shore, handed off from station to station, (a white woman gave me my first directions out), I moved through the underground. As I crossed into the freedom land of Pennsylvania,[9] I had to stop and look myself over—check out my hands and feet and feel my face, for surely there was something different about me. *There was such a glory over everything, the sun came like gold through the trees and over the fields, and I felt like I was in heaven.*[10]

Such a risky journey, but now what? *I was free; but there was no one to welcome me to the land of freedom, I was a stranger in a strange land, and my home after all was down in Maryland, because my father, my mother, my brothers and sisters, and friends were there. But I was free and they should be free.*[11]

I simply would not live out my life in obscurity, hiding from bounty hunters. I could help family and friends, and who better than me? I knew more about slavery and its evils than any abolitionist could.

I made plans to liberate my family. First, I had to have money, so I found work as a domestic and a cook in hotels and homes. Between the free and fugitive blacks and sympathetic communities of Philly, Baltimore, and the like, my contacts and lines of communication grew. When I learned that my niece Kessiah was to be auctioned off in Cambridge in 1850, I put together a scheme to get her out. I arranged to meet her and the others in Baltimore and escort them safely to freedom. Oh, Lordy, it was freezing cold, we had two small children, but we kept on, and we did it! We crossed to freedom. Over the next eleven years I worked my sources through the Underground Railroad, moving back and forth along the ninety miles of the eastern shore of Maryland, thirteen times. I brought seventy slaves to freedom, most of them family and friends.[12] I also gave instructions to about fifty more—supplying them with names, places, and details. Some of them stayed in Philadelphia or moved to places like Auburn and Rochester, New York, but I also took many of them to St. Catharines, Ontario, Canada. I lived there for a time myself.

In 1851 I decided to go back for my husband. I worked, saved my money, bought a suit of clothes for him, and snuck back home. Actually, I wore the suit as a disguise! My sources were old, though; he had gone and married again! There I was, knocking at his door, dressed in his getaway suit, only to find him inside with Caroline. He didn't even recognize me! I felt hard pressed to make a scene, but what would be the point? *If he could do without me, I could do without him.*[13] Not to waste my efforts, I gathered up a few others and took them back home.[14] Many years later that episode made a right good story for my audiences—helped me raise money. (I heard later that John was murdered in a neighbor's quarrel with Robert Vincent, a white man.[15])

Those rescues brought danger to every step. Armed with guns and knives, bounty hunters would follow us with bloodthirsty dogs. The babies had to be drugged with opium to keep them quiet. The scratchy, thin clothes did nothing to protect us from the freezing cold or thorny thickets. Many of us had no shoes. Walking on ice, the sharp sting of marsh grass, or the spiny sweet gum burrs left our feet bleeding or frostbitten. I'd encourage the others: think of freedom just ahead! I recall once having to give away my undergarments in payment for some food—it was all I had to give. Sometimes the trackers, close on our heels, would force us to take evasive action, so a three-or four-day journey could turn into weeks. Five or six of us hiding in potato holes while they passed right by made for some breath-holding moments. Often I had to go out alone, foraging for food. I'd be gone the whole day, returning under cover of the night. And if I couldn't find them, I'd whistle or sing a hymn until they answered:

Oh go down, Moses,
Way down into Egypt's land,
Tell old Pharaoh,
Let my people go.[16]

When I needed to, I felt confident enough to move around in the daytime. I recollect venturing into town once, disguised as an old weary woman with a huge face-hiding bonnet in search of food. I purchased two chickens, and sure enough, there came my old master, and we were about to come face-to-face! Turning the chickens half loose on their bands got them squawking and a-flapping. That gave me a need to bend over and fool with them, so to hide my face. That ole master paid me no mind, brushed right on by! I had a narrow escape with another one, too. I was sitting in the train station when I spotted him. My old master was talking to someone. "Was that Minty?" I heard him say. Grabbing a newspaper—was it even right side up?—I buried my head in it, pretending to read. *But he knew I couldn't read and so didn't suspect me, and the Lord save me that time, too.*[17]

Most often my work to carry others to freedom were not amusing. *I had great confidence that God would protect me in all my perilous journeys, for I never went on a mission of mercy without his consent.*[18]

As a conductor on the Underground Railroad I ran a tight ship, threatening to use my pistol if a runaway needed "encouragement." I never had to use it; just waved it around a might—that pistol and I could be mighty convincing. I preferred moving my passengers in the cloak of darkness, too, and the land protected me. Protected us. Forests, swamps, rivers—they knew me and I knew them.

Cold, damp Saturday nights were the best times to run; not many would follow us on a bone-chilling cold night, even if they saw us. Since a slave's disappearance wouldn't usually be noticed until the next day, and since any work, like the printing of posters, was not allowed on Sundays, running on Saturday night gave us an extra day of getaway. No matter, though; there was always the risk of being recaptured and hanged.

I was living in St. Catharines when I met the abolitionist John Brown. Frederick Douglass, another great abolitionist, told him I could be of great help, what with my knowledge of the territory and the Underground Railroad. Douglass and I advised him some on his plan to attack Harper's Ferry. As I came to see it, Brown was a man of conviction, and I thought highly of him. Brown called me General Tubman and said I was one of the best and bravest persons on the continent![19] Douglass tried to stop Brown—thought his plan was doomed—and my dreams didn't forebode success for him, either. The attack failed, and Brown was hanged.[20] It was one thing for someone like me, a colored woman, to risk my life for my people, but what could be more to admire than for John Brown, a white man, to do so. *He done more in dying than 100 men would in living.*[21]

The fall of Fort Sumter in April 1861 brought the Civil War. From 1862 to 1865 I was a Union spy, filling in also as scout, teacher, laundress, nurse, and cook—whatever was needed. Because the idea of a black man trusting a white man took some getting used to, I was sent out to recruit former slaves to join black regiments.

It also became my mission to lead the Combahee River Raid in South Carolina.[22] General Hunter himself asked me if I would lead it. He had heard that *many times I had penetrated the enemy's lines and discovered their situation and condition, and escaped without injury.*[23] It was June 2, 1863, and under the command of Colonel Montgomery I myself led one hundred fifty black Union soldiers, aboard three gunboats, to specific spots along the shore where fugitive slaves were hiding. We blew up mines in the river and destroyed bridges and railroads. With guidance from God—you can be darn sure of that!—my intelligence enabled us to finish the mission and escape unharmed, transporting 756 former slaves across state lines.[24]

I was with the first black regiment, the 54th Regiment Massachusetts, on that mournful July day in 1863 when they stormed Fort Wagner, South Carolina. We were outgunned and outnumbered—it was a bloodbath.[25] *We saw the lightning, and that was the guns; and then we heard the thunder, and that was the big guns; and then we heard the rain falling, and that was the drops of blood falling; and when we came to get in the crops, it was dead men that we reaped.*[26] As disastrous as it was, the men showed such bravery and valor that many more black men joined and fought—an effort President Lincoln said was key to the Union's victory.

The war freed my people, but there was no outlawing prejudice and bigotry. My battles continued. I turned my efforts to relief activities and joined the women's rights movement. No longer having to hide my identity, I spoke at many women's suffrage conventions. (I'm told I was forceful, charming, and clever.) *I told them of the brave and fearless deeds of women who sacrificed all for their country and moved in battle when bullets mowed down the men. They were on the scene to administer to the injured, to bind up their wounds and tend them through weary months of suffering in army hospitals. If those deeds don't place woman as man's equal, what do?*[27]

I never let my physical condition get in the way. I guess I was used to pain. I once cured an aching abscessed tooth by knocking it out myself—with a rock. (Believe me that aching tooth was worse than any rock!) In the 1890s I couldn't take the pain in my head any longer and walked into Massachusetts General Hospital for brain surgery. I refused anesthetic while they cut open my head—instead bit on a bullet. That's what the solders did—the ones I'd tended to on the battlefields—and it was good enough for me.

Plagued by a never-ending need for money, I'd hire out as a nurse or domestic, raise chickens or pigs, sell vegetables and eggs, and turn to my benefactors for enough money to fund my work. By this time I was living in Auburn, where I bought a home, expecting someday to fulfill my last promise to God, a home for elderly African Americans—which I did, in 1908.[28]

No matter how close I was to the enemy, I never faltered, never feared, because God was with me. *I was at peace with God and all mankind.*[29] God directed my every step; it was his strength that enabled me to deliver his people to freedom. I was ninety-one on March 10, 1913, when I died, surrounded by family. I sang 'til I slipped away—"Swing Low, Sweet Chariot."[30]

I was called Moses. I answered to General. But I was first a soldier, a soldier of God's, and there's no loftier position than that. I fought the good fight, and he was right pleased with me.

◆　◆

"Afterward Moses and Aaron went to Pharaoh and said, 'This is what the LORD, the God of Israel, says: "Let my people go, so that they may hold a festival to me in the wilderness."'"

Exodus 5:1

"Guard my life and rescue me; do not let me be put to shame, for I take refuge in you."

Psalm 25:20

"'Well done, you good and faithful servant!' said his master. 'You have been faithful in managing small amounts, so I will put you in charge of large amounts. Come on in and share my happiness!'"

Matthew 25:23 GNT

- ► It is said that you can feel the energy of Harriet at her home. Visit the Harriet Tubman National Historical Park: https://www .harriettubmanhome.com/.
- ► Legends have grown up around Harriet Tubman and her exploits.
- ► Kate Clifford Larson, PhD, has done extensive research on this American giant. Visit her website at http://www.harriettubmanbiography. com/.
- ► There are many Underground Railroad Museums. The National Park Service has put together a list: https://www.nps.gov/nr/travel /underground/states.htm.

— 9 —

George Washington Carver

1864?–1943

Before George was world-renowned in his agricultural work, he was a slave. One could also say he was a pioneering environmentalist, always looking for ways to befriend the land. He lived within the framework of segregation, yet he broke that barrier with tenderness and goodwill. *It is not the style of clothes one wears, neither the kind of automobile one drives, nor the amount of money one has in the bank, that counts. These mean nothing. It is simply service that measures success.*[1]

I'm told a band of marauders swooped in and kidnapped me when I was a baby, along with my mother and sister. Those who found me got a three-hundred-dollar horse as the reward promised by my owner, Moses Carver. I would say it must have been a very fine horse to command that much money. Mr. Carver paid the reward even though it was for the safe return of all three of us. My mother and sister were never found. Moses had time to hide Jim from the kidnappers, or they surely would have taken him, too.[2]

A Hebrew saying has it that "all beginnings are difficult." I can attest to that one. I was born a slave and kidnapped for ransom. Not to mention that I was born too soon, I think, because my lungs were weak my entire life, and I was never strong enough to do a day's work out in the fields. That weakness, however, turned out to be my strength, as you shall see.

Moses and Susan, my owners, had no one else living in the house. They had no children of their own, but I understand that after Moses' brother died in 1839 they had taken in his three nieces and nephews[3]—who were grown and gone by the time I arrived. A farm needed many hands, and after slavery was abolished in Missouri in 1865 the Carvers kept my brother and me, raising us as their own.

We Carvers lived in a rural settlement near Neosho, Missouri. Because I hadn't the strength for farm work, I tended the kitchen garden; gathered eggs; and learned to wash and iron, embroider, crochet, and cook. Mr. Carver saw that I shared his sense about nature and taught me everything he knew. I did have a green thumb and knew, innately, what would make living things grow—what would make them healthy. My pockets were never big enough to hold my collections of frogs, rocks, and plants. *I wanted to know the name of every stone and flower and bird and beast. I wanted to know where it got its color, where it got its life, and what it could teach me. I loved to think of nature as an unlimited broadcasting station, through which God speaks to us every hour and every moment of our lives, if we will only tune in and remain so.*[4]

I wanted to go to school more than anything else. No school would welcome a Negro, of course, but I was allowed to attend Sunday Bible study. I eagerly memorized Scripture, and my teacher, Mrs. Abbott, helped me pick out melodies on the piano. Mrs. Carver taught me to read and write out of the blue-backed speller.

Mr. Carver was determined that I should get an education, and he actually found a school in Neosho that would take me! Too far away for me to walk there and back every day, I set out, not sure of what I'd do but sure that I'd be in that school when the next bell rang. Shortly after I arrived, Mariah and Andrew Watkins took me in—actually, they found me sleeping in their barn that first night I arrived. Mariah, a laundress, was glad to have my help! As a midwife, she knew a great deal about medicinal uses for plants and was happy to mentor me. We read the Bible together, too. For Christmas she gave me my very own Bible, which I kept for the rest of my life. She would always tell me, "Learn all you can. Go out in the world and give your learning back to our people."[5]

I stayed in Neosho until my teacher had nothing more to teach me. I was fourteen or fifteen when I hitched a ride with a family traveling to Fort Scott, Kansas. Actually, I just got permission to be in their company and walked alongside their wagon for the eighty-mile journey.

I alternated between work and school, saving money to get me through my school days. Content enough, I might have stayed in Fort Scott forever. It was that unforgettable lynching of a colored man—for *being* a colored man—that moved me along. Such hate in the menfolk, and why? After they killed him they dragged him through the streets, beat his head until it split open, and then set his body on fire. The crowd cheered, the blackness of their souls covering everything like a shroud. I couldn't live there one moment longer. I found a school away from there, did odd jobs, and learned to play the accordion. I could make friends with anyone.

By now I was in Minneapolis, Kansas, where I opened a laundry shack and enrolled in school as an eighth grader. I wasn't very tall and looked the age of the younger students, but I was really more like twenty. After four years and a good bit of money saved, it was on to Kansas City and business school. My typing and shorthand skills qualified me to be a stenographer and landed me a job in the Union Telegraph office. My charming and industrious nature certainly helped!

I was ready for college, but no school of higher learning was ready for me. A temporary setback—that's all it was. I worked, and in my spare moments, painted—I was pretty good at it, too![6] I involved myself in any activity that could teach me something. In Ness County, Kansas, the literary society elected me assistant editor, and with that came a bit of a dilemma. There was already a George Carver in town, and so as not to confuse anyone I begin to use a middle initial, "W." Someone once asked me if that stood for Washington. "Sure, why not?" I responded. By this time I had a fair knowledge of geology and botany, and I had a collection of about five hundred plants, neatly organized and catalogued.

To get into college I would have to move east. I was twenty-six, and my first day at Simpson College in Indianola, Iowa—September 9, 1890—was a lovely fall day. I intended to study piano and art. The only Negro student, I knew my place, and I wasn't going to waste any energy dwelling on something that I knew time would take care of. *While hate for our fellow man puts us in a living hell, holding good thoughts for them brings us an opposite state of living, one of happiness, success, peace.*[7] I did my part by being gracious, friendly, and educated. I lived on beef suet and corn meal until I could take in enough laundry to buy better food. *I knew that God had a great work for me to do.*[8]

I loved to paint plants—thought I might make a career of it—but my art teacher, whose father was an agriculture professor, convinced me there was a future in the study of plants. I took her advice and in 1891 transferred to State Agricultural College at Ames, Iowa. I wasn't allowed to sleep in the dorms, so one of the professors let me sleep in his office. Soon they let me eat in the dining hall instead of the basement—it must have been that charm at work again! I had a full life and involved myself in many activities—even joined the football team. Oh, not as a player—would that I could have!—but as a trainer and masseuse. I worked, gave guitar lessons, and continued to paint. One of my paintings, the *Yucca and Cactus,* was even chosen for display at the Chicago World's Fair. I simply ignored the slurs and bad behavior directed my way.

By 1896 I had bachelor's and master's degrees in agriculture. As an interim stop, I immediately enrolled as a graduate student and got a job as the assistant director of the agricultural experiment station at Iowa State.

I never did get that doctorate degree[9] because Booker T. Washington, Tuskegee University's president, made me an offer I couldn't refuse: " . . . we shall be willing to do anything in reason that will enable you to decide in favor of coming to Tuskegee,"[10] he wrote. With the promise of a yearly salary of one thousand dollars plus board, I accepted a professorship at Tuskegee. What really persuaded me was that it was an all-Negro college, students and professors alike, and I was determined to help better the conditions of my people. I took my most valued possessions with me: my Bible, Mother's spinning wheel, and her bill of sale to Moses Carver.

I was in for a bit of a rude awakening. Because I had never lived in the Deep South, some of my colleagues weren't as welcoming. They also didn't like that I was given my own private quarters when they had to sleep two to a room. For some, the ill will never went away, and I will admit that I likely did nothing to assuage their feelings. To others, however, I was loyal, devoted, and a good friend—deeply committed to helping my fellows. In 1897 I was named director of the Agricultural Experiment Station, authorized by the Alabama legislature.

I loved immersing myself in experiments and teaching and spent the rest of my life, forty-seven years, at Tuskegee, splitting my time between teaching and the lab. I did have issues, though, with Mr. Washington—the two of us constantly bickered. I wanted to be left alone to do my work, while he wanted me to write report after report after report. I can't tell you how many times I offered my resignation over it. I was overworked, I'd say. You just need to be organized, he'd say. In reflection, I was too prideful—I didn't like anyone telling me what to do. Somehow we worked things out. I think I just felt underappreciated. Oh, I knew God was in charge of everything, but I still craved attention. Perhaps that was how my feelings of being a Negro in a white man's world manifested themselves. At any rate, anyone's appreciation made me happier than I can tell you. Ah, the foibles of being human.

The center of my world was my beloved laboratory. Oh, what joys it held! I devised specific methods to yield the most sustainable crops. With lectures and agricultural bulletins,[11] I taught people how to tend the land and thus improve the quality of their lives. The bulletins were a lifeline for the farmers too busy to leave the farm. Well, those and the Jesup Wagon.[12] The wagon was my laboratory on wheels, and, oh, how I loved it! With it came a nurse, a demonstration agent, an agricultural agent, and an architect to share the latest techniques with people who lived in rural areas. The earth responds to the love and attention it's given—it doesn't care what color the hand that feeds it. I would tell the farmers, *"Do not get discouraged when you do not seem to accomplish all you wish, sow the seed . . ."*[13]

Through those bulletins, farmers learned how to reduce erosion by laying the crops and plowing in a certain way. They found that adding wild acorns to corn feed increased milk and egg production. I discovered that peanuts and beans would restore nitrogen to the soil, and with that stressed the importance of crop rotation to give them a better crop yield. In one bulletin, I listed more than a hundred recipes using the peanut. Contrary to legend, I didn't invent peanut butter; I only ate it.

It was only a matter of time before the boll weevil insect, making its way from Mexico, began to completely devastate the crops. The beetle, along with soil erosion, soon made the Black Belt—the Southern agricultural region—the most impoverished place to live in the entire country.

> Boll-weevil's coming, and the winter's cold,
> Made cotton-stalks look rusty, seasons old,
> And cotton, scarce as any southern snow,
> Was vanishing; the branch, so pinched and slow.[14]

Black-eyed peas might have been a good substitute, but even better was the sweet potato. Sweet potato production improved dramatically with that phosphate and potash fertilizer I devised, but it was the lowly peanut that raised its head up out of the ground, looked me straight in the eye, and announced, "Here I am! Use me!"

I discovered many uses for the peanut, sweet potato, soybean, and pecan, and they became ingredients in flour, sugar, tapioca, yeast, coffee, axle grease, bleach, cosmetics, ink, linoleum, shaving cream, vinegar, dyes, library paste, ink, shoe polish, paper, shampoo, plastics, diesel fuel, talcum powder, and shoe polish—almost three hundred uses for the peanut alone![15]

The school made its own paint from a formula of mine using the local clay. I found fifty-three uses for poultry feathers! Oh, there's nothing like a challenge! My strengths, however, were in the lab and though I documented much of my research, the follow-through to take it one step further—to bring it to market—always seemed to stay on my to-do list; I was just too excited to move along to the next project.[16]

I often talked about God to my students, telling them that the more they know about nature and plants, the more they would know about the Creator who made those things. (How sad that I wouldn't be permitted to do that in a classroom today.) In 1907 I began teaching a campus Bible study, using plants and drawings to talk about God's creations. I even produced manna for the students—my version of it, anyway! I would impersonate the biblical characters; I'm sure it was a comical scene to see me as Moses, for my voice was high pitched, not deep as would befit a profit who talked to God![17] It wasn't too long before I had a hundred or more students at every meeting—standing room only—for the next thirty-six years or so.

With every class, whether studying the Bible or agriculture basics,

I offered my own set of Be-Attitudes (with apologies to the apostle Matthew's Beatitudes):

- *Be clean both inside and out*
- *Neither look up to the rich nor down on the poor*
- *Lose, if need be, without squealing*
- *Win without bragging*
- *Be considerate of women, children, and older people*
- *Be too brave to lie*
- *Be too generous to cheat*
- *Take your share of the world and let others take theirs*[18]

I recall that a student once asked me if he would ever be able to see God. Pointing to the ever-present flower in my lapel, I explained to the entire class that *"when you look at this flower, you see the Creator. Students who are studying to be electricians, are not able to see electricity, but when they make the proper contact . . . a bulb lights the way, not only for them but for all of us."*[19]

The peanut may have been the means, but it was the House Ways and Means Committee that catapulted me into the national spotlight. In 1921 I was called to give testimony on peanuts and the economy. "Your ten-minute time limit will be strictly enforced," I was told. Since I could show better than tell, I brought my "reasons" with me, showing them what I had made out of peanuts: breakfast cereal, chocolate covered peanuts, peanut hay for livestock, dyes—one thing after another. I'd found one hundred seven uses for the sweet potato, I told them, and here were some more things: instant coffee, buttermilk, and salad oil. *I'm very sorry you can't taste some of these things,* I told the committee, *so I will taste them for you!*[20] They roared with applause, urging me to continue. For over an hour they listened to me. Peanuts were a gift from God, I told them. The newspapers picked up the story, and by the mid-1920s I became the "wizard chemist," the "Columbus of the Soil"—but mostly I was the "Peanut Man."

Because it was difficult for a Negro to travel—having to eat, sleep, and journey in segregated places—I enjoyed being on the radio, especially if there was also a live audience. If I were talking about the peanut, for example, I'd pull out a bottle of peanut milk, and then something else, and then something else. I'd do this a dozen times, and the audience would thunder its approval. I liked to introduce the demonstration with this explanation:

> Years ago, I went into my laboratory and said, "Dear Mr. Creator, please tell me what the universe was made for."
>
> The great Creator answered, "You want to know too much for that little mind of yours. Ask for something more your size."
>
> Then I asked, "Dear Mr. Creator, tell me what man was made for." Again the great Creator replied, "Little man, you're still asking too much. . . ."
>
> So then I asked, "Please Mr. Creator, will you tell me why the peanut was made?" "That's better," he said, "But even then it's infinite. What do you want to know about the peanut?"
>
> "Mr. Creator," I said, "can I make milk out of the peanut?" "What kind of milk do you want," he said. "Good Jersey milk or just plain boarding house milk?"
>
> And then the Great Creator taught me to take the peanut apart and put it together again. And out of the process have come forth all these products![21]

I made several attempts to manufacture some of these products, but investors were put off by my lack of follow-through. Sometimes, when in a rush and in reply to a question about my formulas, I would say *"I have all of these formulas, but I have not written them down yet."*[22] I declined patent rights to all my inventions except for three. Oh, I could easily have been a multi-millionaire, but I had no interest in that. I much preferred to create wealth for others. I wanted to help *the man farthest down.*[23] I felt the same way when Thomas Edison offered me a job—which I didn't take, even at a high salary.[24] We couldn't come to terms over ownership rights; he wanted to make money from the patents, as a businessman would, and I wanted everyone to have free access. To ensure that this scientific work would continue, I endowed a foundation in 1940.[25]

God blessed me many times over. I was an inventor, scientist, educator, botanist, and philanthropist. (I never claimed to have been the first to discover the benefits of the peanut and the sweet potato, but I was a first-class promoter of their value and possibilities.) I could also play the piano well enough to go on tour! I wanted to laugh and make people happy. *I knew that someday I would have to leave this world, and I wanted to have an excuse for having lived in it. I wanted to feel that my life had been of some service to my fellow man.*[26] I also knew that the real value of my accomplishments belonged to the Lord; I was but the carrier of his message.

I cared deeply about raising the standards of poor farmers, and yes, I was a pioneer in agricultural education, but that's not how I'd like to be remembered. More than anything else, my line of sight was fixed directly on our Creator. That is how I'd really like to be remembered. Maybe a peanut man with a halo! Ha!

◆ ◆

"Then God said, 'I give you every seed-bearing plant on the face of the whole earth and every tree that has fruit with seed in it. They will be yours for food.'"

Genesis 1:29

"'I am the vine; you are the branches. If you remain in me and I in you, you will bear much fruit; apart from me you can do nothing.'"

John 15:5

"But we have this treasure in jars of clay, to show that this all-surpassing power is from God and not from us. We are hard pressed on every side, but not crushed; perplexed, but not in despair; persecuted, but not abandoned; struck down, but not destroyed."

2 Corinthians 4:7-9

- ▶ Visit the National Park Service's Tuskegee Institute, which includes the George W. Carver Museum: https://www.nps.gov/tuin/index.htm.
- ▶ George Washington Carver was the first African American to have a national park named after him. It's in Missouri: http://www.nps.gov/gwca/index.htm.

Amy Wilson Carmichael

1867–1951

Amy thought Ireland would always be her home. Her childhood was a happy one—except for those dreadfully painful bouts of neuralgia that plagued her all her life. Otherwise, there was never a spare moment to sit still. Then came that bad fall, leaving her an invalid for twenty years. She made great use of that time. *It is required in stewards that a man be found faithful. Praise God, it does not say "successful."*[1]

God had a specific purpose for me, but my story isn't an easy one to tell, or to hear. There's no sugarcoating what I discovered: culturally sanctioned child prostitution, endorsed by temple priests in the twentieth century. Yet that is the world into which I was to be called.

I'd like you to know that blue is my favorite color—lots of it—everywhere! Admittedly, that may give you pause—why is she telling me that? You will soon see.

Speaking of blue, when I was three years old—oh, I remember it well—I would go to bed at night, praying for blue eyes instead of my brown ones so I could be just like Mother. It never happened, and I was so disappointed. Why would God not answer a child's prayer? Ah, but he did—he said no! Many years later I would understand why God had me hold on to those brown eyes.

I was born in Millisle, a bit east of Belfast in the North of Ireland.[2] Father, a mill owner, gave us a prosperous life. The oldest of seven, I was also the troublemaker in the family—rambunctious and precocious. Like the time I learned of a poisonous plant out in the garden. I convinced two of my brothers to eat it with me! *Let's count how many we can eat before we die,*[3] I goaded, never believing anything would happen. Needless to say, a concoction of a terrible-tasting something was the remedy for the three of us. I was rather wild and reckless, but never with a thought to hurt anyone or anything. I loved being kind.

I loved my family, too. My father taught me never to give in to a struggle, and never, never to nag. Mother let us have endless fun, and later in my life she would heartily support my calling, much to the chagrin of other family members. I loved all things and could not bear to see anything hurting. Live things were infinitely more treasured than my toys and dollhouse full of dolls. *I turned them all out, and filled the rooms with moss and stones and put beetles and even earwigs to live there. Anything alive was far more interesting than those foolish little dolls.*[4]

I remember the first time Mother told me about Jesus dying on the cross. *I rushed out into the garden in a vain attempt to forget the thoughts that were too dreadful to be borne. . . . And there, on the lawn, stood a boy friend, and he had fastened a frog to a monkey-puzzle tree. It looked like a crucified thing.*[5] I could not reach the frog to take it down and ran crying for help. That's when it occurred to me—and I became absolutely convinced of it—that all frogs went to heaven.

Father's mills came into hard times, and we moved to Belfast. It was there that dear, dear father took ill. He died on April 12, 1885. I grew up, it seemed, right then and there. I was eighteen, after all, and Mother needed me. Mother and I became inseparable—even when we weren't physically together—and I helped her raise my brothers and sisters.

Walking home from church one Sunday with the family, we almost bumped into a downtrodden old woman carrying a heavy bundle. She was muddy, dressed in rags, and I had never seen such misery. I went to her aid, of course, but in doing so I realized that everyone in the courtyard was staring at us, and I was crimson with embarrassment at being seen in her company. I hid my face! Oh, was there a speck of goodness left in me? Just as we passed the fountain, I had the strangest sensation. In a blinding flash I heard a voice say, *"Gold, silver, precious stones, wood, hay, straw . . . the fire will test what sort of work each one has done,*[6] and each will be rewarded accordingly." I quickly looked around to see who could be the speaker, but there was no one. I knew those words, though! They were those of the apostle Paul. Paul traveled the known world, spreading the gospel. I knew God, loved God, so what did Paul and his journeys have to do with me?

Still, there was that voice. I shut myself in my room for the *rest of the day, talked to God, and settled once and for all the pattern of my future life.*[7] I would never again aim to please anyone but God, for *nothing could ever matter again but the things that were eternal.*[8]

I would serve God, but I didn't think it would be far from home—I mean, I really didn't have the constitution for anything else. I was always sickly; neuralgia plagued me, sending sharp, shocking pains through me, forcing me to bed for weeks at a time.

I began my service by leading children's meetings, and then, on Sunday mornings, a Bible class for "shawlies." We called our mill workers shawlies because they couldn't afford hats for church and instead would pull their shawls up around their heads. The class became very popular, and soon the room was spilling over with shawlies. We were going to need a bigger place.

Some land and a building would do nicely, I thought, and so I set out, asking people to contribute toward it. That didn't go well at all; many doors were shut in my face. A thought occurred to me. *Why not ask God to make those who love Him want to help the little children whom He loves, instead of asking for help from those who perhaps don't love Him?* I finally settled on this: *it is enough to ask our Father only for money for His work. I had no thought then, no faintest dream, of what He was going to do in answer to prayer like that.*[9] And from that prayer—I won't belabor the details—the building and the land were donated and we had our Welcome Hall for the shawlies.[10]

And that set the pattern for my life. Whenever I needed money for God's work, I wouldn't ask anyone but God for it! I prayed, and it came.

Give me the love that leads the way,
The faith that nothing can dismay,
The hope no disappointments tire,
The passion that will burn like fire;
Let me not sink to be a clod:
Make me Thy fuel, Flame of God.[11]

Robert Wilson had always been a friend of the family, but after Father died he became like my father. I called him *Dear Old Man—D. O. M.*—for short. He was also the chairman of the Keswick Convention.[12] Early on he taught me many truths. I remember a story he liked to tell to illustrate why one must never take credit for saving a soul. (As good as it feels when you do, and as hapless as you feel when you don't, one must always believe that your encouraging words hit the mark.) "'It so happened that a man came upon a stonebreaker squatting beside a pile of stones,' D. O. M. said. 'Admiring his effort, the man said to the stonebreaker, friend, which blow was it that broke the biggest stone?' And the stonebreaker answered, 'The first one and the last one, and every one between.'"[13]

January 13, 1892, is a date I remember well, for I had another encounter with *the voice.* No mincing of words this time—just *go. Go.*[14] I wrote to Mother, summarizing my thoughts with this: *to obey is better than sacrifice,*[15] and I felt compelled to go. Mother wrote back, "Praise the Lord. He has lent you to me all these years. Now, it's your turn. Go."[16]

I was the first person to be sent out as a missionary by the Keswick Convention group. D. O. M. left it to me to decide my destination. It was April 25, 1893, when I arrived in Matsuye, on the west coast of Japan, and there I thought I would stay. But this was not meant to be: I became very sick and left for Ceylon[17] to recuperate. That wasn't any better, and someone suggested that India had excellent weather for my condition. On November 9, 1895, I arrived in southern India and settled into a small mission in Bangalore. Though I didn't know it at the time, I would never again return home, never take a holiday. For the next fifty-five years my life would unfold in ways undreamed of by that young Irish lass of old.

I began my missionary work but wasn't very good at it. I soon realized that people were paying more attention to my Western clothes than to anything I might say. I began to wear only native dress and stained my arms, my hands, and my face with coffee. Remember that blue-eyed prayer? Had I had those blue eyes, they would certainly have made my work more difficult!

I was confident of life's direction. Oh, don't get me wrong, I had no illusions—this was going to be hard work. The segregation required by the Hindu caste system and India's dozens of different languages made communication more than difficult. I did learn to speak Tamil, the official language of my adopted home. Tamil is a hard language to learn, and I had a good laugh during my study when I came across the words of Numbers 22:28: "The Lord opened the mouth of the ass."

In 1901 my life took yet another turn. Little Preena appeared at my doorstep. Sweet little Preena, only seven years old, was a prostitute. Oh, not by her choice—of course not, this innocent child. She told me unbearable tales of sex trafficking, a practice common in the communities as a way to pay temple expenses. A priest paid money to Preena's parents, in essence marrying her to their gods. He then took her back to the temple, where in the name of their "sacred" marriage she was made to fulfill her *wifely responsibilities*, over and over again. Some saw this as a time-honored tradition.[18] What I saw firsthand was that sin, sanctioned by religious custom, is the joy of the devil.

A group of us missionaries formed the Dohnavur Fellowship, and we waged war against this devil. Having moved from Bangalore, my house in Dohnavur became a refuge for these girls. Before our arrival, should a child escape she would run home. Her parents, though, fearing the wrath of their gods and society, would quickly return their daughter to the temple. She would be beaten into submission and branded on the back of her hands, becoming an untouchable except for the act for which she was enslaved.[19] The girls soon learned that if they could make it to any one of our houses they would be safe. They would find sanctuary.

My girls began to call me *Amma*, the Tamil word for mother, and I loved these children deeply, as my mother loved me. But others accused me of kidnapping, and I faced arrest, trials, and threats of imprisonment. Of what did that matter, I was following Jesus, doing his work:

We follow a scarred Captain,
Should we not have scars?

Under his faultless orders
We follow to the wars.
Lest we forget, Lord, when we meet,
Show us Thy hands and feet.[20]

I stood firm, trusting God to clear away the obstacles. I rescued my first boy in 1918, and by 1926 there were more than seventy orphaned or temple boys in the Dohnavur family.

The Dohnavur Fellowship never went into debt. Although we never asked for anything other than volunteers, we grew, blessed through the indisputable belief that God would provide—and he did. Somehow there was always enough money to pay the bills. (Even today there are no fundraising efforts.) The smaller homes led to bigger ones. Working farms were established, each of which includes a dairy and rice lands. Builders, carpenters, and electricians teach their crafts. We built a hospital, and today it serves forty thousand people every year. (Eventually we stopped taking in boys, instead arranging for them to be taken care of elsewhere.)

I'm happy to tell you that my Dohnavur girls still wear blue uniforms!

Cultural traditions change ever so slowly. India outlawed the practice of selling young girls and boys into prostitution in 1956 and strengthened the law in 1986,[21] but the practice very much continues underground. Today, tens of thousands of children are sold every year in India. Nor does this happen only in India—across the world, hundreds of thousands of children are victims of sex trafficking.[22] These precious children need to know they have not been forgotten. Pray for them. Pray for them. Pray for them.

But that isn't the end of my story. I made a habit of asking for God's direction day by day, for that was how God answered my prayers. On the morning of October 24, 1931—another date I remember well—I had a sudden urge to pray this prayer: *Do anything Lord, that will fit me to serve Thee and to help my beloveds.*[23] Later that evening, in the twilight, I stumbled into a newly dug pit that wasn't supposed to be there, broke my leg, and twisted my spine.

That was the end of my walking-around life. I spent the next twenty years as an invalid, rarely able to leave my room. God knew my nature—that I was never voluntarily at rest. After thirty-six years in India without a break, he wanted me to be still so I could write. I had given him permission to do anything that would serve him, and I meant it. I spent the rest of my days confined to bed, reliant upon others, writing. In prose and poetry, I wrote thirty-five books, telling the world of my experiences and of the good people in India.

I died in India in 1951; I was eighty-three. Though I specified no marker for my grave, my Dohnavur family saw fit to ignore my wishes and put a birdbath there. They knew how much I loved the birds, especially the blue ones! It is engraved simply "Amma."

I can't tell you that my life was easy. *Let us not be surprised when we have to face difficulties. When the wind blows hard on a tree, the roots stretch and grow the stronger, let it be so with us. Let us not be weaklings, yielding to every wind that blows, but strong in spirit to resist.*[24]

I heard God's call and obeyed, and he in his turn filled my life with joy. He filled my life with purpose.

◆　◆

"'I am about to do something new. It is beginning to happen even now. Don't you see it coming?'"

Isaiah 43:19 NIrV

"'If you remain joined to me and my words remain in you, ask for anything you wish. And it will be done for you.'"

John 15:7

"For no one can lay any foundation other than the one already laid, which is Jesus Christ. If anyone builds on this foundation using gold, silver, costly stones, wood, hay or straw, their work will be shown for what it is, because the Day will bring it to light. It will be revealed with fire, and the fire will test the quality of each person's work. If what has been built survives, the builder will receive a reward."

1 Corinthians 3:11–14

- ► The Dohnavur Fellowship that Amy established welcomes your donation (remember they never solicit). They are always looking for volunteers. Learn more at: www.dohnavurfellowship.org.
- ► Want to help a child in India? Check out www.charitynavigator.org to find an organization that speaks to your heart.

— 11 —

Mary McLeod Bethune

1875–1955

Mary began life with every worldly circumstance stacked against her. Dirt poor, female, black as ebony in a white man's world, she didn't start school until she was eleven. What she did have, however, was an inner fire to help others. Today there is a university in her name—because she founded it! Oh, and about that cane that became her trademark. She didn't need it—she used it "for the swank!" *I have known no employer but God.*[1]

Well now, greetings! I'm Mary—Mary McLeod Bethune—and when I was a little girl I was a cotton picker! Why, by the time I was nine years old I could pick two hundred-fifty pounds of it a day. I learned how from my mother and father. They were slaves.

I guess you could call that my first résumé. By the grace of God, however, that résumé grew into something a bit more substantial. Who would have ever thought that a poor colored girl, born in 1875 in a log cabin in Mayesville, South Carolina, would have credentials like this?

Education/Experience[2]:

- Graduate, Scotia Seminary, Concord, North Carolina, 1893, and Moody Bible Institute, Chicago, Illinois.
- Twelve honorary degrees.[3]
- Educator
  - » Haines Institute, Augusta, Georgia; Kindell Institute, Sumter, South Carolina; Palatka Mission School, Florida; Founder, Daytona Normal and Industrial School for Negro Girls.
- Founder and president, Bethune-Cookman University, Daytona Beach, Florida.
  - » First black woman to establish a university.
- Director of Division of Negro Affairs of National Youth Administration.
  - » First black woman to head a federal agency.
- Founder, National Council of Negro Women; representative of NAACP to the United Nations.
- Civil rights activist; led nationwide fundraising drive to pay poll tax for thousands of black voters.
- Political advisor to U.S. presidents Coolidge, Hoover, Roosevelt, and Truman.
  - » Coolidge and Hoover appointee to National Child Welfare Commission.
  - » Hoover appointee to Commission on Home Building and Home Ownership.
  - » Special advisor to President Roosevelt on minority affairs.
  - » Truman appointee to Committee of Twelve for national defense.
  - » Truman's official delegate to the second inauguration of president of Liberia, William Tubman.
- Inductee, National Women's Hall of Fame, 1973.

"Unnotable" Events:

- Witness to the lynching of a colored man—for being a colored man.
- Rejected for a missionary job in Africa (Negroes need not apply).

Other:

- Married in 1898 to Albertus Bethune.
- Son Albert—Bert—born in 1899. Husband left to find work in 1907 (never to return).
- Trusted friend and confidante to first lady Eleanor Roosevelt.

Yes, by the grace of God, that was my earthly résumé.

I was the fifteenth of seventeen children; most of my brothers and sisters had been sold into slavery—scattered. Mama and Papa kept track of all of us, knowing exactly who of us had been sold to whom. Our home, a log cabin we called the Homestead, was always neat, clean, and respectable because Mama—Aunt Patsy, as everyone else called her—demanded it. After emancipation, my parents scraped together enough money to buy a piece of land and gathered us all back together, and we stayed a close-knit family. We prayed every night, all of us on our knees. I loved to sing, and when we were working in the fields Papa taught me songs. I must admit that I was a bit of a goodie two-shoes (especially before I became a mischievous teenager), loving it when I could do anything better than my brothers and sisters. Sallie was the oldest. Then came Satira, Samuel, Julia, Kissie, Kelly, Carrie, Beauregard, Cecelia, Rebecca, Maria, Magdalena, William, Thomas, me (Mary Jane), Hattie Bell, and Monday.[4] I was always in the habit of doing for others, and I'd often cajole Mama into making soup for sick neighbors. *Mama had to watch me to keep me from giving away things, like my shoes, that were mine.*[5]

From as far back as I can remember, I wanted to go to school. "Someday you will," Mama assured me. I don't think she ever forgot my tears at the taunts of those two little girls. I was just seven, and Mama left me with them while she delivered their family's weekly washing. Picking up one of their books, I began to look through it. If only I could read, I remember wistfully thinking. "Could you . . . ?" Before I could finish asking, one of them pulled the book out of my hands. "Don't you know reading is for white folks? You can't never read. . . . You're black."[6] *I went away from there determined to learn how to read.*[7]

As young as I was, that was a pivotal event. *It was possibly the first and real wound that I could feel in my soul and my mind—the realization of the dense darkness and ignorance that I found in myself . . . the lack of opportu-*

nity. I could see little white boys and girls going to school every day, learning to read and write; living in comfortable homes with all types of opportunities for growth and service and to be surrounded as I was with no opportunity for school life, no chance to grow.[8]

My parents believed in education, but they were too poor to send all seventeen of us to school. They could send only one, and it was me! I'm not real sure why they chose me, though. Oh, I did have an eye for arithmetic, and Momma had always said I was different. I was more independent, perhaps. Or maybe it was because, out of the seventeen, I was the most homely!

At any rate, I was eleven, thrilled to be a student, and gladly walked the five miles each way, every day. At home I shared everything I learned with my brothers, sisters, and other children in the neighboring farms, opening up our world. Miss Wilson was my teacher. *Miss!* Up until that first day at school I had never heard anyone use a title to address a colored person.

My education, however, was soon to be stopped short, jeopardized by the demise of the family mule. You see, Old Bush, our work mule, the biggest contributor to the family's income, suddenly up and died. The immediate future looked grim: there wasn't a penny left for things like schooling. Besides, I was strong and could pull the plow. Imagine my amazement when, from out of the blue, a complete stranger—a dressmaker from Denver, no less—gifted me with a scholarship! Oh glory day! When I heard the news *I pulled my cotton sack off, got down on my knees, clasped my hands, and turned my eyes upward and thanked God for the chance that had come.*[9]

It was 1887, and I was headed to the Scotia Seminary in Concord, North Carolina, about a hundred-mile train ride to the north. This was a victory for the entire town, *and all of the neighbors stopped work that afternoon, got out the wagons, mules, ox-carts; some riding, some walking. They were going to Mayesville to put me on the train to go to school.*[10] Oh my, what a train it was—*my little heart was going pit-a-pat.*[11] Cushioned red seats, glass windows, and polished ceilings. No one cared where I sat. Oh, was there ever a queen on a throne who had it better than I did? Even more grand was what I saw out the window. I had never seen such wide-open space, and it made me want to see the whole world. My adventure was to be a dream come true, thanks to my sponsor, Miss Mary Crissman, a Quaker from Denver. I'll never forgot that train ride!

My first night at the school was another milestone; I got to sit at a table with a white linen tablecloth and a plate all to myself—I didn't have to share it with anybody! And waiting for me, right alongside that plate—a fork! Never had I laid eyes on one, but I was not intimidated to show my ignorance, for I thought there was only goodness in people. *"You'll have to show me, ma'am*, I said to the teacher sitting next to me. *Forks are just for white folks in Mayesville!"*[12]

I loved life at Scotia and I loved everyone there. Never once having stage fright, I was the spokesperson of the group and the leader of the square dances. I recall one day—I was hanging laundry—when I came to a very profound conclusion about life. If my life were to be filled with love, then I must first give it. I must have been rather mature—or practical—for my age, don't you think? Or perhaps my teachers had taught me well the merits of poise and serenity. I was not an outstanding student in terms of high grades, but Miss Crissman was happy with them, and that's what counted. I was, however, *the prize winner in making breads and cakes; and a fine scrubber. I worked in the big kitchen in the morning, getting in the coal and starting the fires. Nothing was too menial or too hard for me to find joy in doing, for the appreciation of having a chance.*[13]

I went back home for summer break, and with the little bit of extra money I earned I bought a fork and a toothbrush for everyone! Neighbors came from all around, with questions about everything. Did the boiling of water really make it safe? Could I teach them how to trim a hat? Could I teach them how to read the cotton scales so as not to be cheated? There were so many "visitors" that I decided to hold a class one night a week. I would read to them from literature and from the Bible, and we would sing. Oh, what a glorious sound!

By the end of that first summer I had my heart set on going to Africa—to the place where Grandmother Sophie had been born. I would teach people to read and teach them about health and cleanliness. I had graduated from Scotia, and Miss Mary Crissman agreed to continue to support me through the Moody Bible Institute in Chicago. I had been able only to afford travel back home twice during those seven years at Scotia, but I was ready and able to take on a new adventure; I was a different person, educated, worldly, and ready for anything—or so I thought.

And that's when I came face-to-face with Jim Crow.[14]

Jim Crow segregation was hatred, bigotry, and supremacy enacted into state law and sanctioned by the federal government. I could no longer ride in a bus or train with white people, go to school with white people, be treated in a hospital, eat in a restaurant, stay in a hotel, or attend movies with white people. I could not use a restroom or drink out of a water fountain used by white people. I could not be their neighbor. My trip to Chicago was in the baggage car, sitting on a wooden bench. I never forgot *that* train ride, either.

Out of the seven or eight hundred or so students, I was the only American Negro at Moody Bible Institute. Even so, I experienced a racial harmony with my classmates, learning that ignorance was the reason the outside world could not live with the same sense of community. My classmates and I spent the next two years focused on our goals. Every one of us wanted to be a missionary to Africa. Even before we graduated we all knew our mission destinations. All of us did, that is, except me—I did not get an assignment. The Presbyterian mission board denied my request because I was a Negro. [15] Though it hurt me deeply, I knew that God had a purpose for me. What could I do but concentrate on a different future? I trusted that God had something else in mind and would show me in due time. My singing instructor suggested that I could have a good career on the concert stage. I thanked her for the compliment, but I wanted to give back something for all the goodness that had been given to me.

I packed up and went home. Sister Sallie teased me about still wanting to be a missionary. "You've got those *somedays* again," she said. That's all right, I thought, I will always have the *somedays*, wanting a better life for all my brethren.

I was trained to be a teacher, so that's what I would do, right at home. After a year of helping Miss Wilson, I found a position at the Haines Institute in Atlanta, Georgia, a school for Negro girls and boys run by the Presbyterian Church. As it was a mission school, it seemed logical that the first thing I should do was round up the street urchins and bring them in. That's just what I did. [16]

I soon got the *somedays* again. I wanted my own school, and wanted it to be a living part of the community. I dreamed of teaching students a skilled vocation, but also wanted it to be a place where students could learn about the world. Yes, a school that would teach someone how to be a responsible citizen—a place where all people were valued for the content of their character and where Jim Crow was no longer welcome. I'd have to start from scratch, but someday I would have a school—built with red brick—with many students, boys and girls. The dream would have to wait awhile, though; there was a math class to teach.

An opportunity to teach closer to home opened up, and I moved to Sumter. That's where I met Albertus. He charmed me with his sweet poetry and our bike rides. We married in May 1898. Bert, born February 3, 1899, was my parents' ninetieth grandchild.[17]

I knew I was destined for something—I felt it! It was a trip to Daytona Beach that made me think my *someday* had arrived because I discovered a great need for a school among the workmen's families. It was 1904, and I was twenty-nine. With $1.50—and plenty of faith—I opened the Daytona Literary and Industrial Institute for Negro Girls. Lena, Lucille, Ruth, Anna, Celeste—and, of course, Bert—were my first students. In the beginning we dipped our pencils, shaved from charred wood, in elderberry juice to write, my students sat on soapboxes, and my desk was a barrel turned upside down. We didn't mind a bit. *I plunged into the job of creating something from nothing. Though I hadn't a penny left, I considered cash money as the smallest part of my resources. I had faith in a living God, faith in myself, and a desire to serve.*[18]

People saw how determined and industrious we were and pitched in, and I had no problem asking complete strangers to help. Many times we'd find food, flowers, or soap left on the doorstep. My girls and I made sweet potato pies every day and sold them to the workmen. The girls tended the farm animals that provided eggs and milk, and every child had their own garden plot. My students maintained a strict code of conduct. In addition to vocational skills, the curriculum included Bible studies and high-school-level courses in math, English, foreign languages, business, and science. Eventually hospital and nurses' training programs were added.

From five students we grew to one hundred and quickly outgrew our little space; I had to find some property and build. Unfortunately, the only land I could afford was occupied by the town dump. It was called Hell's Hole, for obvious reasons. With the help of others, I bought the place and we cleaned it up, using much of what we found in the dump to build Faith

Hall, one brick at a time—which I sold as an investment in the future at ten cents a brick.

I recall one afternoon that several of my students came to me with some important news. At least it was important to them. They had decided they wanted to concentrate solely on their studies and therefore should be released from their daily, mundane list of menial chores. *"Girls, there is no such thing as menial work,"* I told them, *"just menial attitudes. Remember our Bible verse from last week? For God so loved the world?"* Yes, and they finished it in unison: "that He gave His one and only Son, that whoever believes in Him shall not perish, but have eternal life." *All right,* I said. *God loves you . . . That is where your dignity comes from—not what you do or what you have. Now wash up and let's start these potatoes. I have stories to tell.*[19]

I knew that I would have to have the backing of important businessmen to be successful. It turns out that Daytona Beach was the winter home of many wealthy people. Mr. Gamble (of Procter and Gamble), Mr. White (of White Sewing Machine Company), and Mr. John D. Rockefeller agreed to be trustees of my school. They also invited me up north, where they lived most of the year, to tell my story there. Like a stone thrown into the stream rippling wide, I was able to expand my sphere of influence. One invitation led to another, to another, and to yet another. With their help, we grew to a school of two hundred fifty. My gift, it turned out, was in selling a better way of life. *Any idea that keeps anybody out is too small. . . . Open your heart and let everybody in—every class, every race, and every nation. We must remake the world. The task is nothing less than that.*[20] That was my message. That's what I promoted. To each audience I would begin with *"Here I stand, Mary McLeod Bethune. Let me tell you what I was and what now I am. I am only a humble servant of the Lord. What does He want of us all? With your help other little girls can rise as I have done."*[21]

And to my fellow sisters, so hungry for an education, I would say: *"Go ahead climb. Climb to the very top of your profession. You have every right to be on top but you must remember to lift others as you climb."*[22]

And so it went. Some said it was my fierce determination, courtesy, and goodwill that overcame my encounters with hatred and bigotry. *I was shown goodness in my childhood. My parents believed in me. I learned to believe in other people. To be sure I saw trouble and the way was not easy; but I have thanked God and said Glory Hallelujah!*[23] I walked out of those cotton fields and climbed to the top of the mountain, so to say.

I wasn't the kind of woman to sit back and rest on my laurels. Needs of others became needs of mine, and I championed many causes in the areas of civil rights, women's rights, and education. Colored people couldn't set foot in a hospital—no matter the emergency—so I opened one. I knew that colored boys were also in need of an education, and so after my girls' school was well established, I merged with the Cookman Institute (for men and women) in 1923. By 1941, and with a lot of hard work, our school had grown into an accredited four-year institution. (In 2007 it became a university: Bethune Cookman University in Daytona Beach, Florida—still going strong!) In 1942 I moved on, became politically involved in the fight for equality at the national level.

I traveled all over the world—was even blessed by the Pope! My dreams came true because of Miss Mary Crissman, and, through her, so did the dreams of thousands of others. Could you be a Miss Mary Crissman to someone?

An education had not been available to my mother—and she was of African nobility. She had not been born free, but *I was my mother's daughter, and the drums of Africa beat in my heart. They would not let me rest while there was a single Negro boy or girl without a chance to prove his worth.*[24] *We fought for America with all her imperfections, not so much for what she was, but for what we knew she could be.*[25]

At the end of my earthly journey, the *Atlanta Daily World* pronounced my life to have represented "one of the most dramatic careers ever enacted at any time upon the stage of human activity."[26] Oh, Lordy, you should have seen the grins on the faces of my brothers and sisters up here!

I put my faith and trust in the Lord, and he was right there with me every step of the way. Now that I'm here with him I can look back, graciously, on those early days of picking cotton. I'd be the first to tell you that it's not where you start that counts—it's where you end. Jesus taught me to look back with thanksgiving on those days of picking cotton. He led me from those cotton fields to the top of the mountain. His mountain, so to say.

◆　◆

"Jesus replied: "'Love the Lord your God with all your heart and with all your soul and with all your mind.' This is the first and greatest command-ment. And the second is like it: "Love your neighbor as yourself."'"

Matthew 22:37–39

"For we are God's handiwork, created in Christ Jesus to do good works, which God prepared in advance for us to do."

Ephesians 2:10

"And do not forget to do good and to share with others, for with such sac-rifices God is pleased."

Hebrews 13:16

- ▶ Have a look at her university: http://www.cookman.edu/.
- ▶ Read more about her legacy through the National Park Service, Mary McLeod Bethune Council House: http://www.nps.gov/mamc/index.htm.
- ▶ Dr. Bethune's last Will and Testament is quite inspiring. Read it here: http://www.freemaninstitute.com/bethune.htm.

— 12 —

Aimee Semple McPherson

1890–1944

Who are the best-known people in American history? With whatever list you devise, in the 1930s and 40s Aimee would have been near the top of most lists. In her day, women weren't typically preachers or champions of the poor, and certainly not empire builders, as she was. Not to mention that she cut off her long hair! Scandalous! By doing all those things, Aimee championed a cultural revolution. She felt the love—and the heat. *"Pants don't make preachers,"*[1] she said, and set out to follow God's call.

I was a simple farm girl.[2] Brought up in Ontario, Canada, I loved to parade around the barnyard, bang the drum, and preach Salvation Army messages to the chairs lined up in a row.

Like most teenagers, I thought I knew everything. I was thrown quite a curve, however, that day in school when the teacher spoke of the unfathomable. People evolving from wriggling sea creatures? Of course that couldn't be true! Oh, but what if it were? And if that were the case, what else in the Bible might be wrong? Pressing anyone who would argue the topic of evolution, writing letters about it to the local newspapers, I couldn't quiet my curiosity. I vacillated between believing in God and total disdain of those who did.

It was that little sign in the store window that changed everything. One December morning in 1907, Father and I were in town. "REVIVAL MEETING, Robert Semple, Irish Evangelist,"[3] the sign said. "Let's have a look, Father," I laughed. "Let's go see people who fall down and babble who knows what?" We went, and at first *I giggled with amusement*[4] at the goings on. But then Robert began to preach, and *cold shivers ran up and down my back. . . . The voice of God thundered into my soul*,[5] and I was never the same again.

It didn't hurt that Robert was six-foot-two, charismatic, and good-looking. But more than that, I saw heaven's light reflected in his eyes, and was it not perfect to fall in love with God and Robert at the same time? In 1908 I chose faith, letting the Holy Spirit baptize me with all heaven's angels rejoicing. *"God be merciful to me, a sinner!"* I cried, and *with that a great peace fell over me*.[6]

My faith assured, I fell into a new brand of anxiety. *How can the Lord do so much for me, and I do nothing in return? Lord, what can I do in return for you? And to that I heard a voice, clear and booming: "Now that you, yourself, have been saved—go help rescue others."*[7] But how could I, a woman, be a preacher?[8] Yet God's call was strong, and I would be led. With an innocence regarding life's harsh realities—What does a seventeen-year-old know of the world?—I persevered, never imagining what lay ahead.

Robert and I married later in 1908 in—what else?—a Salvation Army ceremony, his destiny and mine joined in a desire to save souls in China.[9] Just months after we arrived, however, both of us contracted malaria. My sweet beloved Robert died! Our daughter, Roberta, was born soon after his death. It was 1909, and I was far from home, devastated and penniless. Widowed at nineteen, I returned to New York, to Mother, who by that point lived there.

And that's where I met Harold McPherson. In 1912 we married, and a year later Rolf was born. Despite Harold's reluctance, he and I traveled up and down the East Coast on the Sawdust Trail, preaching in tent revival meetings. I often spoke in tongues or interpreted someone else who was doing so—whatever the Holy Spirit called me to do.[10] (Roberta and Rolf stayed with my parents.) Mother promoted our work—she was good at that—and the news spread, filling the huge tents night after night after night.

The crowds loved the gospel message, and I loved preaching. Harold didn't like it, though; he wanted a stay-at-home wife who would raise children, clean house, and have supper ready—that was, after all, what a good wife did in the 1910s. I tried. For four years I tried, but all it brought me was depression, along with mysterious, life-threatening illnesses and surgeries. I kept hearing God ask, "Will you go?" I made excuses. Finally, near death, the doctors called my family in for our final goodbyes. Once again I heard, "Will you go?" This time I said yes. *Immediately new life and warmth surged through my being.*[11] As soon as my will became his, I was healed. Within a day or two I was home.

Harold was finished with the Sawdust Trail, but he said of me: "Darling, I had no idea you could preach like that. You must never stop."[12] He filed divorce proceedings, citing abandonment,[13] and in 1921 the divorce became final.

With two kids in tow, our friend Mabel Bingham, a hundred dollars, and in a 1918 Oldsmobile,[14] Mother and I took to the road. I called the car the Gospel Auto, artfully painting the words "JESUS IS COMING SOON—GET READY" on one side and "WHERE WILL YOU SPEND ETERNITY?" on the other. The convertible was our transportation during the day and our living quarters at night—ours was a gypsy life. I'd stand in the back seat with a megaphone and preach—eight to ten times a day—covering twenty to thirty miles each day. When I wasn't preaching Mother would drive and I'd peck away on the Corona typewriter, typing out sermons or articles for my magazine, the *Bridal Call*.[15] The roads were treacherous or nonexistent—traversable only by trained mechanics. We did it anyway, traveling across the country—four thousand miles.[16] It was mostly believers or seekers at these meetings, but some came to gawk at something they had never seen before: *white and colored attending the same place of worship and glorifying the same Lord side by side.*[17]

Preaching and writing—that's what I did. Healing—that's what Jesus did; I was only the conduit. Above all, I never wanted the physical healing to overshadow the healing of the Spirit. God did *not heal that the sick may take up worldliness and travel in sin again.*[18]

There was another side to this life. Our days were joy-filled with eager crowds. But then everyone would go home, and it would become very quiet. We'd pack up the tents and the gear, shipping them on to the next destination. We'd wash clothes in the streams, spend the night in the car, train depots, or out in the open—if the mosquitos weren't too bad. I would've loved something more than, say, a can of corn for our dinner. The children wanted their own beds.

God knew just how much we could endure and called us to Los Angeles. By now people knew about me—mainly through newspapers and the *Bridal Call* magazine.[19] There we rented the biggest hall we could find—the 3,500-seat Temple Auditorium[20]—and prepared for a full house. Fill it we did; people waited for hours to get in. For every service there was standing room only. Grateful Los Angelinos, wanting us to stay, built us a home. Someone donated the land and volunteers built the house. We called it "The House that God Built."[21]

We were going to need a bigger church—that much was clear. We found the perfect piece of land in Echo Park on Glendale Blvd. Persuading the contractor to accept money as we raised it was a miracle in itself, but that's just what we did. We went back on the road, traveling across the country to raise money—the average donation being about eighty cents.[22] Newspapers would announce my arrival, calling me a "Faith Healer." (I hated being called that and told the newspapers so, but they did it anyway.) We stockpiled the crutches, canes, braces, and eyeglasses from those who no longer needed them. Letters and money flooded in. Donation basket by donation basket, we raised the $250,000 needed to build the temple.

The church's dedication on January 1, 1923, became part of the city's biggest event of the year. We started off the day with a float in the Pasadena Tournament of Roses Parade, winning the Grand Marshall Trophy! An afternoon dedication of the Angelus Temple followed. There was a capacity crowd of 5,300, and we all rejoiced and worshiped with music and prayer.

To become a winner of souls, you first had to get their attention. *If you want to make rabbit stew, first you have to catch the rabbit.*[23] Every Sunday in the Angelus Temple we gave the congregation illustrated sermons using huge moving sets, a cast of hundreds, live animals, a fifty-person band, and worshipful singing—whatever it would take for them to remember and to think. No nodding off, that's for certain! Writing and preaching ten to fifteen sermons a week, performing weddings and funerals, and taking care of business—it was a good thing I only needed four to five hours of sleep a night.

Wherever we went, whether in a temple or a tent, the place would be packed. Loudspeakers outside quieted overflowing crowds. Police would have to clear folks away from the doors or tent openings after each service just so those inside could get out. At the temple we'd have to search everywhere after the last service to find those hiding in the closets, bathrooms—every nook and cranny. They wanted to spend the night and so assure themselves of a seat inside for the next day! These crowds weren't rare; this happened all the time. In 1924 Echo Park was jammed with 50,000 people a week. We loved that people who vacationed in Los Angeles put Angelus Temple on their must-see list. That meant they would return home carrying the gospel message—that Jesus is Savior, Healer, Baptizer, and Coming King—back with them to their own church—or, not having one, would write to Angelus Temple asking about a church in their community. Hallelujah!

Mother also helped the newspaper reporters document healings and identify the pretenders and con artists. Recording names and addresses, the reporters would conduct interviews before and after each service. Some concerned physicians recruited the American Medical Association to send in doctors undercover to authenticate the healings.[24] What did they see? *"In the name of Jesus Christ of Nazareth, Rise up and walk,"*[25] I would command. The lame walked, the deaf heard, and the blind saw. Broken bones were healed, bruises receded, and children walked out of there, cured of polio. Not everyone was healed; I had no control over that. I did know that *if the eyes of the people were set on ME nothing would happen. I would pray and believe with others who pray and believe, and the power of Christ worked the cure.*[26] I was scared to death over what was expected of me. Would the ever-increasing crowds[27]—as many as fifty thousand at a time filling the auditoriums, theaters, opera houses, pavilions, and boxing rings—give credit where credit was due—to God? Often my work took me into the midnight hours. I became so exhausted that I couldn't sleep. *Severe insomnia set in and plagued me for the rest of my life.*[28] The doctor prescribed one nightly sleeping pill as a remedy.

Race, creed, or someone's place in society was of no concern to me, and I used contemporary stories to replace the condemning fire-and-brimstone rhetoric of the day. *Look at the plight of the elderly Negro man who wanted to worship in the big beautiful city church, I'd say. Stopped at the door, he was not allowed in but directed instead to a smaller church—for 'his kind.' Too weary to go on, he sat on the church steps, weeping. A stranger approached and put his hands on his shoulders. 'Don't be sad,' he said. 'I too have been trying to get inside for many, many years.' The old man looked up and into the compassionate face of Christ beside him.*[29] I'd let that sink in, and then tell them that no one has to be shamed—If anyone thinks they're broken beyond repair, let the love of Jesus Christ heal. For if God be for us, who can be against us?[30]

I used every opportunity to make a point, even at my own expense. The newspapers once made great jest over a speeding ticket—thirty-one in a twenty-mile-an-hour zone. The next week, congregants saw a long, winding road across the back of the church, a lone cross at the intersection, and me, sitting on a motorcycle in a policeman's uniform, holding up a sign saying "STOP! You're speeding to ruin." *If Christ were alive today, I think he'd preach modern parables about oil wells and airplanes—the things you and I understand. Things like being arrested for speeding.* Blasting the motorcycle's siren, I went on to preach of everyone's need to slow down when going past the cross. *Let him set the joy bells in your heart.*[31]

People may have come to see me—I knew that and promoted it. But I made sure they left seeing Jesus. They knew me by the long, navy blue cape I always wore, the red roses carried to every sermon, and the lilt in my voice. Some complained that for a preacher I had an inappropriate sexual aura about me—but, as someone jokingly observed, I didn't have to look like last years' warmed-over biscuits. (The culture was such that I once cut my hair, and some were so shocked that they left the church!) Others would say, "Never did I hear such language from a human being as flowed from the lips of Aimee Semple McPherson. . . . She would talk for an hour and a half, holding her audience spellbound."[32] I do think I had an innate gift of persuasion in which the love of Jesus showed through. I knew what people needed to hear. My agnostic friend Charlie Chaplain put it another way: "Half your success was due to your magnetic appeal, and half due to the props and lights."

The *Bridal Call* was distributed worldwide, 12.7 million people read my nationally syndicated weekly newspaper column, and in 1924 I built and operated radio station KFSG, it's signal reaching Australia. My voice became familiar. *"Lord, bless us and give us a soul shaking revival tonight. Let everyone in Angelus Temple, and listening over the air, the ships at sea, and wherever they may be, feel God's motivating power."*[33]

It was May 18, 1926, and I wanted to finish working on the day's sermon at the beach, so my assistant Emma Schaffer and I went to Ocean Park (near Venice Beach). I took a break to go for a swim, and Emma went to make a phone call. When Emma returned, I was gone, nowhere to be found. Over the ensuing days thousands swarmed the beach, and all-day, all-night vigils were held to search or mourn. The water was dynamited to raise my body from the depths. The only thing that surfaced, besides dead fish, were rumors: I was undergoing plastic surgery or having an affair, a baby—or even an abortion! (Never mind that it was public knowledge that I'd had a hysterectomy years earlier.) Nothing more than a publicity stunt, some insisted. Newspapers assigned fifty reporters to the story, including chartering two planes with photographers to scan the sea. They printed pictures of the "very spot" where I had dropped my robe to walk into the ocean. Nothing was sacrosanct; the type of lingerie I wore was hotly debated. A silent film was made. I was seen simultaneously, sometimes as many as sixteen times a day, all over the country. The former mayor of Venice suggested that a mysterious, thirty-five-foot long monster had swallowed me. The papers printed all of the rumors as though they were gospel truth.

On June 25, 1926, Mother opened a ransom note signed by the "Avengers." Out of the envelope fell a lock of my hair and a letter demanding $500,000.[34] In it they said that delivery instructions for the money would be sent a week later. What the kidnappers didn't know, however, was that I had already escaped. We were in a desert shack, and when they left me alone I freed myself by rubbing my wrist-bound ties against a rusty tin can and escaped into the desert, reaching the authorities in the Mexican border town of Agua Prieta. After spending time in a hospital across the border in Douglas, Arizona, I returned home.[35] Fifty thousand people greeted me at Central Station in Los Angeles.[36] Scores of firemen in parade uniform were there, and an airplane flew low overhead, dropping roses over the crowd.[37] *Imagine, if you can, the joy of that reunion between pastor and people, the reuniting of the little under shepherd and the flock.*[38] I thanked God that he had spared me.

The Los Angeles newspapers saw this as an opportunity to make lots of money and increase their subscriber base—they made me daily front-page news. The *Los Angeles Examiner* offered ten thousand dollars for information leading to an arrest (not to solve the case but to fuel the fire). The Chamber of Commerce, embarrassed by the wrong kind of attention, sought to discredit me by claiming I had faked a kidnapping to cover up an adulterous affair. The district attorney convened a grand jury. Twenty-three days of testimony and eighty-eight witnesses later, Judge Blake issued a stop order in the search for kidnappers and instead held me over for trial on charges of criminal conspiracy to commit acts injurious to public morals and to prevent and obstruct justice.

Fueled by the newspapers, the public hung onto every word. Grandstands were erected in the courtroom; letters to the editor burned from one direction or the other. Preachers weighed in, some for me and some against. Vendors sold souvenirs on the street. The hearing lasted for a good six months and cost half a million dollars.[39] (Too bad they didn't spend that much time, energy, and money on finding the kidnappers. And how ironic that the *New York Times* devoted as much ink to the trial as they did to the Scopes Monkey trial.) For weeks on end I was vilified—called every name conceivable. I never changed my story, though the prosecution couldn't keep theirs straight. There was no evidence whatsoever—not even a fingerprint at the supposed love cottage in Carmel.[40] Finally, all charges were dropped. It was January 1927.[41]

That hearing was much more than about the *violation of public morals*—I knew that. Women were meant to stay in the background—a woman preacher, in the minds of many, so inappropriate as to be out of the question. But did not the prophet Joel prophesize that "the LORD will pour his Spirit on all people. Your sons and daughters will prophesy?"[42] And what is prophesy? The apostle Paul says, "Everyone who prophesies speaks to men for their strengthening, encouragement, and comfort."[43] And I also stand by Paul's directive to pray for one another. *Well, I'm one, . . . and you're another!*[44]

The hearing was also about politics and envy. In three-and-a-half years our church, the International Church of the Foursquare Gospel, had grown to epic proportions, while attendance at other churches in the area had declined, their income and prestige threatened. Politicians and educators vehemently opposed my opposition to evolution. Powerful criminal organizations didn't want me shining light on their drug trafficking, prostitution, alcohol, and loansharking activities. I had powerful enemies.

It was 1931, and my mother and children had all married and moved out of the parsonage, and I found myself completely alone.[45] There can be such an aching loneliness in the spotlight. *At the end of each day, our dear people and my children would go to their homes arm in arm, with their tender words and little caresses, while I would sit in silence, watching the last light extinguished in the big auditorium and the last happy couple disappear in the darkness.*[46] Loneliness was poor grounds for a marriage, I'll admit, and my 1931 marriage to actor and musician David Hutton ended a year later. Some said I had no right to marry another while Harold was still alive. I reasoned (rationalized?) that since Harold's subsequent marriage constituted infidelity, for which cause the Bible allows the dissolution of a marriage, I had not sinned. For some, however, the remarriage was scandalous.

Still I persevered. Angelus Temple had a duty to teach *and* to serve. A twenty-four-hour commissary fed anyone who walked in, no questions asked, and when it came to feeding the hungry all were treated equally. We fed and clothed a million and a half people in the 1930s and early 40s, far more than the city ever could have done or did.[47] In addition to the Bible college, which opened back in 1923, we added a laundry, nursery, sewing rooms, and employment programs. All in all, we had thirty-five separate working ministries (e.g., prison work, choir, lonely committee, missionary, and automobile club [providing transportation for anyone]). KFSG stayed on the air until 2003.

During my lifetime I baptized thirty-eight thousand at Angelus Temple alone, and we collected about twenty thousand prayers a month (all were followed up to ascertain and record results).[48] The museum at Angelus Temple houses crutches, braces, canes, eyeglasses, and wheelchairs discarded by those who were healed. (Go and see them.) The International Church of the Foursquare Gospel[49] today has eight million members worldwide, with eighty-six thousand churches and meeting places in one hundred forty-six countries.

On September 26, 1944, I was in Oakland—with ten thousand people expected for the next day's dedication of the new church. I spoke at the

Oakland Civic Auditorium Theater that evening and went home, excited about the next day. *The love of winning souls for Jesus Christ sets a fire burning in one's bones.*[50] During the night, however, my adrenal gland burst from a bacterial infection, and my nightly sleeping pill[51] went directly into my bloodstream instead of being oxidized through the liver, resulting in respiratory failure. I was fifty-three.[52]

I did live a very full life. I was human and made my share of mistakes, but I never lost sight of Jesus. He never changes; he is alive always for you and for me. After all, *Jesus is the great I Am, Not the great I Was.*[53]

◆ ◆

"Like the appearance of a rainbow in the clouds on a rainy day, so was the radiance around him. This was the appearance of the likeness of the glory of the LORD. When I saw it, I fell facedown, and I heard the voice of one speaking."

Ezekiel 1:28

"All of them were filled with the Holy Spirit and began to speak in other tongues as the Spirit enabled them."

Acts 2:4

"I commend to you our sister Phoebe, a deacon of the church in Cenchreae. I ask you to receive her in the Lord in a way worthy of his people and to give her any help she may need from you, for she has been the benefactor of many people, including me."

Romans 16:1–2

"Jesus Christ is the same yesterday and today and forever."

Hebrews 13:8

- ▶ See Aimee in action: https://vimeo.com/47660280.
- ▶ The Angelus Temple was once one of the top destinations for visitors in Los Angeles. It is open for services on Thursday evenings and Sundays. http://www.angelustemple.org/.
- ▶ Kathie Lee Gifford produced a Broadway play about Aimee titled *Scandalous*. Hear her talk about it here: http://www.playbill.com/video/exclusive-who-was-aimee-semple-mcpherson-kathie-lee-gifford-and-carolee-carmello-of-scandalous-explain.

— 13 —

Corrie ten Boom

1892–1983

How could one woman who lived her first fifty years above her watch repair shop in Haarlem, the Netherlands, reach millions of people with her message of faith? Well, she might say: *Three men, building a wall, were asked what they were doing. One said "I'm building a wall." One said "I'm earning money." One said "I'm building a cathedral." Have a vision, change the world.* [1]

Most everyone, at some time or another, has played the childhood game of hide-and-go-seek: run, hide, hold stock-still until it's safe to come out—oh, what cloak and dagger fun! In the 1940s world of Nazi occupation, though, this was a real-life "game" and no fun at all. Fraught with danger, your life depended on how well you could hide—in plain sight or otherwise. Your life depended on the secrets you could keep.

Living in Haarlem, the Netherlands, we ten Booms were a devout Christian family, and we considered it our privilege to pray for our Jewish brethren. For generations we prayed every evening for them.[2] We always helped everyone in need, too, believing everyone to be part of God's family.

The first floor of our home—our Beje—was the watch repair shop; we were watchmakers by trade—me, my father, and his father before him.[3]

Our shop was always a center of social activity, especially with all the go-ings on of our foster children. I enjoyed spending time with disabled chil-dren, too. I was an ordinary, everyday sight around our neighborhood. For fifty years mine was a very happy life. *We were not rich in money but in all other things, because the Lord was always with us—he was a member of the family.*[4] Life was pleasant.

Soon, however, nothing was ordinary, or pleasant. The shadow of the Second World War fell across us. Germany invaded the Netherlands in 1940, and I can still remember *the boots marching over the streets, thump, thump, thump.*[5] By 1942 we decided to become part of the underground. Fa-ther, sister Betsie, and I risked our lives every day to conceal Jews from the Nazi secret police, the Gestapo.[6] We tried to act normally, but these were frightening times. Strangers around our place were common enough not to arouse suspicion, and that was a good thing. Nazi informants, however, could pretend to be customers, or people needing help, and we had no way of knowing the difference. Even our neighbors didn't know what we were doing. It was just a good thing there were two entrances to our house. The one in the alley allowed people to come and go without being readily seen.

The everyday uncertainty and tension became too much for me, and I would often console myself with Daddy's comforting words to me when I was a child. "When you and I go to Amsterdam," he would say, "When do I give you your ticket? Three weeks before we go? One week?" *"Oh, no Daddy,"* I would say. *"Just before we get on the train."* "Exactly," he would respond. "And our wise Father in heaven knows when we're going to need things, too. Don't run out ahead of him, Corrie. When the time comes he will give you the strength you need—just in time."[7]

It was our faith that kept us strong and determined—what else could it have been? We never hesitated to help others, not for a moment. We became part of the Haarlem underground, working side-by-side with some eighty others to protect fugitives and resistance workers. We built a secret room upstairs, within the walls, for fugitives to hide in, no bigger than a small clothes closet. Reachable only on hands and knees, it had room for a jug of water, hardtack, and some vitamins. Everyone prac-ticed hiding drills all day and all night. We practiced until we could get the outsiders into the secret room within two minutes. In our nighttime drills we had to make sure we turned over the mattresses so there would be no warm spots. Imagine so many people coming and going from a house everyone knew to be home to just an old watchmaker and his two spinster daughters.[8]

Since I was a familiar face out and about, my task was to collect donated food ration cards and seek out courageous Dutch families willing to hide refugees. Some eight hundred people moved safely through our underground network. Everywhere suspicious eyes. Every moment filled with fear.

One day Jan Vogel walked into our shop. He was a Dutch informant, though I didn't know it at the time. He told me that his Jewish wife had been imprisoned for helping Jews, that he had arranged to bribe a prison guard six hundred guilders to set her free, and that he had come asking for help with the money. I told him to come back and I would give him everything I had. He did, and five minutes later—it was closing time on February 28, 1944—the Gestapo burst into our home and arrested everyone they could find—some thirty people. As hard as they searched, however, they never found the secret room. Oh, they knew it was there, somewhere. I heard one officer say to the others, "If there's a secret room here, the devil himself built it." It was there, all right, but the devil surely didn't build it. That hiding place, the one in which huddled those six terror-stricken fugitives and resistance workers, was pitch black and so small that all they could do was stand. They didn't dare move for fear of making a noise and being discovered. They didn't dare move until it was safe to come out. For forty-seven hours they didn't dare move.[9]

We ten Booms weren't so lucky. We were imprisoned. A Nazi officer offered freedom to Daddy if he would stop what he was doing. "If I go home today, tomorrow I will open my door to anyone who knocks for help. . . . It would be an honor to give my life for God's ancient people,"[10] he told them. Daddy, dear Daddy, died in prison ten days later. He was eighty-four.

I hated Jan Vogel.

Because I had been sick with a hacking cough, they had separated me from Betsie and put me in solitary confinement for three months in a dark, dismal cell. When well enough, I was summoned for interrogation. I told Lieutenant Rahms only that I had worked with the disabled. He sneered, telling me they had been "mercy killing" that kind for years. I looked him straight in the eye and said to him, *"In God's eyes a half-wit may be worth more than a watchmaker. Or—a lieutenant.*"[11] I was lucky, I guess, that I wasn't shot right then and there.

Betsie and I, now reunited, were put on a train, packed in like cattle, and after three days arrived at Ravensbrück, the women's death camp north of Berlin. Desperately hungry and frozen to the core, we were marched into the camp. The locals watched, but they never dared look us in the eye. Eventually we were taken to our barracks—there were dozens of them—but only after spending two nights outside on the ground, pummeled with the pouring rain from the violent thunderstorms. Betsie and I were assigned to Barracks 28, already overflowing with women. Built to hold four hundred, did they care when our numbers swelled to four hundred plus one thousand more?

As newcomers, we were forced to remove our clothing, throw our few possessions into a great growing pile, and parade naked in front of the leering guards. Panic stricken at the approaching discovery of my hidden treasure, my pulse raced as we inched forward in the line, fear clutching at my heart. What was I going to do with the small Bible hidden in a pouch hanging down my back—how was I going to get it by them? Betsie, scared to death, felt a sudden need for the toilet, and an annoyed guard let us out of line. "Use the drain holes," he snapped. "And then get back in line."[12] There was a bench in the shower room, and I hid the pouch underneath. On impulse I threw a little bottle of vitamin drops in with it, and retrieved the pouch later. (Little did I know how important that act would become to everyone in our barracks.)

They moved us to the showers, we dressed in flimsy prison garb, and once again the pouch was safely around my neck. Even though it was probably visible through my thin dress, I thought it was safe. But then they performed a second body check! Filing past the guards once again, they felt our bodies everywhere to make sure no contraband was smuggled past them. *Lord, make your angels untransparent,*[13] I prayed. A strange request, but God was way ahead of me. Systematically searching everyone else, the guards acted as though I wasn't even there; they didn't see me or touch me! The angels covered me, rendering me, and my precious contraband, invisible—I'm as sure of that as I have ever been of anything.

At Ravensbrück our days were the same.[14] Tens of thousands of us, standing at roll call attention for three hours in the pre-dawn cold. You didn't dare move. Then hard labor in gang details, all day long. You didn't dare stop. *Vernichtung durch Arbeit*—extermination through work—was the camp's operating principle. It didn't matter our age. I was in my fifties. If work—or the gas chambers—didn't kill us, disease, starvation, the cold, or despair would do its best.

The female guards were unbelievably cruel; they hated us for their own miserable lives. Hatred filled their eyes and spewed from their lips. Accompanied by dogs and zealous SS troops with whips, they needed only a little provocation, usually imagined, to unleash the dogs or beat us viciously.

We were subjected to unspeakable living conditions and obliged to witness depravity of the worst kind. Every cell, every barracks was crowded and filthy beyond belief. The straw mats were dirty, foul smelling, and scratchy, and there were so many of us we slept touching shoulders. The rooms jumped with bedbugs and fleas. Rats and roaches scurried across our bodies at night. The lice crawled across our faces and burrowed into our skin. The bugs were so bad that the guards wouldn't set foot past the barracks doorway, no matter what was going on inside. "The bugs," Betsie would say, "are a blessing!" I looked at her as though she were crazy. "How else," she smiled, "could we have gotten away with reading your purloined Bible aloud to the others?" We read it secretly every night, and soon the entire barracks began to listen, women translating the words into languages others could understand: German, French, Polish, Russian, and Czech. *Our Bible became the center of an ever-widening circle of help and hope.*[15]

Do you remember that little bottle of vitamin drops I also managed to sneak in? It was a little dark bottle; I never could see how much was left. Betsie was so weak that I wanted to save it all for her—to dole it out one drop at a time. But Betsie would share it with everyone, and soon a dozen or so would get their drop each day. *I knew about the oil in the Bible that never ran out,*[16] *but could this happen to us? And yet it happened, that day, and the next, and the next, until an awed little group of spectators stood around watching the drops fall on the daily rations of bread. Every time I tilted the little bottle, a drop appeared at the top of the glass stopper.*[17]

Many times I felt the Lord's companionship in a way I had never felt before or since Ravensbrück.[18] Sometimes I experienced times of hatred

127

and resentment. *I remember once I said, "Oh Lord all the stars are in your guidance, but have you forgotten your child Corrie ten Boom. But I read in the Bible that even the hairs of our head are numbered and God has all the Universe in his hands. That means that God has a telescope and a microscope."*[19]

Betsie taught me many things about forgiveness, and so even in the worst circumstances Betsie and I were able to show others that the one thing our torturers wanted to strip from us, yet couldn't, was God's love. We taught our fellow inmates that whenever they didn't feel like praising Jesus they were to ask him for the power to praise, for that is how circumstances are changed. Betsie and I practiced forgiveness with everyone. Others began to do likewise, and life in our barracks—Barracks 28—became a little more bearable—a little more civilized. Instead of fending for ourselves we began to look out for each other—not one of us was alone. Barracks 28 became known as the *crazy place, where there is hope.*[20]

As for the guards, we forgave them, too. Oh, we knew that forgiving another does not condone what they have done. The consequences, whether in this life or the next, are in God's hands.

Ravensbrück saw almost one hundred thousand women to their death. My sweet Betsie was one of them. Betsie somehow knew I would survive, though I had my doubts. Before she died she told me, "Corrie, your whole life has been a training for the work you are doing here in prison—and for the work you will do afterward."[21] She was right, I thought. *No athlete complains when the training is hard. He thinks of the game, or the race.*[22] With her last breath, on December 16, 1944, she extracted a promise from me to tell the world of the healing power of forgiving another—a power that is possible when one leans on God.

I knew that God could make a way when there was no way, but I would surely need a miracle to keep that promise! And that is just what happened. Three mornings after Betsie's death I was standing in my place for the 4:30 a.m. morning roll call when I heard my "name": "66730! Come forward—wait over there!" For three hours I stood in the freezing wind, not knowing my fate. I heard someone whisper the words "death sentence." But no, I was to be released! No one knew how or why. I was no one special, and even the SS officers themselves were baffled. What's more, a week after my release all woman fifty years of age and older were forced to walk into the gas chamber to make room for others. I was fifty-two.[23]

I would often reflect on those days in the camp, remembering how I had gazed bleakly out the window of Barracks 28 at the crematorium's smokestack. Oh, how we had longed to see colors! All those days of wondering when I would be one of the six hundred women who would daily walk into that death room were over. As I readjusted to life outside of the barracks, I became mindful of an old German motto: *What I spent, I had; what I saved, I lost; what I gave, I have.*[24] In my newfound freedom, though, I was surrounded by people who cared for everyday things, which were no longer important to me. I felt myself a stranger in my own land. And what would I do without my dear Betsie?[25]

Betsie had seemed mercifully oblivious to pain and despair.[26] At fifty-nine, she had been the kindest, gentlest person—yet she had died a prisoner, forgiving everyone who had put her in that situation. And with her death, God in his infinite grace had given me a gift that sustained me all my years. They didn't allow me to be at the hospital with her, so she died without me. I was outside when I heard the news and ran to her window to have a look whether I could see her, even though the pane was almost opaque with dirt. At first I wasn't sure it was her at all—why was an ivory statue lying there in her bed? But it was indeed Betsie, and I watched as two nurses folded her up in a sheet and took her away. I ran to where I thought I would find her, and I did. She had been skin and bones, but *there was my Betsie, her eyes closed as if in sleep, her face full and young. The care lines, the grief lines, the deep hollows of hunger and disease were simply gone. . . . Even her hair was graciously in place as if an angel had ministered to her.*[27]

I kept my promise to Betsie. Even though humanity's free will causes much pain in the world, as Betsie always said, *"there is no pit so deep that God's love is not deeper still."*[28]

At the heart of healing is forgiveness. The inability to forgive is a strange thing, built upon a foundation of stubbornness and wounded pride. One has every reason, should one so choose, to be nothing more than an interesting invalid, full of self-pity and self-righteousness. But *those who were able to forgive their former enemies were able also to return to the outside world and rebuild their lives, no matter what the physical scars. Those who nursed their bitterness remained invalids—prisoners. It was as simple and as horrible as that.*[29]

I also learned that just *forgiving* was not enough. I had to bury the sins of those who had hurt me in the deepest sea, never again to be dredged up. I could never have done that by myself.

I learned that unforgiveness would do more harm to me than the guard's whip,[30] and every time a remnant of bitterness returned I dealt with it anew. *So many times, we wonder why God allows certain things to happen to us. We try to understand the circumstances of our lives, and we are left wondering. But God's foolishness is so much wiser than our wisdom.*[31] *He has a purpose for those who know and trust Him. God has no problems—only plans!*[32] Whenever I would have hatred in my heart and think it would be impossible to forgive someone, I would pray: *Thank you Jesus that you have brought into my heart God's love through the Holy Spirit and thank you Father that your love in me is stronger than my hatred.*[33] And because I believed that with all my heart, I could forgive.

Betsie was certainly right about God preparing me for my life's work, even though I was approaching sixty. For *the coming decades* I lived out of a suitcase, traveling to sixty-four countries—from big cities to huts far back in the jungle—with our message of reconciliation and forgiveness. I also wrote many books. All I had to do was tell of my reality.

On February 28, 1977, exactly thirty-three years to the day after my family had been taken away by the Gestapo, I moved into a house in Placentia, California. People said, "Oh, you're going to retire?" And I said, *Yes! I will have new tires!*[34] The Lord had promised me that I would write more books and help to produce several films from that house, and because of that our message would reach more people than I had been able to do crisscrossing the world, meeting people face-to-face. I was so happy to be at rest. I had a bed to make in the morning! I named my house Shalom.

The Hiding Place[35] became both a bestselling book and a movie. Just as Betsie had envisioned, I helped to open rehabilitation homes for war victims, their disabled children, and perpetrators. The nation of Israel, newly formed, bestowed upon my Father, Betsie, and me the title of "Righteous Among the Nations." Born on April 15, 1892, I died to the earth on the same April day, ninety-one years later.[36]

Many times during my ninety-one years I found myself recalling the events of the past and contemplating what God had done for me and through me. *Such memories are the key not to the past, but to the future,* I thought. *I know that the experiences of our lives, when we let God use them,* become the mysterious and perfect preparation for the work He will give us to do.[37] Looking back enabled me to see forward. I could see eternity through the rearview mirror.

After the war I had heard that Jan Vogel had been caught and sentenced to death for causing the deaths of many Dutch people. I wrote him a letter—it was June 19, 1945—that said: *"Your betrayal meant the death of four of my family. I myself suffered very much in three prisons,[38] but I have forgiven you because the Lord Jesus is in my life, . . . and this is a fraction of the love and forgiveness that awaits you when you ask Jesus to come into your heart and confess all your sins. . . . And when they kill you—perhaps very soon—you can know that Jesus will have a house ready for you."* Jan wrote me back. "I was so amazed that you could forgive me . . . and because of that I have said yes to Jesus."[39] A week later he was indeed put to death.

There is a postscript to my story. While on the lecture circuit I discovered that I had more to learn about forgiveness. As I was finishing my story one particular time, I watched a man walk down the aisle toward me. Tears streaming down his face, he asked me to forgive him! He told me who he was, but he didn't have to—this former Ravensbrück guard I believed to have been responsible for my Betsie's death—I remembered him. *I stood there, the coldness clutching my heart. But I knew that forgiveness is an act of the will, and the will can function regardless of the temperature* [coldness] *of the heart. Jesus, help me! I prayed silently. I am human and all I can do is lift my hand. You do the rest. Woodenly, mechanically, I thrust my hand into the one stretched out to me. And as I did, an incredible thing took place. The current started in my shoulder, raced down my arm, sprang into our joined hands. And then this healing warmth seemed to flood my whole being, bringing tears to my eyes. I forgive you, brother! I cried. With all my heart!*[40]

Jesus can give you that same power—his supernatural power to forgive—and that's no secret. No secret at all.

◆　◆

"You are my hiding place. You will keep me safe from trouble. You will surround me with songs sung by those who praise you because you save your people."

Psalm 32:7 NIrV

"'If you do not forgive others their sins, your heavenly Father will not forgive your sins.'"

Matthew 6:15

"Hope does not put us to shame, because God's love has been poured out into our hearts through the Holy Spirit, who has been given to us."

Romans 5:5

"Do not be anxious about anything, but in every situation, by prayer and petition, with thanksgiving, present your requests to God. And the peace of God, which transcends all understanding, will guard your hearts and your minds in Christ Jesus."

Philippians 4:6–7

- ▶ Visit the Corrie ten Boom House in Haarlem, Holland.
- ▶ You can continue the ten Boom tradition of praying for the Jewish people and take a virtual tour of the ten Boom house: https://www.corrietenboom.com/en/home.
- ▶ Read of hope, forgiveness, Satan and his demons, living the single life, and chocolate (!) in Corrie ten Boom's uplifting book *Tramp for the Lord.*
- ▶ Learn more about the courageous people who risked their lives to help Jews during the Holocaust: http://db.yadvashem.org/righteous/search.html?language=en.

C. S. Lewis

1898–1963

"You'll never get to the bottom of him"[1] is how the Lord of the Rings author and good friend Tolkien characterized C. S. Lewis. Spontaneous and delightful, Lewis brought vitality and sensitivity to his work. He was a good listener, too. In his deep, rich voice he would regale his listeners with stories of wit and humor. One to never betray a confidence, he was a man of honor and a man of God, even if he was a most reluctant convert. *I believe in Christianity as I believe that the sun has risen: not only because I see it, but because by it I see everything else.*[2]

M y friends called me Jack, though I was born Clive Staples.[3] When I was five, my dog Jacksie died. He was my best friend at the time, and I thought it fitting to become Jack in his honor, refusing to answer to anything else.

I grew up loving words. Reading took me out of myself and became for me a world of great adventure. I became fascinated, too, at how weaving together just the right words could precisely express a thought that made logical, mystical, and spiritual sense. I had a flair for teaching the complicated in an uncomplicated way—a good thing because I wasn't much good at anything else.

I was born in 1898 in Belfast, Ireland, though I wasn't Irish—*I was more Welsh than anything.*[4] I had quite the imagination, and even as a child wrote lots of stories—some rather heady, others about animals that talked. I was a happy child, too, . . . and then quite suddenly I wasn't. Mother died. I had prayed in great earnest for her to get better, but she didn't, and at the time thought no more about it. And therein might have been the germ of my unbelief, for at ten years old I had a sense that life without her would be impossible.

By the time I was fourteen, I was convinced that the world was not a friendly place to live and that God didn't exist. I was one with the Roman poet Lucretius: "Had God designed the world," he said, "it would not be a world so frail and faulty as we see."[5] (Later, as an adult, I realized that part of my problem *was my deep-seated hatred of authority, my monstrous individualism, my lawlessness.*[6] I would not be interfered with, and I would *call my soul my own.*)[7]

I hated the school Father sent me to, and I didn't have a particular string of wonderful boyhood memories. There were exceptions, of course. When at home, my brother Warnie (Warren), who was my best friend and ally, and I didn't mind that Father was gone all day at his law office and that we didn't have any outside playmates. Maybe it was, for me, because what I loved to do was read—more than anything else—and I devoured every book I could get my hands on. Our house, Little Lea, was stuffed with books (my parents were bookish and clever), piled high on every table, corner, and shelf, for there were nooks and crannies, secret rooms, and passages everywhere—like a medieval castle! Even at a young age my heart and mind were filled with the imagery, poetry, and thoughts of the literary giants.[8] Greek literature and nature especially fascinated me. I became enthralled with Norse mythology—their gods more important to me than my *steadily growing doubts about Christianity.*[9]

When Father finally understood how awful school was for me, he sent me to private tutors. My teacher, Dear Old Knock, as I called him, properly engaged my brain, sharpening my skills in logic, reasoning, and debate. And it was Smugy, as I nicknamed another teacher, who taught me to love poetry, to read it as though it were song. Keats, Shelley, Wordsworth, Chaucer—it was all so marvelous. I especially loved heroic poetry, the deeds of aristocratic warriors and rulers taking me to faraway places. As I thought back on what gifts Smugy and Dear Old Knock had given to me, I realized *there are some experiences that paralyze you. You feel so much that you can't speak.*[10]

In the fall of 1916, I was awarded a scholarship to Oxford! I was sure I didn't do well on the exams but was told I had potential. Before that I had gone away to boarding school, and the only good memories that clung to me from there were the enlightening conversations with my friends. I remember one specifically, because it was probably my first metaphysical debate: *Was the future like a line you can't see, or like a line not yet drawn?*[11]

It's a good thing I had an almost photographic memory because I was too clumsy for anything but the intellectual. The coordination required for sports activities, driving, and even typing utterly eluded me. I once bought a car and attempted to learn to drive but could never get the hang of it. (Both Warnie and I loved being chauffeured.) Typing was altogether foreign—I never mastered it and wrote everything by hand. I did love to walk, though—daily contemplative walks and walking vacations—by myself or accompanied. Now if one could call skinny-dipping a sport, then by all means I was an enthusiast. The Kilns, where I lived from 1930 on, had a pond, and I would skinny dip every day. Even though the pond was somewhat dirty, I always came out clean! Oh, and I could also eat faster than any other human being.

Every place I lived was in constant need of repair. I didn't care about the state or quality of any household furnishings, either—which aligned with my nonexistent fashion sense. Nor were social skills particularly important to me—perhaps because they too required a degree of nimbleness. I could even posit that my *physical-ness* (or perhaps the lack thereof) determined my career, for all I could really do well was think and write.

As I said, I did have a love of words, and from an early age I displayed the gift of repartee. Father liked to tell of the time when, after a family holiday in France—I was about eight and rather immature—I told him *I had a prejudice against the French*. Father asked me what had brought that on. *"If I knew why,* I told him, *it would not be a prejudice."*[12]

Sometime during my late childhood I became acutely aware that there should be more to life than what I knew—what I *felt*. It was like thinking about a journey, one yearned for but not yet taken. This feeling was very real, but just out of reach—almost mystical, like a sense of things changing, yet not changing. Do you know what I mean? Like a feeling one might associate with happiness or pleasure, but certainly something more. I came to call this *something* "joy." Even more perplexing was that I came to think it might be the desire itself rather than the object desired. I thought that joy, in part, *must have the stab, the pang, the inconsolable longing*,[13] and I wanted "it." I was surprised by joy, and in the back of my mind somewhere—a glimpse perhaps—I thought God—if he existed—might be in the middle of it all.

I was seventeen, and the Oxford scholarship meant that I would be moving to England. (Such strange accents there—to my ears the locals sounded demonic!) On March 4, 1916, while waiting for a train home at the Great Bookham Station, I picked up a book at a nearby bookstall. It was *Phantastes* by George MacDonald, and I was anxious for a weekend of endless reading. Little did I know what I was in for. I remember the date well because the power of MacDonald's fantasy introduced profound new thoughts into my mind. His writing, so light-hearted, contained nothing of the dark elements of my favorite romanticists, and I found that righteousness didn't have to be dull! As I read, I inexplicably had those mystical thoughts again, that sense of things changing, yet not changing. *My imagination was, in a certain sense, baptized; the rest of me, not unnaturally, took longer.*[14] Was it joy, this something more than happiness and pleasure? This *thing* eluding me was almost otherworldly, much like a permanent longing, bittersweet in its sense of a transforming joy and fear and longing and pain rolled into one.[15] But I didn't believe in God, so what could this be? I'm getting ahead of myself, but this was, I would come to realize, a spiritual hunger, planted by God to point us to his Son. I would come to know this joy as *holiness*.[16]

I didn't have much time to settle in at college; by nineteen I was on the front lines in the Somme Valley in France, commissioned as a second lieutenant in the Somerset Light Infantry. It was 1914, and in the beginning, before the fighting, I had many a conversation with my friend Collins. With *whiskey on the table, the kettle on the hob, and our pipes drawing evenly*, we would talk all night, *reconstructing post-war heaven*.[17]

But then life became dangerous. This was World War I trench fighting at its worst, and its evil only strengthened my now full-blown atheism. My good friend and roommate, Paddy Moore, was killed in battle, and the sergeant who had earlier saved my life was blown up before my eyes. My wounds sent me to hospital, after which I finished out my service away from the battle lines until 1916. My thoughts were so conflicted: *I was very angry with God for not existing. I was equally angry with him for creating a world.*[18] *Why should creatures have the burden of existence forced on them without their consent?*[19]

It seems that I myself didn't know this Jack, but God did. He had other plans for me.

Back at university, I lost myself in school. Despite depression and homesickness, I excelled, taking the school's highest honors.[20] I was a writer. Disciplined. Precise. Particular in the use of each word. Expressing myself through the written word was something I could do in solitude, and that was good for me. I had no thoughts of God's role in my life. *The trouble about God is that he is like a person who never acknowledges your letters and so in time you come to the conclusion either that he does not exist or that you have got his address wrong.*[21]

I kept returning to MacDonald's words as ideas began to grow and take shape within me. I decided to pay attention to some of the things my friends were saying, who, apart from their Christianity, had always been exemplary. People like Owen Barfield, J. R. R. Tolkien (Tollers) and Hugo Dyson. I read the works of G. K. Chesterton, always longing for that something—just beyond my reach. I came, slowly, to realize that my desire was for *something* no human could fulfill, that my life had been all about limiting liabilities to avoid suffering. In the end, all that did was limit delight. Coming to a different conclusion about God was in no way what I wanted to do—but then again, as I would later find out, I was not in charge.

Paddy had asked me to take care of his mother if he were to be killed in action. This was a promise I was happy to keep. Mrs. Moore and her daughter Maureen lived with Warnie and me from 1921 on. We—Mrs. Moore, Warnie, and I—jointly purchased The Kilns, very close to Magdalen College at Oxford, in 1930. I wanted to be near Magdalen because in 1925 I had been elected a Fellow at Oxford! I was elated, and so was Father, bursting into tears of joy at the news. (While this meant the end of poverty for me, the frugal habits that had been required to get along stayed with me.) I served there as a tutor in English Language and Literature until 1954, when I left for Magdalene College, Cambridge.

My conversion to Christianity *was no sudden plunge into a new life but rather a slow steady convalescence from a deep-seated spiritual illness of long standing.*[22] I had come to distrust psychology and occultism and longed for an objective, traditional morality. In 1929 I realized that it was atheism that didn't make any sense. I knelt before God and gave myself over to him. I was a resistant, prodigal son, *kicking, struggling, resentful, and darting my eyes in every direction for a chance to escape.*[23] Two years later, on September 22, 1931, I took the next step and willingly surrendered to Jesus and Christianity. Oddly enough, this happened while I was on the way to the zoo with Warnie. He was on his motorcycle, as usual, and I was in the sidecar. I left not believing Jesus Christ was the Son of God, and when we arrived I did. And that was that. It was *like when a man, after long sleep, still lying motionless in bed, becomes aware that he is now awake.*[24]

There I was—practically a recluse, and then, almost suddenly, . . . I wasn't. *To believe in God and to pray were the beginnings of my extroversion. I had been taken out of myself.*[25] Together Warnie and I broadened our circle of friends. We called ourselves The Inklings, and we acted as buffers for each other against modernism—the philosophy of the day—which allowed no room for God. Just a few of us at first, and always on Thursday nights. Through the years there were about nineteen of us, coming and going. *My happiest hours were spent with three or four old friends . . . sitting up to the small hours in someone's college room talking nonsense, poetry, theology, metaphysics over beer, tea and pipes.*[26] We challenged ourselves. "Let's see who can write the best story from a single word picked out of a hat," we decided. I drew "space." Tollers drew "time." From that he wrote his Lord of the Rings trilogy and I my space trilogy.

It was 1939, World War II was raging, and all hands were needed. Well, apparently not *all*, as my re-enlistment attempt was denied. Instead I joined the Oxford City Home Guard Battalion. We also welcomed child evacuees into our home. Never having been around children, I welcomed this chance to make their acquaintance. One of the girls wondered what might be behind that big old wardrobe pushed close up against the wall. Hmmm, I mused. There might just be a story in that . . .[27]

Even though I didn't like radio and television, I realized its value in reaching people who would listen but not read, and I broadcast two years of weekly radio talks about God. Originally, it was just to be a few talks, but servicemen and civilians alike clamored for more. (Those talks were later compiled into a book, *Mere Christianity*.)

My teaching career at Oxford and Cambridge spanned nearly forty years. I was rather prolific, producing seventy-four books, selling one million copies in forty-seven languages. In fiction, nonfiction, and poetry I wrote essays, autobiographies, children's literature, poetry, satire, allegory, apologetics, science fiction, and literary criticism. The Chronicles of Narnia, a series of seven books targeting young readers but savored by an adult audience as well, became very popular. The first in the series was *The Lion, The Witch, and the Wardrobe*. (Remember the little girl's query?)

I was a former atheist with a love of logic, characteristics that helped me explain theology to both skeptics and believers.[28] For example, when people asked me to explain the divinity of Jesus, I would give them three choices—Jesus was either a lunatic, a liar, or Lord[29]—and explain the implications of each. I'll have to say, though, that the sterling defense of my choice (hint: Jesus was not a lunatic or a liar) really left no other option![30]

It's like salt—this faith business. Your first taste of pure salt, likely on the tip of your finger, would leave no doubt that it would overwhelm any other taste. You soon learned, though, that salt actually enhances other flavors. If belief in Jesus is overwhelming at first, trust that he will bring out the best in you. Let me tell you about a *post-Lewis* "Tom" and his taste-of-salt experience. One day Tom Monaghan, the founder of Domino's Pizza, picked up a copy of *Mere Christianity*. Reading that book caused him to rethink everything about his life, and he realized that his desire for wealth was grounded in pride—spiritual cancer at its worst. Then and there he changed and became a new man,[31] vowing to dedicate his money and his energy to pro-life causes and Catholic education. He sold his worldly passions, which included the Detroit Tigers baseball team, two hundred forty-four classic automobiles, and a thirty million dollar resort and dedicated the proceeds to his chosen causes.

My inspiration for the magical elements came from authors I had grown up with. There were plenty of unsavory characters in stories like Milton's *Paradise Lost* and von Goethe's *Faust*. These literary traditions influenced the creation of the Screwtape demons, though I must say that looking through the evil lenses needed to write *The Screwtape Letters* left a very bad taste in my mouth. In *The Screwtape Letters* I enlisted a senior demon named, oddly enough, Screwtape, to teach his nephew, Wormwood, about the best methods to secure a human soul. Screwtape counsels Wormwood that the process is quite simple and points out that there is no need to resort to frightful, evil behavior when gentle encouragement is far more effective. *The safest road to Hell is the gradual one—the gentle slope, soft underfoot, without sudden turnings, without milestones, without signposts.*[32] (By the way, Screwtape didn't get away with his bad behavior. He received painful punishment from Satan for revealing to Wormwood the truth of God's genuine, faithful love for us humans.) I once read a *New Yorker* magazine article (yes, we have access here) in which the U.S. Supreme Court Justice Antonin Scalia[33] surprised the interviewer when he told her he believed in the devil. "Haven't you read the *Screwtape Letters?*" he asked her.[34]

Then came another Joy altogether: Helen Joy Gresham. She wrote to me from America, and as was customary with anyone who sent me correspondence, either Warnie or I wrote back. Joy, this poet and writer, like me an atheist-turned-Christian, kept writing, and I kept answering. She came to visit, and then Warnie and I invited her and her sons, Douglas and David, to the Kilns for Christmas. We became friends—she even helped me move my office from Oxford to Cambridge. Soon we were meeting every day, collaborating on whatever it was I was working on. Our friendship became such that I was able to solve a thorny problem for her. Her visa was about to expire and would not be renewed unless she married an Englishman. Purely legal marriages were common—this is what our civil ceremony was—and we continued our separate living arrangements. It was 1956.

A few months later doctors diagnosed Joy with cancer. Thought to have originated in the breast tissue, it was terminal bone cancer. The finality of that diagnosis made us both realize what we meant to each other. We loved each other—desperately so—and remarried later that year in a Christian ceremony. At her hospital bedside, we asked the priest to include healing prayers in the wedding wows. I pleaded with God to take away her excruciating pain—to put it on me if that would make her well.

We waited—her death expected in days, or perhaps only hours. But quite suddenly and unaccountably she was healed! The doctors had never seen anything like it; a cancer-decimated pelvis simply doesn't rejuvenate itself. She came home, and *we feasted on love. Every mode of it.*[35] How could I, a bachelor of almost sixty, have discovered love—a love the likes of which I had never known, a love that suffused me with an insatiable desire for another human being?

Joy wasn't the only one who had been ill. By seeming coincidence, I was diagnosed with a bone disease myself: osteoporosis. A great deal of pain came with it, and I became unable to walk without a brace to protect my weakened spine from fracture. *The intriguing thing was that while I (for no discernible reason) was losing the calcium from my bones, Joy, who needed it much more, was gaining it in hers.*[36] Even more incongruous, however, was that by 1958 neither of us was in pain. It was a glorious time.

But then, three years later, Joy's cancer returned. She forced me to confront the suffering that would ensue once she died, to acknowledge that our very joy together would make the sorrow worse—it was part of the equation, a *universal and integral part of our experience of love.*[37] And though the anguish I experienced could not begin to approximate the unremitting physical agony she endured, her death brought me unbearable, inconsolable grief. [38] *No one ever told me that grief felt so like fear.*[39] I came through it, but it was difficult. *Her absence was like the sky, spread over everything.*[40]

Warnie and I together raised David and Douglas. To survive the pain of her death, I returned to my writing, and it was during this period that I wrote *A Grief Observed.* I couldn't bear to share my pain with anyone else, so I first published the work under a pseudonym: N. W. Clerk. Ironically, many well-meaning people insisted that I read it as a way to confront my own grief!

I never needed much money and remained frugal by habit. I lived on my salary as a university professor and directed the royalties from the sale of millions of my Christian books into a foundation to assist orphans, poor families, and others.

Three years after Joy died I was diagnosed with renal failure. Warnie became my constant companion and cared for me as only a brother and best friend could. We had many reminiscent conversations about long-forgotten days. He was too distraught to attend the funeral. I would have pointed out to him that I most certainly would have gone to his.

I left the earth in obscurity—and that was quite all right—for the world was busy elsewhere. Another Jack, also of Irish descent, took center stage, tragically, on that same 22nd day of November 1963. On that day the American president Jack Kennedy was assassinated.

A last word about my unending search for that elusive something I called "joy": it happens that I didn't give it much thought after I became a Christian—I didn't have to. *It was valuable only as a pointer to something other and outer.*[41] Suffice it to say that before you can know yourself, you first have to know God.

◆ ◆

"The heavens declare the glory of God; the skies proclaim the work of his hands. Day after day they pour forth speech; night after night they reveal knowledge. They have no speech, they use no words; no sound is heard from them. Yet their voice goes out into all the earth, their words to the ends of the world. In the heavens God has pitched a tent for the sun."

Psalm 19:1–4

"You will seek me and find me when you seek me with all your heart."

Jeremiah 29:13

"Though you have not seen him, you love him; and even though you do not see him now, you believe in him and are filled with an inexpressible and glorious joy."

1 Peter 1:8

▶ Visit the Kiln's, the Lewis residence in Oxford: http://www.cslewis .org/ourprograms/thekilns/kilnstour/.
▶ *Shadowlands*, starring Anthony Hopkins and Debra Winger, is a movie about the relationship between Jack and Joy. (Keep in mind, however,

that the real Jack did not have the stereotypical British demeanor displayed in the film, but a jovial, booming voice and a personality to match.)

► Rediscover the Chronicles of Narnia with a walk through CS Lewis Square in Belfast: https://visitbelfast.com/see-do/partners/cs-lewis -square.

► Wheaton College's Marion E. Wade Center is a marvelous resource for information: https://www.wheaton.edu/academics/academic -centers/wadecenter/authors/cs-lewis/.

— 15 —

Gladys May Aylward

1902–1970

As a young girl, Gladys wanted to be an actress. She gave up that idea to do something better and in the process became a superstar of sorts, her work becoming a cause célèbre. *My heart is full of praise that one so insignificant, uneducated, and ordinary in every way could be used to His glory and for the blessing of His people in poor persecuted China.*[1]

What a mess I was in. There I was, forced off the train in the middle of nowhere—in Siberia—thirty miles from the nearest outpost! I stood there, my back to that idled hulk, and all I could see were grey foreboding skies dimming into night, a dark forest blanketed in white, and the railroad tracks disappearing from sight. Oh, the icy wind whipped across my face. How bitter cold it was. What was I ever to do?

Life had begun simply enough. Born in Edmonton, London, I left school at fourteen to take employment as a parlor maid to help support my struggling family. Not at all fond of school, that was perfectly fine with me, especially since what I wanted was a life of excitement and adventure—as an actress! My dreams of holding audiences spellbound, me in the limelight, forever intact—or so I thought. I could work during the day and take drama classes at night. Oh, yes, life was working out just the way I'd planned.

Drama was to be in my life, all right, but nothing like I had envisioned.

I attended Sunday school as a child, but as I grew older *I became impatient with anything to do with religion.* You would never find me in a church, that's for sure. *One night, for some reason I can never explain, I went to a religious meeting. There, for the first time, I realized that God [and Jesus] had a claim on my life.*[2] My friends thought me barmy.

How serendipitous that at about the same time a *Young Life*[3] magazine article about China caught my eye. It staggered me to think that millions of Chinese might never have the opportunity to hear the Word. *I felt that sorely we ought to do something about it.*[4] I began urging my friends to go to China, but everyone thought I was crazy. I tried to talk my brother into it. "Not me," he said. "That's an old maid's job. Why don't you go yourself?" Old maid's job indeed, I thought angrily. *But the thrust had gone home. Why should I try pushing other people off to China? Why didn't I go myself?*[5]

One thing led to another, and there I was, resolved to abandon those acting dreams (gladly) for something better, to spread the gospel in China. Never mind that I had never even seen a Chinese person. Father was extremely perplexed!

China's missionary services, however, would have nothing of me. Oh, I was accepted into the Women's Training Home, but just months of it revealed my inadequacies. My language skills were barely tolerable, and approaching thirty I was too old, they said. I know they thought I was just too ordinary. Well, I guess I was, but that wasn't going to stop me. I would make my own way to China. A train ticket to Tientsin, China, was forty-seven pounds.[6] I saved every penny I could, and in less than two years I had my ticket.

Just where exactly I would go, I had no idea—yet, but I had better prepare for whatever lay ahead. I looked at my Bible. What was I thinking? *I don't really know enough about this to start preaching to other people,* I said to myself. *Maybe I ought to set about really getting to know it.*[7]

I started reading, now with determination and purpose: sermons, stories of missionaries, and about China in general. I read how God told Abraham to leave everything, every comfort he knew and go, and off he went. "Obey me," God said to Moses, "and leave Egypt." It was Nehemiah, however, who really spoke to me. He was an ordinary person, a kind of a butler, and he left his comfortable surroundings to rebuild the walls of Jerusalem. *As if someone was in the room, a voice said clearly, "Gladys Aylward, is Nehemiah's God your God?" Yes, of course!* I replied. *"Then do what Nehemiah did, and go." But I am not Nehemiah. "No, but assuredly, I am his God."*[8]

And then I realized I had no experience in preaching. So up on the soapbox I went, every free moment spent in Hyde Park. People going home from work walked by with nothing more than a curious stare, but I didn't care. I needed practical experience, too, and spent time wandering the streets at night near the docks in South Wales, talking to the homeless and the prostitutes, taking them back to the mission hostel when they'd let me.

China is a big place. Where should I go, Nehemiah's God?

A woman told me about a missionary in China who needed help. That was my cue. I wrote to this Mrs. Lawson and received an encouraging reply: "I will meet you in Tientsin if you can find your way out."[9]

My family helped me pack. My ticket, passport, Bible, Mrs. Lawson's letter, a fountain pen, and two one-pound traveler's checks went into special pockets mother had sewn into my underclothes. Some pennies went into my pockets. In a borrowed suitcase (needless to say it went unreturned) went a few clothes; crackers; cookies; hard boiled eggs; tea; and tins of meat, fish, and baked beans. I also had a bedroll, teakettle, saucepan and a fur rug that Mother had made out of an old, falling apart fur coat. I had nothing else—that would have to last.

I was ready. Family and friends[10] took me to the train at the Liverpool Street station. It was Saturday morning, October 15, 1932. I settled into a window seat and slowly waved goodbye to them as the train chugged away from the platform. Like Abraham, Moses, and Nehemiah, I left everything behind, trusting God to provide. I crossed the English Channel and boarded a Trans-Siberian train at The Hague.

This five-thousand-mile adventure would take me through Holland, Germany, Poland, and Russia to Tientsin, China, where I would be taken to Mrs. Lawson in Yangcheng in the mountainous province of Shanxi. Not even the lack of a sleeping car, which I could not afford, could dampen my enthusiasm. The long days were lonely, though, especially in Russia, for I didn't know the language, and no one else could speak English. On the ninth day—we were two days into Siberia by then, and oh, was it cold!—the train filled with Russian soldiers. I had been warned that Russia and Japan were at war and that this might compromise my journey, but I hadn't worried.

"Everybody off except military! Everybody off," the announcements rang out. Stopped at the Chita railway station, I think that's what I was hearing. But I had a ticket and was staying put—after all, I was a much-needed missionary! I later found out they didn't run me off because they thought I was a much-needed machinist![11] It turns out that a clerk in England had thought the word "missionary" on my passport was a typing error and changed it. I never noticed it.

Twenty days from departure, thirty miles outside of Chita, the train stopped, and there it would stay—the end of the line (beyond was the battlefield). Discovering my *real* occupation, and with no regard for my vigorous protests, a soldier shoved a hot cup of coffee into my hands, marched me off the train, and left me there! I was nine hundred miles from my destination.

And that is how I came to be standing all alone on those awful railroad tracks. What *was* I ever to do? Really now, I had no choice, did I? Strengthening my resolve, I wrapped that fur rug about me and began to walk, following those tracks the thirty miles back to Chita. Four hours into it I had to stop, eat, and sleep some. I drifted off to the sounds of howling animals, *wondering who let all those big dogs out at this time of night?*[12] (It's a wonder I didn't freeze to death.) I later learned that I was likely hearing a pack of wolves! Another day of walking, and I was back in Chita, weary, but safe and sound. A month's journey by boat, bus, and mule train got me, finally, to Tientsin. It was a physically rough journey, and *I thought I should be all broken in little pieces, but when I reached Yangcheng and found my arms and legs were still where they should be I thanked God for all his goodness to me. Mrs. Lawson was pleased to see me.*[13]

The long and short of it is that I devoted my life to helping others, giving them hope and strength to endure those hardships of war and poverty, and had quite a life of excitement after all. My story was even told in a movie starring the Academy Award-winning actress Ingrid Bergman:

The Inn of the Sixth Happiness.[14] (I was horrified by it. They renamed our inn, and I was told they glossed over the obstacles and challenges, Ms. Bergman was much too tall to be playing me, and they had me abandoning my children for a love interest! Never would I set my eyes upon it.)

But I'm getting ahead of myself. Arriving in Yangcheng in November 1932, Mrs. Lawson's *mission* was nothing more than an old, run-down house. She had just rented it, and we decided to turn it into an inn for the caravans of mule keepers.[15] We spent months cleaning it up, making repairs, and bringing in provisions. It had to have a grand name, of course, and so The Inn of the Eight Happinesses it became. We took care of the keepers and their mules—my reticence over tending to those nasty mules soon dispelled. We enraptured our guests with Bible stories at dinner. I became a storyteller! It was a time of endless adventure, and I was happy to be part of something bigger than myself. Despite the fact that the townspeople thought Mrs. Lawson and I were foreign devils, I knew that perception would change with perseverance and patience on our part. I could see myself happily spending the rest of my life there.

This was not to be. I had barely a year with Mrs. Lawson before she died. "God called you to my side, Gladys, in answer to my prayers," she told me on her deathbed. "He wants you to carry on my work here; He will provide. He will bless you and protect you."[16]

But what could I do? It would certainly be a lonely life (I had dearly wanted a husband and children), and I was the only European woman in that part of China. We had existed on Mrs. Lawson's small pension, and that was now gone.

As I saw it, God had brought me there, and it was up to him to fix it. The *fix* came with a knock on the door—a most unusual visit from the Mandarin of Yangcheng, a powerful imperial official. All that ceremony and grandeur—what would he ask of me? "Miss Aylward, I need your help because you have such big feet," he said. I looked down at my size three feet. (It turns out my feet *were* big because they weren't bound according to their ancient, excruciatingly painful custom of breaking and binding the feet of young girls.[17]) Their feet, sir? I asked. Yes. He needed me to travel throughout the countryside and examine girls' feet to assure the palace that the practice had been stopped. A man could not examine a woman's feet; I was the only one to do it. Well, I said—feeling a little like a movie

149

director—yes, provided I be allowed to speak of my faith. Accompanied by two guards for safety, I became the official Government Foot Inspector. How's that for a starring role! Along with that I was given a new name—a stage name, yes? I became Ai-weh-deh, meaning virtuous woman.

I was quite outspoken with my new title behind me. *"Listen,"* I would tell the women: *"If God intended little girls to have horrible stubby little feet, he'd have made them like that in the first place, wouldn't he? Feet are to walk with, not to shuffle up and down with, aren't they? I don't care if the husbands say you should do it or not. They should try it sometimes, and see if they like hobbling about on little club feet. Any man who tells you to do it goes to prison at once; that's the law now."*[18] It was delightful to watch the girls unbind their feet, wiggling their toes. They saw I was right, and that gave me much face, which is key to the Chinese spirit. I never tried to impose my Christian morality, either—just told them of Jesus's love for them. I let the limelight shine on Jesus and honed my storytelling skills, spellbinding the peasants of Shanxi. Slowly, one or two in a village would accept my faith, and a house church would be created. Through the years the gospel was preached and foot binding ceased. Eventually Ru Mai, a young Chinese widow with three children, would take over for me.

No longer the foreign devil, I became, in every sense, a Chinese woman. I wore their clothes, ate their food, and spoke their language with ease (me, who could not learn a thing out of a book!)—not to mention that I could spit with the best of them! In 1936 I gave up my English passport, became a citizen, and made an official petition to change my name. A stage name no longer—I was Ai-weh-deh.

God had even bigger roles in mind for me. I vividly recall when a wretched woman accosted me alongside the road. Would I buy her child! Outraged, I paid the nine cents for her—she was probably about four years old—adopted her, and named her Ninepence.[19] I nursed her back to health, news spread, and soon I had an orphanage full of bought-and-paid-for children. (Along the way, I gathered some adults to help.)

I had many talks with the Mandarin, and we became good friends. He didn't understand my faith, though, and was sure China's culture would never change to accommodate it. "We will always be a nation of peasants," he said, "miserable in our poverty because it is the will of the gods. Your God will be as a pebble in the great ocean." *Jesus Christ, I told him, the son of*

God, was born two thousand years ago. He was a Baby born of a humble mother in a stable in an insignificant village. Yet, because of the ripple he created, I am here, many thousands of miles away from my own land. "Ah," he said, "Is this why you care for the sick, midwife to the mothers, visit our criminals, and mother the unwanted?" *Yes,* I told him. "This must be a strong faith of yours, Ai-weh-deh," he marveled.[20]

It was 1938, and Japan and China became engaged in an eight-year battle. Japan invaded, and with a scorched earth policy burned, looted, and bombed their way across China, killing millions of civilians.[21] Because I was a woman and a missionary, no one paid attention to me, which meant that I could easily spy for the Chinese nationalists. Our mission was bombed, and people were killed and maimed. Everyone fled to the hills. It was heartbreakingly horrible! Our little town changed hands four times. With all that, there was still a most blessed moment. My friend the Mandarin became a Christian!

Early in the war I was able to send children away to various Christian homes in the surrounding countryside. But as the war dragged on, neglected children would find their way to my door. Soon I had about a hundred children and only myself to beg for food in the town while a few elders cooked in the bombed out mission.

I stubbornly refused advice to leave—until I was shown a wanted poster with my face on it. (My espionage efforts had been discovered.) "Wanted for high treason," the poster said—with a 100-pound reward from the Japanese High Command.[22]

Obviously, if I wasn't safe my children weren't either. Fearing for our lives, my *bei*[23] of children—twenty-seven were between eleven and fifteen, and the rest were between the ages of four and eight—and I, with a whistle, fled on foot. What chance did we have? No money and barely any food—certainly not enough to last the journey—and safety in Sian (Xi'an) lay a hundred miles away. Each child had a bowl, chopsticks, a face towel, a little quilt, and that was it. We couldn't travel the main roads; the Japanese army controlled them. The only route left was over the mountains, which also meant crossing the wild and untamed Yellow River. Although the town's mayor thought I was crazy, he gave us enough grain to last until the next town, and two men to carry it. "I admire your courage," he said. "But it is very foolish."[24]

We made our way from town to town, begging for food. Sometimes we slept in temples, rats and all, but usually it was alongside the road, sleeping in tight bundles for warmth. What in the world was I thinking? I don't know how many miles we walked—I only counted days—up and over the mountains. After twelve long days and nights of walking, toddlers carried by older children, we came to that mighty Yellow River. "Don't worry," I assured the children. "The people here will feed us and carry us across." But no, the town was empty. Evacuated. For three days we waited, always searching for boats on this mile-wide, frightening river, not knowing where to go, where to turn.

Again doubt tempted me. *If only I wasn't saddled with all these children,* I thought. *Nobody else bothered about them, why did I have to get myself and them into this mess?*[25] In the midst of my frustration and despair, *I heard God's voice: "I died for these children. I loved every one of them. I gave them to you to look after."* One of my children prodded me to just act like Moses and part the river! *"Oh child, I am not Moses."* "Of course you're not," she said, "but Jehovah is still God!"[26]

She was right, of course, and I prayed, humbled by this child's faith. *Please God, open the way for us, for only you can save us.*[27] I opened my eyes to see a Chinese soldier watching me. "Are you mad? What are you doing here with all these children?" he asked. Enemy planes with machine guns are on patrol, and you know they shoot anything that moves!" At that he whistled, a boat appeared from around the bend, and we were ferried safely across that mighty river. The townspeople there fed my children until their tummies were full!

We continued our journey, trekking over the mountains—sometimes forming a human chain to navigate the treacherous paths. I felt bad for the teenage girls who had to hobble (even though it had been years since their feet were unbound)—but what else could they do? Once we were able to travel some distance in a coal car, crouching atop the coal, not uttering a sound lest they find us and throw us off. It was a journey of twenty-eight days to the safety of an orphanage in Fu-Feng, a day's journey from Sian.[28] I had the children sing unceasingly, for that was the best way to dispel the fear and the hunger. I was the only adult,[29] and I hardly ate—the food was for the children. The trek nearly killed me—I didn't even remember that last day at all. Suffering as I was from severe malnutrition, pneumonia, and typhus, my survival was a miracle. I spent months in a hospital, in and out of consciousness, and it was many more months after that before I recovered. When the doctors found out who I was and how much I had been through, they couldn't fathom how I had survived it all. But I knew God had more work for me to do—of that I was sure.

I did things I wouldn't have done on my own because I knew God was with me, and because of that my life was full of amazing adventures. I continued my work in missions, leper colonies, and prisons.

I went back to England in 1948 and stayed there until 1957, becoming an ambassador for missionaries in China, raising awareness and money in a whirlwind of speaking engagements all over the world, especially for the refugees fleeing from Communist China. I was interviewed on the BBC radio, lunched with Queen Elizabeth, met with the Archbishop of Canterbury, and appeared on the television program "This Is Your Life." What a surprise that was!

The public seemed to be fascinated by the experiences of such an unassuming looking woman, even though I thought I had done nothing that was especially interesting. After all, I was just the vehicle for God's work. Author Alan Burgess seemed to be enthralled by my account of the prison uprising. A riot had broken out, and the guards, overwhelmed and outnumbered, would not go in. The governor of the prison summoned me and ordered me to go in (by myself!) and stop it! *"Are you mad—they'll kill me!"* I said. "But how can they kill you? You have been telling everyone that you have the living God inside of you. . . . If your God protects you from harm—then you can surely stop this riot." This was a challenge I could not ignore if I were to ever save face and continue my ministry. Horrified and scared out of my mind, I walked into the courtyard to find fifty or sixty men screaming, yelling, and fighting. Without any plan I did the only thing I could think of. I yelled at the wildest man in there—the one with a hatchet hacking people to death!—and demanded he hand it over. He took two paces forward toward me, his eye wild and bloodshot, and suddenly he stopped, looked at me, and meekly handed it over. Just like that! It's a fairly long story, but I got them all quiet and asked a spokesman to tell me what had happened. The conditions in the prison were inhumane. I persuaded the governor to give them jobs and see that they had food.

After years in England, I yearned to return to my people. The Chinese government, now Communist, refused my entry, and so to Taiwan I went, opening an orphanage in 1958. I died there in 1970; I was almost sixty-eight.[30] *I had been a fisher of men. I went to China because God asked me. I did not have missionary training or missionary status. I was answerable to Him and no one else.*[31]

I was small by human definition—four feet ten. But God gave me the strength to be huge; I think even Goliath would have cowered. It was the role of a lifetime. Or should I say, the role *for* a lifetime.

◆ ◆

"'Be strong and courageous. Do not be afraid or discouraged.'"

1 Chronicles 22:13(b)

"He said to them, 'Go into all the world and preach the gospel to all creation.'"

Mark 16:15

"'For I will give you words and wisdom that none of your adversaries will be able to resist or contradict.'"

Luke 21:15

- ► Enjoy a recording of Gladys telling of her experience—quite a sense of humor! https://youtu.be/3_xngUfIL6U.
- ► Hear about Gladys's amazing adventures here: https://www.youtube .com/watch?v=4isJi7ALHCc.
- ► Australian Greg Pringle has put together a wonderful pictorial essay of the Inn of the Eight Happinesses as it stands today. Visit his website, CJV Lang, here: http://www.cjvlang.com/Photos/yangcheng/small woman.html.

► Breaking and binding the feet of young women was a status symbol among the socially elite and wealthy Chinese. For more information, visit the Smithsonian website at: http://www.smithsonianmag.com/ history/why-footbinding-persisted-china-millennium-180953971/.

— 16 —

Louis Zamperini

1917-2014

As a child, Louie was dirt poor and could barely speak English. He grew into a teenage thug with poor prospects, mad at everyone. But he had a lot of goodness in him. All he had to do to bring it forward was to be cast adrift at sea, rescued, imprisoned, tortured, forgiven, and adored. It was an up and down rollercoaster.

If you cling to the axe you're grinding, eventually you'll only hurt yourself. [1]

I led a charmed life, answering to Lucky Louie as far back as I can remember, surviving more crazy stunts and shenanigans, scaring Mother out of her wits. As a kid growing up in Torrance, California, [2] I was an outsider—a delinquent—a smoker at five and a drinker at eight! I could barely speak English, and that made me an easy target for the bullies. My life became about getting even. *Every recess I was surrounded by jeering, kicking, punching, and rock-throwing kids. The idea was to make me crazy so I'd curse in Italian.* [3] To protect myself, Father taught me the fine art of the punch and jab, followed by a quick right cross. And because we were dirt poor, he taught me other survival skills, like how to put food on the table. *I'd shoot swamp ducks, mud hens, or wild rabbits for dinner.*[4] As defiant and hardheaded as one could be, I became the neighborhood thief, stealing anything and everything I could get my hands on—the act greater than the prize. Well, that and I was just hungry, pilfering food out of kitchens and restaurants. I mastered the art of self-preservation early on.

Close to being kicked out of school, I was instead denied participation in sport activities. That didn't matter to me, but Pete, my brother, talked the principal into letting me play something, convincing him it was the only way to redeem me. I found something to do that didn't cost a thing. Run! Actually, that particular sport wasn't my idea. At first it was a way to get the attention of the girls, but Pete saw something in me and made me run—every day. Soon my dislike gave way to anticipation. Then it became all I did. No more thieving, no more drinking, no more smoking. Pete was my trainer; he took my bicycle away and made me run through my newspaper route. At the community pool in Redondo Beach I worked to increase my lung capacity—I could stay underwater for three minutes and forty-five seconds! I broke course records and became the fastest high school miler in American history, running right into a place in the 1936 Olympics.[5] The *Torrance Tornado, as they called me*, I became the youngest American ever to have qualified for the long distance race: 5,000 meters. (Little did I know that *going the distance* would become a major theme in my life.)

Training for the Olympics was a dream come true; I thought I'd died and gone to heaven! ("Not so fast, Louie boy," Jesus might have said.) And then there was the transatlantic journey to the Munich games! So much food on the ship, and it was all free. *I had not just one sweet roll, but about seven every morning, with bacon and eggs. My eyes were like saucers.*[6] There's no free lunch, though, as they say. That *lean machine* suddenly wasn't so lean. With nine days of non-stop eating I arrived at the games twelve pounds heavier, and my running time suffered—this *favored son* came in eighth. *I didn't win the 5000-meter race, but making the team and not winning is like going to the moon and stumbling over a rock and falling. So what? You're still on the moon.*[7]

I caught a glimpse of Hitler's evil during those 1936 games, and by 1941 it was clear that the United States was headed into war. Commissioned as a second lieutenant, I became a bombardier in the Army Air Force, stationed at Oahu's Hickam Field. It was November 1942, eleven months after the Japanese bombed Pearl Harbor. We named our B-24 Liberator *Super Man* and readied ourselves for combat, eager to display our prowess against the enemy. While waiting for orders to fight, we would often be assigned to rescue missions. In addition to our missions and endless training, I took classes in survival, wound care, and fighting off sharks. One of our great successes was the bombing of Wake Atoll on December 24, 1942. Twenty-six B-24s took off from Midway Island and dive-bombed[8] Wake Island with 75,000 pounds of bombs, and all returned unharmed.

In a later battle we weren't so lucky. *Super Man* was badly damaged over Nauru. Japanese Zeros, bullets, and shrapnel were everywhere. We were successful as far as the mission went—the island was destroyed—but Brooks and Pillsbury were hit. Our plane was hit many times, too, and we were looking at a five-hour flight back to Funafuti. *Super Man* landed way too fast—110 miles an hour—without any landing gear, flaps, or brakes, and skidded to a halt with no runway left. The ground crew counted the holes in the plane: 594. Pillsbury recovered. Brooks did not. *Super Man* did not. It was April 1943.

May 27, 1943, was a fateful day, seared into memory. I awoke for an early morning run, found someone in a jeep, and asked him to clock me. I ran that mile in four minutes and twelve seconds! It was a record! Who needs wings to fly? That was also the day of the *Green Hornet*. Our crew was assigned to undertake a rescue search for survivors of a plane downed in the open sea. Unfortunately, the *Green Hornet* was the only plane left on the tarmac that morning. It was a miserable looking, ramshackle, broken down B-24 that had become good only for errands. It was so worn out that ground crews thought of it more as a replacement parts store. If it had been anything but a rescue mission, we would have balked.

How bad could it get, anyway? We soon found out. Engine failure. Then another engine failure, both on the left side. Efforts to restart them were futile, and the right engines caused the plane to roll onto its left side. Far south of Hawaii, the *Green Hornet* slammed into the ocean.[9] *The crash forced me forward and down into the sea. I blacked out momentarily from the impact and found myself entangled in coiled wires and cables that wound around me like metal spaghetti.*[10] The last thing I remember was that I must have been twenty feet under because that's when ears pop, and that's what mine did, just before I lost consciousness.

I awoke into total darkness. Was I dead? No, but I was still underwater. Miraculously, that metal cage of chains fell loose, and I pushed my way through a jagged hole in the fuselage, my lungs screaming for air. I pulled on the strings of my Mae West vest, it inflated, and I raced to the surface, exploding out of the water into a sea of flames, an inferno of fire and smoke fueled by the gasoline-soaked air, burning my every breath. I found two life rafts and pulled two others into them—the only others I could find. Of eleven crewmembers only Phil, Mac, and I survived.

We did a lot of praying in those canvas and rubber boats. *Of course, on life rafts that's what you mostly do: you pray.*[11] I had so many questions. All those boyhood stunts—narrowly escaping death and disfiguring injuries—for this? But we were alive and thanked God for that. (I don't think I would have been so grateful, though, had I known what was coming . . . .)

In the rafts I found some chocolate bars, metal bottles of water (about half-pint size) a mirror, flare gun, sea dye, fishhooks, fishing line, two air pumps, and a pair of pliers. That was it. No other food, first-aid kits, whistle, compass, or knives! No tarps for shade, no bailing buckets, no sail, and nothing to distill the salt water.

I got pretty good at catching albatross that landed on our boat (I had scars on my knuckles from their razor-like beaks). As hungry as we were, the first one's insides smelled so bad we threw it overboard, keeping some of it for bait. The second and third we managed to eat—they tasted so good, like a hot fudge sundae![12] I caught a small shark and we ate its liver. We captured rainwater to drink, using the canvas casing that the pumps were in. Drifting along on the high seas for some two thousand miles, we endured punishing storms—surviving a typhoon by lashing ourselves to the raft using the raft cord—achingly cold nights, and mercilessly hot days. Our lips became so swollen that they pushed up against our nostrils. Our skin cracked and salt sores appeared up and down our bodies. Our skin turned yellow, absorbing the dye of the yellow rafts that were disintegrating under the scalding sun. We'd take turns using the pumps' canvas covers to shade ourselves. From the sea came the sharks, always the sharks, toying with us, rubbing their backs against the bottom of the rafts. We had visits from a Great White that was at least twelve feet long. We would beat them back with the oars.

We heard the airplane! Frantically we shot off our flare guns and stained the water with dye. It saw us, but it wasn't our rescuers—it was our executioners. A Japanese plane, its machine guns firing, made eight passes at us, dropping a depth charge on the last run! They missed every time—not a bullet found our bodies. A very inept crew, . . . or a miracle? I couldn't understand either. "If the Japanese are this inept," Phil said, "America will win the war."[13] That was the twenty-seventh day.

We managed to patch the fifty or so holes on the one raft, but the other was useless; we stripped it and used it for shade.

Phil and I were sure we'd survive no matter how long it took, but Mac felt doomed from the moment I picked him out of the water. He held on for thirty-three days. We'd heard stories of cannibalism, of eating dead bodies to survive, but that never entered our minds. We buried him at sea.

Phil and I kept ourselves lucid by talking. We quizzed each other about trivia, described in detail each meal we'd *cooked*, each detail of the recipe explored. We recounted events in our lives over and over. We memorized things just to keep our minds sharp. We both prayed. *I promise to seek you and serve you if you just let me live*, I prayed.[14]

I was completely lucid when I heard the *voices*. I saw the outlines of twenty-one people floating in a cloud above me, singing the sweetest sounds one could hear. They sang until I had the melody memorized, and then they were gone. Phil heard nothing, saw nothing. It was the fortieth day.

July 14, 1943, myself some fifty pounds lighter and Phil just as skeletal, we reached shore, only to find our Japanese captors waiting. Forty-seven days at sea, we had drifted two thousand miles to an atoll in the Marshall Islands. Could it get any worse?

Yes. Prisoners of war now, we soon found out firsthand that cruelty has no limits. Those first few days in the infirmary we were treated humanely, but that was the last of it. Thrown into individual cells, not much bigger than the size of a coffin except that there was a thatched roof about seven feet up, we found the darkness disorienting. In this little cell was a latrine hole covered by swarms of files and mosquitoes. Three times a day bits of hardtack and rice were thrown into the cell onto the dirt floor. A cup of tea would appear on the ledge. Two sips of water a day. *Sometimes they'd reach into the slop bucket, squeeze together a gob of rice the size of a golf ball, and throw it at me. That usually meant an hour or two spent crawling around in the half-light, on the dirty floor, trying to find every grain while the guards howled with delight.*[15] I wished for the openness of the raft. Somewhere in that misery, though, I heard those same heaven-sent voices. No people this time, just the voices singing that same melody. I hung on, singing it over and over, hope renewed.

After about a week the interrogations began, complete with beatings, pelting with stones, and a few medical experiments thrown in for good measure. Getting nothing out of us, they shipped us off Execution Island[16] on August 26, 1943, six weeks after the rescue. After a three-week journey we docked at Yokohama, Japan. We were taken, not to a POW camp, but to Ofuna, an interrogation camp just south of Yokohama where there were no international rules of conduct.[17] Because they did not register us as POWs, they could do anything they wanted and no one would ever know. Meals consisted of broth and a half bowl of rice. No protein, maybe a few vegetables, but plenty of rat droppings, maggots, and grit. Sometimes they'd give us fish, but as often as not they would be covered in pulsing maggots, overpowering in their stench. We were starved.

I never recognized how important dignity is to the human soul until it was stripped away from me. Could a human life really be so worthless?

Even so, I would do my best to lift the spirits of my fellow prisoners. I'd tell them about my favorite Italian food, complete with recipes—anything to keep their minds off the real food.[18]

We were beaten for any reason. Folding our arms, talking in our sleep, and moving our eyes resulted in beatings. There were long periods of confinement when the lifting of one's gaze earned another agonizing beating. One man's infraction meant a dozen others were beaten. The guards wielded absolute, brutal power. I ate my dinner alone in my cell, after which I was not allowed to speak, make a noise of any kind, or look out the window. I was at Ofuna for a little over a year.

On June 27, 1944, the families of the *Green Hornet* crew were notified that we were all officially dead, declared so on May 28, 1944. My parents, Pete, and sisters Virginia and Sylvia didn't believe it for a moment.[19]

In September 1944 a few of us were moved to Omori just outside of Tokyo. We were told it was a real POW camp, which meant rules of humane treatment. They lied. The real pain and terror were yet to begin. At Omori was Sergeant Watanabe, nicknamed "Bird"[20] by the prisoners.

Because I was an officer and an Olympian—a prized specimen—I became the prime target for Watanabe, and he took a sadistic, personal interest in me, determined to break me. Sometimes Watanabe pummeled me with his fists; other times he'd use a ball bat or a heavy stick. He liked to use his steel-buckled belt to crack me full across my temple. Most every day it was a ruthless beating of some kind. He delighted in beating everyone, actually, but he concentrated on me. Sometimes he would beat someone for hours, leave, and return to apologize, vowing never to do it again—and with the words still fresh in his mouth resume the beating.

Omori was a slave camp. We worked ten to twelve hours a day, every day. It was backbreaking work, too, shoveling coal and sand, working in the rail and shipyards. Because the food was devoid of calories and nutrition, dysentery was common to all nine hundred of us. Officers were assigned to empty the latrines. Pits, called benjos, is what they were. We would empty the pits into buckets using big dippers and carry them to cesspits. Unless you've done it, you can't imagine how nauseating that was. The Bird took delight in our misery. To thwart him, we acted like it was the most fun we'd ever had. It wasn't so fun, however, when he forced us to do pushups over the pits, or lick our boots clean after a pit run. If he wasn't beating us physically, he would emotionally torture us—I'm not sure which was worse.

At the end of 1944, Watanabe was transferred out of Omori. Hooray! Life became somewhat bearable. The reprieve was short-lived, however, as a few months later fifteen of us were transferred to the other side of the island to a camp called Naoetsu. Awaiting us was the Bird! Omori seemed like a picnic compared to this. Watanabe continued his beatings and aberrant, mania-like behavior. Conditions in camp were worse than at Omori. High in the mountains, we—the seven hundred of us—almost froze to death in the winter—no way to keep warm. The temperature inside the ramshackle buildings was not much different from what it was outside. With the summer nights came huge, biting rats, and *the sand fleas were so thick that the earth itself seemed to be crawling, undulating like waves . . . but bugs were the least of our torments.*[21] *By this time I was having about twenty bloody bowel movements every day.*[22]

On September 4, 1945, after the bombings of Hiroshima and Nagasaki, Japan surrendered. I flew home in a B-24. It was October when I was reunited with my family following two years and three months of imprisonment.[23] Awarded a Purple Heart and the Distinguished Flying Cross, I returned home to a hero's welcome: received thousands of letters, countless awards, and delivered at least a hundred speeches. Yet I felt terrible. *Heroes are guys with missing arms or legs—or lives—and the families they've left behind. All I did in the war was survive.*[24] How does one go on after that? My behavior spiraled out of control—no purpose or path, just drinking, mainly drinking. I was still an outsider.

But then I met Cynthia. Ten days later I proposed. Her mother tried to talk her out of it; it was all too sudden. I was an Italian; weren't they only good for pushcarts or neighborhood restaurants?[25] But we both knew we were meant for each other. Forgoing the big wedding plans, we married on May 25, 1946. The next day we told our parents.

On January 7, 1949, Cissy was born. By the end of the year, Cynthia knew she'd made a mistake. My sorrow, anger, and bitterness consumed me, and I wasn't easy to live with. The money I'd saved had run out, and I couldn't keep a job.[26] *I'd failed her. I'd failed my family. I'd failed myself.*[27]

The Bird was still tormenting me. He never left me alone, my nightly nightmares filled with his tyranny and humiliation. I became convinced that the only way to be at peace with myself was in revenge, and I hatched a plot to murder Watanabe. If this were possible, my soul became even darker, murder ever on my mind.

I frightened Cynthia so much that she decided to divorce me. But then a friend took her to a Billy Graham tent meeting. It was September 1949. I had been out drinking—could barely walk when she told me about it—but would I go with her to listen to him? What could he do for me, this preacher who talked about Jesus and how much he loved us? What could he know? When she got home I was ready for a fight, but she wasn't. In fact, she decided she no longer wanted a divorce. There was something different about her, too, all calm and smiley. I wanted her to just stop talking, but then she stopped me with these words: "I've accepted Christ as my Savior."[28] I looked at her and went to bed.

She talked me into going. Dragged me was more like it. Billy spoke of the strength that comes when we forgive others. Had he been through even a little of my torments? I was a *half-lapsed Catholic*,[29] sure, but I was righteously angry at Billy's highfalutin preaching. I had earned every right to be bitter, and I would never let go of what my captors had done to me. Despite my resistance, though, his nonsense talk crept into my brain and began to take root. Cold fear replaced my anger, and I ran—right outta there into the night. A few days later Cynthia insisted I return.

"What God asks of men is faith," said Graham. "His invisibility is the truest test of that faith. To know who sees him, God makes himself unseen."[30] I don't know how to say it other than that something miraculous happened to me under that tent. My head began to spin, and in an instant I saw the truth—that forgiveness isn't possible on one's own; it takes a partnership with Jesus. Mr. Tough Guy died. That long-forgotten promise made to God back in that life raft—to serve him—surfaced through that wall of dissolving hatred. I felt, once more, a favored son.

I made that walk to the altar call. I lifted up my hands and just . . . let . . . go. I willingly surrendered—not to an enemy, but to the One who could give me freedom. *For the first time in my life I truly humbled myself before the Lord.*[31] I prayed for forgiveness—and for the strength to forgive others. I said many things on my knees that night, and when it was over I felt a peace I had never before known. What I knew was that Jesus—his grace—was now a part of me. Never again would I be on the outside. Always I would be at peace.

My nightly terror-filled dreams evaporated; I never suffered another nightmare or migraine, never felt the need to smoke a cigarette or take a drink. Instead, I spent the rest of my days *going the distance* for God. In 1952 I went to Japan to address the war criminals at Sagamo prison. I also met with many of them personally, to forgive them.[32] Four days before my eighty-first birthday I was in Japan, carrying the Olympic torch for the Nagano games in Takada, near the site of that prison camp. Running between rows of one hundred twenty Japanese soldiers, gratitude ran both ways. They honored me, and through Jesus I found kindness and compassion. Watanabe would not meet with me, even though it was not my intent for him to ask me for forgiveness. I'd already forgiven him. *The one who forgives never brings up the past to that person's face. When you forgive, it's like it never happened. True forgiveness is complete and total.*[33]

Cynthia and I were married for fifty-four years, and we had another child, Luke. I lived for ninety-seven years,[34] honoring my God who had taught me about unconditional forgiveness. Jesus and I have had some great talks along the way. I've even thought about challenging him to a foot race—though I thought better of it. *That* would most certainly have been pushing my luck.

◆ ◆

"'And when you stand praying, if you hold anything against anyone, forgive them, so that your Father in heaven may forgive you your sins.'"

Mark 11:25

"Do you not know that in a race all the runners run, but only one gets the prize? Run in such a way as to get the prize."

1 Corinthians 9:24

"Blessed is the one who perseveres under trial because, having stood the test, that person will receive the crown of life that the Lord has promised to those who love him."

James 1:12

- ▶ Watch Louie read his letter of forgiveness to Watanabe: https://youtu .be/BEyqbSK-XIQ.
- ▶ Watch a video of Louie telling his story: https://youtu .be/ mkR4TVKKJQM.
- ▶ Here's a link to the Louis Zamperini Youth Ministries: https://www .zamperini.org/.
- ▶ For a compelling, page-turning account of Louie's survival, read Laura Hillenbrand's *Unbroken*, Random House Publishers, 2010.

— 17 —

Johnny Cash

1932–2003

Johnny was a superstar, yet he identified with the broken. A social reformer, he used his music to fight injustice and never hid from his need for grace (getting what he didn't deserve) and mercy (not getting what he did deserve). *Being a Christian isn't for sissies. It takes a real man to live for God . . . a lot more man than to live for the devil, you know? If you're going to be a Christian, you're going to change. You're going to lose some old friends, not because you want to, but because you need to.*[1]

Daddy always said what was on his mind: "It should've been you. He took the wrong son."[2] I can't say I blame him; everyone loved Jack, and grief has a way of messing with you.

I was twelve when Jack died. He was sawing wood and the circular blade got away from him—sliced him deep up the middle. He was my hero, and we were as close as two brothers could be. Jack had plans to be a preacher. One of the last things he said to me was, "Can you hear the angels singing?"[3]

I helped dig his grave.

My earliest good memories were of Mama's singing. She loved to sing Gospel. I sang every song in the hymnal with her—memorizing came easily—and listened to the battery-powered radio every chance I got. We sang our way through the cotton fields, and every night we sang 'round the piano until bedtime. Mama kept me thinking about singing. "J. R.," she would say, "*God has his hand on you. You'll be singing for the world someday.*"[4]

We had moved from Kingsland, Arkansas, to the Dyess Colonization Project when I was three.[5] Like everyone else during the Great Depression, Daddy was looking for a new beginning. The government gave us twenty acres in a New Deal housing project.[6] (It wasn't welfare; Daddy had to repay the government from crops sold.) First Lady Eleanor Roosevelt, who came to dedicate the new buildings, shook my hand; I never forgot that. Before we could farm, though, we had to clear a tangle of trees, bushes, and vines. I helped as I could. But when it started raining, it seemed as though it wouldn't stop.

How high's the water, mama?
Two feet high and rising
How high's the water, papa?
Two feet high and rising

Well, the hives are gone
I've lost my bees
The chickens are sleeping
In the willow trees
Cow's in water up past her knees
Three feet high and rising[7]

Up rose the Mississippi and Tyronza Rivers, breaching, forcing our little town to evacuate. Higher and higher the water rose, washing away (or so I thought) my parents' hopes for a new start.

How high's the water, mama?
Four feet high and rising
How high's the water, papa?
Four feet high and rising

Well, the rails are washed out north of town
We got to head for higher ground
We can't come back till the water comes down
Five feet high and rising
Well it's five feet high and rising[8]

Mama always told us to look for the good in adversity. Two weeks later, we returned home to find our land covered in rich black bottom dirt. From the bounty sold, Daddy was able to pay back the loan.

I had picked cotton with Daddy and Mama from the time I was five years old. Then the cotton was gone and Daddy hopped freight trains looking for work. It was tough raising us seven—no, six—kids.[9] I tried to please him my whole life. I may have needed to prove to Daddy that I was a good boy, but because of Jack I somehow knew there was someone who loved me, and I didn't have to earn it. In his last hours, Jack kept telling us he could see the light, and that's where he was heading. *I made my choice after his death which way I was going to go . . . I accepted Jesus Christ as savior.*[10]

I joined the army in 1950, and a lot of study earned me a spot with an elite group of radio intercept operators. After basic training I was assigned to intercept Soviet Army transmissions with the 12th Radio Squadron Mobile at Landsberg, Germany. That's where I bought my first guitar. That's where I wrote my first songs. That's where I first saw a movie about a prison called Folsom.

But it was back in San Antonio—at the skating rink—that I first saw Vivian Liberto. I hadn't left for Germany yet—was still in basic training in Texas, but I knew she was the one. Over the course of daily love letters—at least a thousand pages worth[11]—we were both sure. One month after I got out, on August 7, 1954, we were married by her uncle and settled down to raise a family. I worked as an appliance salesman but was lousy at it, really lousy. What I really wanted to do was sing, and Gospel was my favorite.

Then I met Sam Phillips. He had this little place, Sun Records,[12] and I talked my way into an audition. We—Marshall Grant, Luther Perkins, and I—sang our favorite Gospel songs. "Gospel doesn't sell," Sam said. "What else you got?" He liked "Hey Porter" and said he'd record it if I wrote another song for the flip side. Oh man, I had a contract! It was 1955 and we—Johnny Cash and the Tennessee Two[13]—were on our way. Boom Chicka Boom![14]

The rest, as they say, is history. In 1954 I was making about twenty dollars a week selling appliances. In 1955 I got my first royalty check: $2.41.[15] In 1959 I made two hundred and fifty thousand dollars.[16] Oh how I loved to play the crowds. The spotlight played across the stage, dancing with my silhouette.

Hello, I'm Johnny Cash.

Everyone knew that silhouette, it seemed, for I was to record ninety-six albums and hundreds and hundreds of singles. I wrote thousands of song lyrics and performed in front of millions of people worldwide, had my own television show, starred in movies, and received thirteen Grammys and nine CMA awards[17]—all a gift from God. I would later team up with Kris Kristofferson, Waylon Jennings, and Willie Nelson to form the Highwaymen. I had way more than my share of the good life.

It was back in 1956 that I had heard what would become life-changing words (backstage at the Grand Ole Opry): "Hello, I'm June Carter." Little did I know that she would eventually become the center of my life. (Many thought June was the reason for my divorce from Vivian; she wasn't—too many other self-inflicted faults before she even came along claimed that failure.)

While I was a spiritual man, I was also a wild man, and the *biggest sinner of them all.*[18] In the beginning all I did was tour. Traveling and singing. Singing and traveling. Anywhere from two hundred to three hundred concerts a year. It got so *I could wake up anywhere in the United States, glance out the bus window and pinpoint my location within five miles.*[19]

I was exhausted. Something had to give.

I was introduced to amphetamines on the road back in 1957. *One pill was too many and a thousand wasn't enough.*[20] Many of my sins were played out on the world stage: drugs, alcohol, adultery, and divorce. For years the addictions overshadowed everything. I still worked, but sometimes the pills brought me laryngitis, glazed eyes, and a skin-and-bones appearance. Seven arrests and seven nights in jail[21] attested to my legendary mood swings. Cancelled recording sessions and concerts became the rule rather than the exception. *Sometimes I was two people. Johnny was the nice one.*

Cash caused all the trouble. They fight.[22] I wrote about the accolades and the sins in my autobiographies. I'd tell people they could overcome any obstacle. What a hypocrite. I was the one dancing with the darkness, I was the one who saw the darkness, and you could hear the pain of it all in my lyrics. It's a wonder I didn't kill myself. It wasn't for lack of trying.

My marriage to Vivian had been over for years; I was really sorry about that. A legal divorce was only a matter of time.[23] And when I fell in love with June, she wouldn't have me until I could clean up, and I didn't think I'd have the strength for that. I was shattered and feeling too lost to save. It was October 1967 and I was heavily into the drugs—hadn't slept or eaten in at least three days.

The beast in me
Is caged by frail and fragile bars
Restless by day
And by night rants and rages at the stars
God help the beast in me.[24]

My mind was crazy for relief. There was only one way out, and I chose the Nickajack Cave as the place to end it all. I knew that if I crawled deep into the cave—crawled until the flashlight batteries died—I'd never be able to find my way back. After two or three hours the batteries did die, and the darkness was so complete I couldn't tell up from down. Yet *I felt something very powerful start to happen to me, a sensation of utter peace, clarity, and sobriety. I didn't believe it at first. I couldn't understand it. How, after being awake for so long and driving my body so hard and taking so many pills—dozens of them, scores, even hundreds—could I possibly feel all right? I became conscious of a very clear, simple idea: I was not in charge of my destiny. I was not in charge of my own death. I was going to die at God's time, not mine.*[25]

Slowly and carefully I crawled out in whatever direction I was being led, but the biggest hurdle was yet to come: getting clean. It was a withdrawal of extreme pain—everything you've always heard about and then some. Glass shards seemed to explode out of my body; it was as though the excruciating pain of it would go on forever, but I got through it. Stayed clean—for years. *The greatest joy of my life was that I no longer felt separated from Him. Now He is my Counselor, my Rock of Ages to stand upon.*[26]

Addictions, compulsions, drugs, they haunted me all my life—they were the thorn in my side. Yet with the help of Jesus I could beat back the demons—staying clean for years at a time. It was an up and down rollercoaster, spiritually and physically. I didn't have to pretend when singing

> The beast in me
> Has had to learn to live with pain
> And how to shelter from the rain
> And in the twinkling of an eye
> Might have to be restrained
> God help the beast in me.[27]

Nor did I have to pretend that I didn't know the consequences. I did. It was a torment that kept me in the cycle of drugs. I knew there'd be a price I couldn't pay.

> There's a man going around taking names
> And he decides who to free and who to blame
> Everybody won't be treated all the same
> There'll be a golden ladder reaching down
> When the Man comes around.[28]

I included Gospel songs in most of my albums and sang them in my concerts and on television. I loved the old favorites and wrote many of my own. I loved singing for the crowds at Billy Graham Crusades, which I did dozens of times. That gave me a chance to tell everyone that *Jesus Christ was Lord in my life.*[29] One of my most successful songs was "I Walk the Line," and it was more than a love song; it also spoke to my spiritual side. *Sam [Phillips] never knew it, but "I Walk the Line" was my first gospel hit.*[30]

> I keep a close watch on this heart of mine.
> I keep my eyes wide open all the time.
> I keep the ends out for the tie that binds
> Because you're mine I walk the line.

You've got a way to keep me on your side
You give me cause for love that I can't hide
For you, I know I'd even try to turn the tide
Because you're mine, I walk the line.[31]

My family was everything to me, but in the fifties and sixties I was too consumed with myself to pay attention to them. I tried to make up for it in the second half of my life—with my children Rosanne, Kathy, Cindy, Tara, and later with June, John Carter, and June's girls, Carlene and Rosie. I made some lasting friends along the way, too: Johnny Horton, Billy Graham, Bob Dylan, Jerry Lee Lewis, Roy Orbison, Hank Williams Jr., Merle Haggard, Carl Perkins, Bono, and Sheryl Crow, to name a few.

I proposed to June in 1968 on stage in front of a crowd in Ontario, Canada. (We were married for thirty-five years, and very much in love. Four months after June died, so did I. They said it was complications of diabetes. They were wrong—it was my heart, broken.[32])

I'd like to think I did a few things right. I was a champion of the poor and oppressed. Do you know why I always wore black?

I wear the black for the poor and the beaten down,
Livin' in the hopeless, hungry side of town,
I wear it for the prisoner who has long paid for his crime,
But is there because he's a victim of the times.

I wear the black for those who've never read,
Or listened to the words that Jesus said.
About the road to happiness through love and charity,
Why, you'd think He's talking straight to you and me.

. . . I wear it for the sick and lonely old,
For the reckless ones whose bad trip left them cold,
I wear the black in mournin' for the lives that could have been,
But 'til we start to make a move to make a few things right,

. . . Ah, I'd love to wear a rainbow every day,
And tell the world that everything's OK,

But I'll try to carry off a little darkness on my back,
'Till things are brighter, I'm the Man In Black.[33]

I helped total strangers, remembering how poor I once was. I wrote songs for the downtrodden and imprisoned because I could relate to them. (While I might have promoted an outlaw image, I never did hard prison time—just overnights in jail—but I could still relate.) I was heartsick about the treatment of Native Americans, especially by our government. I performed on Native Lands, told stories, and produced albums to benefit the American Indian.

You may know the "Ballad of Ira Hayes." In it I sought to bring justice to the United States Marine, a Pima Indian, who raised the flag at Iwo Jima. Even though he was a hero, he could never get over the guilt of surviving when so many of his buddies didn't.

At a U.S. Senate subcommittee hearing, I presented specific proposals for prison reform and continued to support and encourage reform whenever I could. From the many letters I received, I know that my concerts provided hope and encouragement to prisoners through dozens of prison concerts: Folsom (California), San Quentin (California), Huntsville (Texas), Cummins Unit (Arkansas), and Ostraker (Stockholm), to name a few. Inmate Merle Haggard, that Okie from Muskogee, was in the audience at San Quentin when I performed there on January 1, 1958. Serving what would be two years of a fifteen-year sentence for burglary, Merle credited me (bless his heart) with setting him on the right path. He went on to a career that included thirty-eight number one hits on the country charts. "Johnny was a mean mother from the South who was there because he loved us,"[34] Merle said.

"Folsom Prison Blues" had been rolling around in my head since Germany:

I hear the train a comin', it's rolling 'round the bend
And I ain't seen the sunshine since I don't know when
I'm stuck in Folsom prison, and time keeps draggin' on
But that train keeps a rollin' on down to San Antone.

When I was just a baby my mama told me, "Son
Always be a good boy, don't ever play with guns"

But I shot a man in Reno just to watch him die
When I hear that whistle blowing, I hang my head and cry.

. . . Well if they freed me from this prison,
If that railroad train was mine
I bet I'd move it on a little farther down the line
Far from Folsom prison, that's where I want to stay
And I'd let that lonesome whistle blow my blues away.[35]

The seventies was a decade of contradiction. There were the good times: my thriving relationship with June, the birth of John Carter; I was blessed with abundant riches—spiritually and materially. Bible study became very important to me, and June and I embarked on a three-year course of study from the Christian International School of Theology. June and I together worked on our biblical studies on the road, on planes, on the bus, and at home. I graduated from there with an associate of theology degree and became an ordained minister.[36] June and I went to Israel and filmed a movie about the life of Jesus. *The Gospel Road* was my proudest work, even though it wasn't a hit with my fans. Billy Graham bought the rights to the movie and let it be shown, free of charge, in churches across the country. You know about the bad times, the addictions and everything that came with them. Through no one's fault but my own, my career stumbled. Beginning in the seventies and continuing into the eighties, record sales plummeted. *I became invisible on the charts.*[37]

And then Rick Rubin entered my life. Formerly at Columbia Records, he was the cofounder of Def Jam Records. He helped hip-hop become a household word with the Beastie Boys and worked with such groups as Red Hot Chili Peppers, Public Enemy, and Tom Petty and the Heartbreakers. At first June thought I was crazy to even think of working with a heavy-metal producer. But Rick and I, we had a chemistry, and my career, which had had one foot in the grave, revived. He helped me push new boundaries, brought back the vulnerability, and gave me the confidence to put my heart back into the music, and I became a hit with a new generation. I recorded a video with Rick: *Hurt*, lyrics by Trent Reznor. *I think Hurt was the best anti-drug song I ever heard. If it doesn't scare you away from taking drugs, nothing will. I never did the needle, but I did everything else.*[38]

One of *my* heroes was the apostle Paul. I read everything I could find about this man who went from persecuting the followers of Jesus to being one himself, and I decided to write a novel about him. I read first-century historians Josephus and Pliny and Suetonius, and every other book on first-century Judea that I could find. I read many, many books and commentaries about Paul. It took me almost a decade, but I finished it in 1986. The *Man in White*, a historical novel, covers a six-year period in Paul's life. Paul wrote of the thorn in his flesh. We'll never know exactly what his thorn was, but I sure knew what mine was—the drugs—and he taught me to deal with it. *Jesus Christ told us how to live. The apostle Paul showed us how the plan works.*[39]

All I know is that without God's grace I'd have been one sorry son of a gun. He blessed me in spite of my sin. Did I ever feel bad about all the bad things I'd done? Of course, *but I forgave myself. When God forgave me I figured I better do it too. So, everything's all right.*[40]

God forgave my sins, of course, but they weren't without consequences; I spent the second half of my life in physical pain. Neuropathy and diabetes plagued me. I had surgeries on my heart and knees. A dental surgeon accidentally broke my jaw, and even with sixteen subsequent surgeries it never healed; the intense pain never left—except when I was on stage. I prayed for that, and I was grateful.

I've tried drugs and a little of everything else, and there is nothing in the world more soul-satisfying than having the kingdom of God building inside you and growing.[41] In my last interview, one month before I died, I was asked, *"Where do you expect to go when you die." "Well, we all hope to go to heaven,"*[42] I said.

I'm there now, by the grace of God. Have been since 2003.[43] You'll know me by my silhouette, all in white.

Hello, I'm Johnny Cash.

◆　◆

Inscribed on Johnny's gravestone: "Let the words of my mouth, and the meditation of my heart, be acceptable in thy sight, O LORD, my strength, and my redeemer."

Psalm 19:14 KJV

Inscribed on June Carter Cash's gravestone: "Bless the LORD, O my soul: and all that is within me, bless his holy name."

Psalm 103:1 KJV

"In order to keep me from becoming conceited, I was given a thorn in my flesh, a messenger of Satan, to torment me. Three times I pleaded with the Lord to take it away from me. But he said to me, 'My grace is sufficient for you, for my power is made perfect in weakness.' Therefore I will boast all the more gladly about my weaknesses, so that Christ's power may rest on me. That is why, for Christ's sake, I delight in weaknesses, in insults, in hardships, in persecutions, in difficulties. For when I am weak, then I am strong."

2 Corinthians 12:7–10

► Hear some of Johnny's best:
  ► *Hurt*, at. https://youtu.be/vt1Pwfnh5pc;
  ► *Ring of Fire* at https://youtu.be/It7107ELQvY;
  ► *Folsom Prison Blues, Live at San Quentin* at https://youtu.be/ wGofS4DoGUc;
  ► *Man in Black* at https://youtu .be/t51MHUENlAQ ?list =RDi1zRFnw4jOU;
  ► *The Highwaymen:* https://www .youtube .com/watch ?v =mwq7NxGQeOw;
  ► *Jackson, with June Carter, Live at San Quentin:* https://www .youtube.com/watch?v=M51MPPaDc2M
► *Walk the Line* is a movie about Johnny. It stars Joaquin Phoenix and Reese Witherspoon.
► Johnny's sister Joanne, along with her husband Dr. Harry Yates, founded the Nashville Cowboy Church. Learn more about it here: http://nashvillecowboychurch.com/.

18

Your Name Here

Simple faith, extraordinary works. With boldness, not arrogance, these seventeen lived lives of purpose, fulfillment, and joy. (Joy and happiness are not always interchangeable; sometimes they go together, sometimes they don't.) And you too can have such a life. It's never too early—nor is it ever too late.

Everyone has a role to play. Do you want to be an eighteenth?

If you haven't done so yet, what do you think would happen if you were to make the conscious choice to totally trust God and honor his divine appointments? Sometimes it's good to be reminded that life isn't about what we can do for God (he is, after all, God). Nor is it necessarily about what God does for us (because he loves us). Isn't it really about what God wants to do through us?

Whether you positively change the world for one person, for a nation, or for the world, the outcome will be a noble and glorious reality. The future is not an open book (and isn't that a blessing!?), but just as we have looked in the rearview mirror to see God's hand in the lives of these seventeen world-changers, so you too can look back and see how God has prepared you for the unique work that lies ahead. If you can't decipher the direction of his call, then maybe the lives of these seventeen, and others like them, can inspire and encourage you.

God never promised freedom from pain and adversity (does anything of value come easily?) or that you will not have a cross to bear—but he promises to give you the strength you need when you need it—if you will reach out and accept it. You can't earn your way into God's heart—you're already there. He is the God of second chances, too, wherever you are in life.

You needn't overthink this—it's a matter of simple trust and faith. Let go of the need to control, if that's where you find yourself. (What you'll find is that when you lose yourself you'll find yourself. Like I said, don't overthink this!) Let go of the need to figure out the *why*; there are mysteries you won't solve on this earth. Do you want to trust him to shape your destiny? You should, because he can do things in your life you could never dream of.

Here's another way to look at it: imagine a symphonic performance without its conductor. The concertmaster (first violin) would take the lead, but the musicians, not familiar with his cues and standards, would not perform well.

Now the symphony's conductor, who is also the composer, arrives. He walks onto the stage amidst eager applause, acknowledges the concertmaster, readies the musicians with a steady eye, and raises his baton. All eyes rest upon him, waiting. On his mark the sound of music fills the air, rising, falling, reverberating with harmony and dissonance. The music caresses listeners and musicians with a complexity of emotions as anticipation, delight, and sometimes bittersweet remembrance waft through the senses. The heart fills with wonderment, the soul yearns for more, and the mind, seeking to reason, cannot. The composer/conductor knows to create intervals of rest, for without them music has no meaning. Each musician uses their gifts to enhance the quality of the whole, creating a sense of family and communion. And then there is the finale. Will it be peaceful and contemplative contentment, or a thunderous, heart-pounding ovation? Perhaps it will be, mysteriously, both.

What have I been talking about? A relationship with God, of course. He will sustain you through life's refrains, embolden your sound, and give you your best self—one that can give away everything and lose nothing at all.

What is your story, dear Number Eighteen? Are you a C. S. Lewis, struggling to escape God's presence only to surrender to what becomes the thrill of a lifetime? Are you a Corrie ten Boom, thanking God in all circumstances—even for the fleas? Maybe you're a George Washington Carver who sees only the goodness in mankind, or a Mary McLeod Bethune whose passion is to right wrongs.

Or maybe you are or will be the wind beneath someone else's wings. God could bless you as he did Felix Mendelssohn, Stephen Grellet, Mr. Wagenen, Miss Mary Crissman, Betsie ten Boom, and George MacDonald—without whom, respectively, J. S. Bach, Elizabeth Fry, Sojourner Truth, Mary McLeod Bethune, Corrie ten Boom, or C. S. Lewis might not have changed the world.

Whatever your story, what you'll have in common with these world changers is a simple faith: a passion and capacity to love God and to love others. That's it. God will do the rest.

Think you're too ordinary? Think again. Tomorrow needs you. Be the Eighteenth.

◆　◆

"I lift up my eyes to the mountains—where does my help come from? My help comes from the LORD, the Maker of heaven and earth."

Psalm 121:1–2

"For you created my inmost being; you knit me together in my mother's womb.

I praise you because I am fearfully and wonderfully made; your works are wonderful, I know that full well."

Psalm 139:13–14

"Faith is being sure of what we hope for. It is being sure of what we do not see."

Hebrews 11:1 (NIrV)

ACKNOWLEDGMENTS

I could say thank you a hundred times, and still I'd want to say it again. To those who were once strangers, through our mutual admiration for these world changers we are now friends in truth. Although they graciously reviewed and provided comment in their particular areas of expertise, they are in no way responsible for any inadvertent errors in this book. The guilt is solely mine. My profound thanks to:

Dr. Maurice A. Finocchiaro, Distinguished Professor of Philosophy (Emeritus), University of Nevada Las Vegas and author of nine books on the life, work, and significance of Galileo.

Peter Bach Jr., great, great, great grand cousin of J. S. Bach, creator of www.bachonbach.com, a children's coloring book about J. S. Bach, and producer of Bach-inspired calendars.

Marylynn Rouse, author of *365 Days with Newton* and *Ministry on My Mind* and Director, The John Newton Project in Kettering UK, www.johnnewton.org.

Deborah Riddle, Executive Director, Elizabeth Fry Society Peel-Halton, Ontario, Canada.

Wendy Sinton, member, Sojourner Truth Memorial Committee, Florence, Massachusetts.

ACKNOWLEDGMENTS

Leslie Podell, Director, The Sojourner Truth Project, San Francisco, California, https://www.thesojournertruthproject.com.

Samuel Wheeler, PhD, State Historian and Director of Collections for the Abraham Lincoln Presidential Library, Springfield, Illinois.

Elizabeth Burgess, Collections Manager, Harriet Beecher Stowe Center, Hartford, Connecticut.

Diane Miller, National Program Manager, National Underground Railroad Network to Freedom, National Park Service, Harriet Tubman Underground Railroad Visitor Center, Church Creek, Maryland.

Shirley Baxter, Park Ranger, National Park Service, Tuskegee Institute National Historic site, George Washington Carver Museum, Tuskegee, Alabama.

Mrs. Lark Sessions, Honorary Secretary, Dohnavur Fellowship Corporation, U.S.A.

Dr. Rosie Saunders, Secretary, Dohnavur Fellowship Corporation, U.K.

Whitney Barrett, Archivist, Bethune-Cookman University, Daytona Beach, Florida.

Charles Broadwell, Curator, Sumter County Museum, Sumter, South Carolina.

Steve Zeleny, Archivist, International Church of the Foursquare Gospel, The Parsonage of Aimee Semple McPherson, Los Angeles, California.

Frits Nieuwstraten, Director, Corrie ten Boom House Foundation, Holland.

Steve Elmore, Vice President, Events and Communication, The C. S. Lewis Foundation, Redlands, California.

ACKNOWLEDGMENTS

A special thank you to Bob Adam, who was invaluable in helping me find the rest of the story, and for giving me the idea of the *Eighteenth*. Thank you to my agent, Karen Neumair, who spent countless hours refining this project. Thank you to Donna Huisjen, my editor. Donna, you pull out the best in me! Thank you, too, to Tim Beals at Credo House Publishers for your steadfast encouragement.

Closer to home, to my wonderful husband of thirty-four years and daughter, Amy. I can't say enough about how you fill my heart. To Jane Allen and Shelly Pinomaki, who listened to my rewrites over the many years and provided invaluable feedback—thank you both; I love and appreciate you more than you know. I can say the same for Marilyn Wyman and Ruth Frost; they are world changers in my book. And I must say a heartfelt thank you to those in my Bible studies. Your prayers and encouragement mean the world to me.

I want to say a very special hello to my Watoto child, Annet Musabyimana. Living in Uganda, you are far from ordinary, and you too can be a world changer, for the Holy Spirit resides within you, dear one.

PERMISSIONS

(listed in order of chapters)

Out of the Depths, John Newton. Used by permission of Moody Publishers, Chicago IL. All rights reserved.

"November Cotton Flower." From *CANE* by Jean Toomer. Copyright 1923 by Boni & Liveright, renewed 1951 by Jean Toomer. Used by permission of Liveright Publishing Corporation.

Permission for use of quotations by Aimee Semple McPherson and information about the International Church of the Foursquare Gospel provided courtesy of the International Church of the Foursquare Gospel, Los Angeles, California.

Edges of His Ways by Amy Carmichael, ©1955 by the Dohnavur Fellowship. Used by permission of CLC Publications. May not be further reproduced. All rights reserved.

Amy Carmichael of Dohnavur by Frank Houghton, ©1955 by the Dohnavur Fellowship. Used by permission of CLC Publications. May not be further reproduced. All rights reserved.

"Make Me Thy Fuel," from *Mountain Breezes* by Amy Carmichael, ©1999 by the Dohnavur Fellowship. Used by permission of CLC Publications. May not be further reproduced. All rights reserved.

"Royal Scars," from *Mountain Breezes* by Amy Carmichael, ©1999 by the Dohnavur Fellowship. Used by permission of CLC Publications. May not be further reproduced. All rights reserved.

Mary McLeod Bethune transcripts courtesy of State Archives of Florida.

Copyright permission from the C. S. Lewis Company for the following extracts:

The Weight of Glory by C. S. Lewis © C. S. Lewis Pte. Ltd. 1949.

Surprised by Joy by C. S. Lewis © C. S. Lewis Pte. Ltd. 1955.

Mere Christianity by C. S. Lewis © C. S. Lewis Pte. Ltd. 1942, 1943, 1944, 1952.
The Screwtape Letters by C. S. Lewis © C. S. Lewis Pte. Ltd. 1942.
A Grief Observed by C. S. Lewis © C. S. Lewis Pte. Ltd. 1961.
C. S. Lewis *Essays by C. S. Lewis* © C. S. Lewis Pte. Ltd.
Warren Hamilton Lewis, *C. S. Lewis: A Biography.* Unpublished typescripts in the Marion E. Wade Center, Wheaton College, IL.
Albert Lewis, ed. *The Lewis Papers*, 11 volumes. Letter from Clive Staples Lewis to Albert Lewis, Leeborough Press, Wheaton College, IL.
Tramp for the Lord by Corrie ten Boom, © 1978 by Corrie ten Boom. Used by permission of CLC Publications. May not be further reproduced. All rights reserved.
Gladys Aylward: The Little Woman, Gladys Aylward and Christine Hunter, © 1970. Used by permission of Moody Publishers, Chicago IL. All rights reserved.
"The Beast in Me" song lyrics written by Nick Lowe ©1994 New Sea Gayle Music (ASCAP). All Rights Reserved. Used by Permission. International Copyright Secured.
"Five Feet High and Rising" words and music by Johnny Cash. Copyright © 1959 (Renewed) Chappell & Co., Inc. All Rights Reserved. Used By Permission of Alfred Music.
"The Man Comes Around" words and music by John R. Cash. Copyright © 2002 Song Of Cash, Inc. All Rights Administered by BMG Rights Management (US) LLC. All Rights Reserved Used by Permission. *Reprinted by Permission of Hal Leonard LLC.*
"I Walk The Line" words and music by John R. Cash. Copyright © 1956 House Of Cash, Inc. Copyright Renewed. All Rights in the U.S. Administered by BMG Rights Management (US) LLC. All Rights outside the U.S. Administered by Unichappell Music Inc. All Rights Reserved Used by Permission. *Reprinted by Permission of Hal Leonard LLC.*
"The Man In Black" words and music by John R. Cash. Copyright © 1971 Song Of Cash, Inc. Copyright Renewed. All Rights Administered by BMG Rights Management (US) LLC. All Rights Reserved Used by Permission. *Reprinted by Permission of Hal Leonard LLC.*
"Folsom Prison Blues" words and music by John R. Cash. Copyright © 1956 House Of Cash, Inc. Copyright Renewed. All Rights Administered by BMG Rights Management (US) LLC. All Rights Reserved Used by Permission. *Reprinted by Permission of Hal Leonard LLC.*

NOTES

1. C. S. Lewis, *God in the Dock: Essays on Theology and Ethics* (Grand Rapids, MI: Wm. B. Eerdmans, 1972) p. 93.

Introduction

1. C. S. Lewis, *Mere Christianity*, Complete C. S. Lewis Signature Classics (New York: Harper One, New, 2002), p. 75.

2. Ibid., p.76.

Chapter One—Galileo Galilei

1. Galileo Galilei, "Letter to the Grand Duchess Christina" (1615), *Modern History Sourcebook* (Fordham Univ.), http://sourcebooks.fordham.edu/mod/galileo-tuscany .asp. Note: There's an Italian saying, "Traduttore, traditore," meaning that translators are traitors. This speaks to the difficulty in conveying the exact meaning of the original, and one is cautioned to review more than one translation. Concerning Galileo's biblical interpretations, quoted are several translations from two sources: "Letter to Castelli (1613)" and "Letter to the Grand Duchess (1615)."

2. Atle Naess, *Galileo Galilei When the World Stood Still* (Berlin: Springer, 2005), p. 17.

3. Note: Galileo made many discoveries and observations, the subjects of which included Earth's orbit, scientific method, the principle of the pendulum, comets, the law of falling bodies (inertia), mathematics as nature's language, mechanics, military science, tidal movement, floating objects, the flight path of projectiles (ballistics), magnets, motion, the force of friction, the gravitational center of solids, the invention

of the military compass, the thermometer, irrigation devices, navigational aids, and improvements to both the telescope and the microscope.

4. James Reston Jr., *Galileo, A Life* (Harper Collins, 1994), p. 14.

5. Note: What are the qualities of a genius? There are many, but geniuses all share an insatiable curiosity, are open-minded, and are creative.

6. Stillman Drake, *Discoveries and Opinions of Galileo* (Anchor Publishing, 1957), p. 134.

7. Galileo Galilei, *Il Saggiatore* (*The Assayer*) (Rome: Giacomo Mascardi, 1623), trans. by Stillman Drake (Anchor Pub., 1957), pp. 237–38, paraphrased.

8. Note: Vincenzo Viviani, one of Galileo's pupils, insisted that Galileo performed this experiment from the top of the tower for his students. This assertion is puzzling, however, because Galileo didn't write about it. Galileo scholars surmise that Viviani, a great admirer of Galileo, fabricated the story.

9. Note: This is a linear magnification of thirty times.

10. James MacLachlan, *Galileo Galilei* (University of California Press, 1953), p. 406.

11. Ibid.

12. Shaun Usher, ed., *Letters of Note, An Eclectic Collection of Correspondence Deserving of a Wider Audience* (San Francisco: Chronicle Books, 2014), pp. 124–25.

13. League of Everyday Doxologists, http://www.doxologists.org/galileo-galilei/. Note: Galileo was not the first to make these observations. Hariot, Marius, Scheiner, and Castelli each recorded these things before he did.

14. Note: Galileo did posthumously succeed in persuading Church officials of later times, e.g., Pope Leo XIII in 1893 and Pope John Paul II in 1979.

15. Note: Father Orazio Grassi, an Italian Jesuit priest, was a mathematician, astronomer, and architect who was very critical of Galileo. He wrote under the pseudonym Sarsi.

16. Mordechai Feingold, Ed. The New Science and Jesuit Science: Seventeenth Century Perspectives. Springer Science+Business Media Dordrecht 2003. P. 153. Note: Father Grassi wrote this in a letter Girolamo Bardi dated September 23, 1633.

17. Note: Interestingly enough, Galileo's theory that the ebb and flow of tides provide evidence of a revolving earth has come to be known as Galileo's Big Mistake because that theory proved to be false.

18. Note: The Church ruled that until Copernicus's book *On the Revolutions* was corrected, it was to be placed on the *Index of Prohibited Books*.

19. Note: The Assayer in Italian: *Il Saggiatore*.

20. Galileo Galilei, "Letter to the Grand Duchess Christina" (1615), in *The Essential Galileo*, ed. and trans. by Dr. Maurice A. Finocchiaro (Indiana: Hackett), p. 119.

21. Note: In the events that led up to the trial, Galileo attempted to explain how he had "misunderstood" the mandate not to defend the Copernican system. In a 1953 edition of *The Dialogue*, Albert Einstein wrote about this in the foreword, saying, in essence, good try, but not convincing: "a downright roguish attempt to comply with this order in appearance and yet in fact to disregard it. Unfortunately, it turned out

that the Holy Inquisition was unable to appreciate adequately such subtle humor," For more information: http://www.pbs.org/wgbh/nova/earth/galileo-big-mistake.html.

22. Note: To say that the sun sets in the west, for example, does not imply a belief that the sun actually moves. Scripture was not written as a scientific treatise, and imagery and personification were often used. Here are some Scriptures that, if not understood within their literary genre, would seem to support an earth-centered theory: Joshua 10:12–14, 1 Chronicles 16:30, Psalm 93:1, Psalm 96:10, Psalm 104:5, Ecclesiastes 1:5, Isaiah 38:8.

23. Note: It was not until 1822 that the Church acknowledged that passages in the Holy Bible referring to the earth as immovable are phenomenal statements, i.e., statements experienced through the senses and meant as imagery.

24. Maurice A. Finocchiaro, "Galilei, Galileo," *Biographical Encyclopedia of Astronomers*, ed. Thomas Hockey (New York: Springer, 2014), p. 401.

25. Note: Giordano Bruno was passed over for the position offered to Galileo at Padua. Bruno was arrested in 1592 for heresy and blasphemy. His court trial lasted seven years. He was convicted, and on February 17, 1600, he was hung naked, upside down, and burned at the stake.

26. Note: Galileo's verdict was classified as an intermediate category of theological crime.

27. Maurice A. Finocchiaro, *The Essential Galileo* (Hackett Publishing, 2008), p. 294. See pp. 293 and 294 for a transcript of Galileo's statement.

28. Note: In 1992 the Catholic Church formally recognized its error, asserting that Galileo was right in adopting the Copernican astronomical theory.

29. Note: The Penitential Psalms are the Psalms of Confession—6, 32, 38, 51, 102, 120, and 143—that are often recited during Lent. Galileo's daughter, Sister Celeste, received permission to assume that duty.

30. Note: Galileo's other daughter, Livia, who took the name Sister Arcangela, was ill throughout most of her life. She was not particularly agreeable, and Galileo kept abreast of news of her through Maria.

31. Galileo Galilei, 1634 letter to Elia Diodata in Paris, in Dava Soble, *Galileo's Daughter, A Historical Memoir of Science, Faith, and Love* (Bloomsbury, 2009), Kindle Location 4190.

32. Ibid., Location 4173. Note: The actual quote, written to Signor Geri, reads as follows: "I feel immense sadness and melancholy, together with extreme inappetite: I am hateful to myself, and continually hear my beloved daughter calling to me."

33. Note: Some suggest that Galileo also had glaucoma. Do not believe the urban legend that he went blind (at the age of seventy-two) from looking at the sun through his telescope. His observations of the sun were made twenty-five years earlier. Even then he looked at the sun near sunrise and sunset, or by projection.

34. Note: Genesis 1 summarizes God's perspective on the origin of the heavens and the earth as "And God saw that it was good."

Chapter Two—Johann Sebastian Bach

1. William J. Federer, "The Aim and Final End of All Music," *American Clarion*, March 21, 2012, http://www.americanclarion.com/2012/03/21/aim-final-music-2-4710/.

2. Note: Bach's compositions, more than a thousand, included concertos, cantatas, fugues, passions, chorales, canons, masses, four-part chorales, songs, and arias. Complex and detailed, some of the pieces were three hours in length.

3. Note: The seventh and youngest child, Bach was born on March 21, 1685, in Eisenach, Germany, and was baptized Johann Sebastian. Sebastian was the name of a forester by that name who stood as a witness at the baptism. (Paul Elie, *Reinventing Bach* [New York: Farrar, Straus and Giroux, 2012], Kindle Location 341.) He was nine when his mother died, and his father died just before his tenth birthday.

4. Bach Necrology/Obituary, https://www.bachonbach.com/johann-sebastian-bach/the-life-of-johann-sebastian-bach-facts-biography-video/johann-sebastian-bach-necrology-obituary-1750-1st-bach-biography/.

5. Christoph Wolff, *Johann Sebastian Bach, The Learned Musician* (New York: W. W. Norton, 2013), p. 58. Note: Bach retained this ability for eight days, during which he could neither speak nor sing except in octaves. At the end of those eight days he lost his fine soprano voice altogether.

6. Note: Improvisation is the spontaneous performance of music. Keyboard compositions in the 1700s were often not written down. Everything was improvised, played from a voice score. Bach could improvise a six-voice fugue—an ability almost unheard of.

7. Hans T. David and Arthur Mendel, ed., revised and expanded by Christoph Wolff, *The New Bach Reader, A Life of Johann Sebastian Bach in Letters and Documents* (W. W. Norton, 1998), p. 329. Note: This statement was written by the German classical scholar Johann Matthias Gesner in a letter dated 1738 to Marcus Fabius Quintilianus. Animals known as Arioins in Greek mythology were said to be divinely bred, extremely swift, immortal horses endowed with speech.

8. Note: The Coffee Cantata, BWV 211, was performed in 1735 at Zimmerman's coffee house in Leipzig. The song is about a father who wants his daughter, Aria, to stop drinking so much coffee. She rebels with that stanza. (BWV stands for Bach-Werke-Verzeichnis and is a catalogue, first published in 1950, of his compositions.) http://www.openculture.com/2014/06/j-s-bachs-comic-opera-the-coffee-cantat.html.

9. Note: Bach took an active interest in genealogy, tracing the beginnings of his clan to Herr Veit Bach in 1550; Veit Bach was a baker who had to flee Hungary because he was a Lutheran. The English translation of the name *Bach* is a brook, a tiny river, or a creek. In the words of Ludwig van Beethoven, "Bach, this ocean, is endless and unfully utilized in his wealth of ideas and harmonies! He is the prime father of harmony."

10. Christoph Wolff, *Johann Sebastian Bach, The Learned Musician* (New York: W. W. Norton, 2013), Kindle Location 252. Note: In 2005 Bach's earliest music manuscript was discovered. Clean and error free, it is called the Weimar Organ Tablature. It demonstrates his technical competence at the very young age of thirteen or fourteen.

11. Ibid., p. 3.

12. John Eliot Gardiner, *Bach, Music in the Castle of Heaven* (Alfred A. Knopf, 2013), Kindle Location 3947. Note: According to Gardiner, there is enough evidence to assume that Bach was a teenage thug.

13. Note: The stops, or set of pipes, an organist chooses determine the sound at any given moment. A manual is a keyboard.

14. Note: A Danish ducat would have been worth about $2.00 in today's dollars. Two ducats would have been enough for a feast and money for a future trip.

15. Christoph Wolff, *Johann Sebastian Bach, The Learned Musician* (New York: W. W. Norton, 2013), p. 63.

16. Ibid., p. 96.

17. Note: In 1703 Bach was appointed court musician in the chapel of Duke Johann Ernst III in Weimar. There his reputation as an organist spread, leading to his appointment as the organist at the New Church in Arnstadt. In 1707 he moved to Mühlhausen, accepting a position as organist at the Blasius Church. In 1708 he returned to Weimar as court organist and director of music; he stayed there until 1717. From 1717 to 1723 he was in Köthen, and from 1723 until his death in 1750 he was in Leipzig.

18. Christoph Wolff, *Johann Sebastian Bach, The Learned Musician* (New York: W. W. Norton, 2013), p. 307.

19. Ibid., p. 183. Note: Bach was confined to the county judge's place of detention on November 6 and freed on December 2, 1717.

20. Hans T. David and Arthur Mendel, ed., revised and expanded by Christoph Wolff, *The New Bach Reader, A Life of Johann Sebastian Bach in Letters and Documents* (W. W. Norton, 1998), p. 93. Note: The wine cost more than a fifth of Bach's annual salary (Christoph Wolff, p. 218). I wonder if there was any left over.

21. Note: Bach's children with Maria: Catharina, Wilhelm, Maria (d. one month), Johann (d. at birth), Carl, Johann, and Leopold (d. 9 months). With Anna: Christiana, Gottfried, Christian, Elisabeth, Ernestus (d. 2 days), Regina, Christiana Benedicta (d. 3 days), Christiana Dorothea, Johann Christoph, Johann August (d. one day), Johann Christian, Johanna, Regina Susanna. For more detail, see Wolff's *Learned Musician*, pp. 396–98.

22. Note: A cantor is the chief singer and instructor in a church. He is also responsible for the choir and the preparation of liturgy (pattern for worship). This was considered a prestigious office. A cantor had to choose and conduct the vocals for the choir.

23. Christoph Wolff, *Johann Sebastian Bach, The Learned Musician* (New York: W. W. Norton, 2013), p. 225.

24. Note: A fugue is a composition in which a short melody or phrase is introduced by one part and successively taken up by others and developed by interweaving the parts.

25. J. S. Bach, letter to friend George Erdmann October 28, 1730, in Alpert Schweitzer, *J. S. Bach*, trans. Ernest Newman, vol. I (London: Adam and Charles Black, 1905), p. 137.

26. Note: "For ye suffer fools gladly, seeing ye yourselves are wise" (2 Corinthians 11:19 KJV).

27. Sojourn Website, http://www2.nau.edu/tas3/wtc/sdg.html.

28. Note: The numerical symbolism to which Bach refers is called gematria—a system by which Hebrew letters correspond to numbers. Each letter is represented by a number. One can calculate the numerical value of a word, and the method was sometimes used to support biblical exegesis—interpretation.

29. Note: That note was written by Bach in his Bible, next to 2 Chronicles 5.

30. J. S. Bach, letter to friend George Erdmann October 28, 1730, in Alpert Schweitzer, *J. S. Bach*, trans. Ernest Newman, vol. I (London: Adam and Charles Black, 1905), p. 122.

31. Note: Some English translations of this incident relate that Geyersbach was a bassoonist. He was not. The confusion comes from the similarity between the name Fagotist, which is used here, and the word *fagottist*, which means bassoonist. Zipple-Fagotist actually means something akin to *jerk* or *idiot*.

32. Hans T. David and Arthur Mendel, ed., revised and expanded by Christoph Wolff, *The New Bach Reader, A Life of Johann Sebastian Bach in Letters and Documents* (W. W. Norton, 1998), p. 47.

33. Charles Sanford Terry, ed., *Johann Sebastian Bach; His Life, Art, and Work*, translated from the German of Johann Nikolaus Forkel (1749–1818) (London: Constable, 1920), p. 106, footnote. Note: This quote has many variations. The quotation in this book is in response to someone who praised his skill on the organ. Bach: *There is nothing wonderful about it. You merely strike the right note at the right moment and the Organ does the rest.*

34. Bach Cantatas Website, http://www.bach-cantatas.com/Topics/Personality.htm.

35. Hans T. David and Arthur Mendel, ed., revised and expanded by Christoph Wolff, *The New Bach Reader, A Life of Johann Sebastian Bach in Letters and Documents* (W. W. Norton, 1998), p. 346.

36. Note: Luke 4:24.

37. Note: Bach taught Luther's Small Catechism. Bach's edition of Luther's Bible is located in the Concordia Seminary Library of St. Louis. It was gifted by the Reichle family of Frankenmuth, Michigan, in the 1930s; see https://www.csl.edu/campus-life/music-arts/bach-at-the-sem/bach-bible/. The story of how it came to rest in St. Louis is fascinating. The owners, who lived in the U.S., didn't want it to get into Hitler's hands. Read more about it here: http://www.bachbijbel.nl/english/the-history/.

38. John Eliot Gardiner, *Bach Music in the Castle of Heaven* (Alfred A. Knopf, 2013), Kindle edition, Location 3058.

39. Note: Bach's two major Passion oratorios are those of St. Matthew and St. John. Passions are the reading of the Gospels—the journey of Jesus to the cross—accompanied by instruments. St. John's Passion follows chapters 18 and 19 of John's Gospel. St. Matthew's Passion sets chapters 26 and 27 of Matthew's Gospel to music and is regarded as a masterpiece of classical sacred music.

40. Note: This notation can be found in his Bible alongside 1 Chronicles 25; see http://www.bachbijbel.nl/english/bach-writes-in-his-bible/.

41. Note: The stroke was likely brought on by diabetes mellitus.

42. Note: In 1850 the Bach Gesellschaft was created to collect and publish his music—a fifty-year project. This Bach renaissance also created a desire (see endnote 43) to find his grave, and in 1894 an anatomy professor was commissioned to identify Bach's remains. Bach had been buried in an unmarked grave, and then to facilitate a church enlargement was reburied elsewhere on the grounds. Based on oral tradition, Bach's grave was "six paces away from the south portal." Click here for a dissertation on the subject, which concludes that the skeleton buried at St. Thomas does not likely belong to Bach: https://www.mja.com.au/journal/2009/190/4/are-alleged-remains-johann -sebastian-bach-authentic.

43. Note: Bach and his work went unappreciated until another man's work caused the world to recognize the genius of Bach. In 1829 the great composer and conductor Felix Mendelssohn Bartholdy performed Bach's *St. Matthew Passion* for the first time since its original world premier one hundred and one years earlier (to the very day, Good Friday). It was only then that the world recognized the genius of Bach.

44. Note: The Golden Records are aboard the Voyager Spacecraft, launched in 1977. There are two records, and they are part of a time capsule intended for any extraterrestrial life form or future humans. To see a list of the songs, go to NASA's site, here: https:// voyager.jpl.nasa.gov/golden-record/whats-on-the-record/music/.

45. Frank R. Jacobson, producer, *Jesus Is Victor: A Personal Portrait of Corrie ten Boom* (Worldwide Pictures), https://youtu.be/vylsn89ypWo.

46. Aaron Copland, "The Pleasures of Music," in *The Saturday Evening Post* (Philadelphia: Curtis Publishing, July 4, 1959) http://www.saturdayeveningpost.com/wp -content/uploads/satevepost/the_pleasures_of_music_by_aaron_copeland.pdf. or here: http://archive.org/stream/coplandonmusic031152mbp/coplandonmusic031152mbp _djvu.txt.

47. Note: This quote is commonly attributed to Bach; however, I could not find its source.

48. Note: Peter Bach Jr. pointed me to a similar quote from the theologian Karl Barth: "It may be that when the angels go about their task of praising God, they play only Bach. I am sure, however, that when they are together en famille they play Mozart.

Chapter Three—John Newton

1. John Newton, *Out of the Depths: Autobiography of Rev. John Newton, letters written to Rev. T. Hawei*, first published in 1764 (Chicago: Moody Pocket Books), p. 129.

2. Note: Newton's words of "Amazing Grace" speak to a much bigger picture than atoning for the sins of his slaver days; they speak of life on earth in a fallen world.

3. John Newton, sermon notes, January 1, 1773, "#1 Who Am I?" The John Newton Project, https://www.johnnewton.org/Groups/231011/The_John_Newton/new_menus /Amazing_Grace/sermon_notes/sermon_notes.aspx.

4. Note: John Newton was born July 24, 1725 (Old Style) in Wapping, London,

United Kingdom. He was the only child of John and Elisabeth. Dates given in the Old Style refer to the Julian Calendar. The New Style, referring to the Gregorian Calendar, was adopted in Britain by omitting the eleven days from September 3–13, 1752. From then on Newton regarded his birthday as being on August 4. (The Julian Calendar had miscalculated leap years, and dropping those eleven days was necessary to get the calendar back in synch.)

5. Note: Press gang, also called impressment or being shanghaied, is the act of taking men, ages eighteen through fifty-five, into a military or naval force by compulsion, with or without notice. The British Royal Navy began using it in 1664 as a means of crewing warships.

6. John Newton with Richard Cecil, *The Life of John Newton* (Edinburgh: Johnstone and Hunter, 1779), p. 25.

7. John Newton, *Out of the Depths* (Chicago: Moody Pocket Books), p. 64.

8. Note: Jonah being swallowed by the big fish is a story of God's grace. Jonah disobeyed God's direct order to travel to Nineveh to warn the inhabitants of their impending doom unless they mended their ways. Jonah didn't like the Ninevites and wouldn't have minded their destruction, so instead he boarded a ship heading in the opposite direction. The ship ran into a great storm and was in danger of sinking. Jonah, realizing he was the cause of the ship's troubles, instructed the captain to throw him overboard, and the sea at once was calmed. God gave Jonah a second chance; he was swallowed by a great fish that the Lord had "prepared." Jonah prayed a masterful, beseeching prayer of thanksgiving and repentance, and the Lord heard him and caused the fish to vomit Jonah upon the dry land. God told him again to go to Nineveh, and this time he went! The Ninevites listened to Jonah, and Nineveh was spared (760 B.C.).

9. John Newton, *Out of the Depths* (Chicago: Moody Pocket Books), p. 68.

10. Ibid., p. 69.

11. Ibid., p. 70.

12. Ibid., p. 71.

13. John Newton, sermon notes, January 1, 1773, "#1 Who Am I?" The John Newton Project, https://www.johnnewton.org/Groups/231011/The_John_Newton/new_menus/Amazing_Grace/sermon_notes/sermon_notes.aspx. Note: One of the verses in "Amazing Grace" is rogue, written decades after Newton's death: "When we've been there ten thousand years, bright shining as the sun, we've no less days to sing God's praise than when we'd first begun."

14. March 10, 1745 Old Style (OS). March 21, 1745 New Style (NS).

15. John Newton, *Out of the Depths* (Chicago: Moody Pocket Books), p. 90.

16. Ibid., pp. 91, 92.

17. Jonathan Aitken, *John Newton: From Disgrace to Amazing Grace* (IL: Crossway Books, 2007), p. 101.

18. John Newton, *Thoughts upon the African Slave Trade* (London: J. Buckland, 1778), p. 3. Note: It was not until ten years later, in 1758, that any concern over the immorality of slave trading and ownership was voiced, and only then by a small group of Quakers.

19. Note: Extracts from Newton's diaries provided by Marylynn Rouse, The John Newton Project, United Kingdom.

20. Jonathan Aitken, *John Newton: From Disgrace to Amazing Grace* (IL: Crossway Books, 2007), p. 148.

21. Note: The Newton household also included Betsy Catlett, adopted in 1774. She was a five-year old orphaned niece. In 1783 the Newtons adopted Eliza, another orphaned niece, who came to them at the age of twelve and died two years later. Newton wrote an account of her death, which was included in his published *Works*. They had no children of their own.

22. Jonathan Aitken, *John Newton: From Disgrace to Amazing Grace* (IL: Crossway Books, 2007), p. 195.

23. John Newton, *Out of the Depths* (Chicago: Moody Pocket Books), p. 143.

24. Ibid.

25. John Newton, sermon notes, January 1, 1773, "#1 Who Am I?" The John Newton Project.

26. Note: 1 Chronicles 17:16–17:

"Then King David went in and sat before the LORD, and he said: 'Who am I, LORD God, and what is my family that you have brought me this far? And as if this were not enough in your sight, my God, you have spoken about the future of the house of your servant. You, LORD God, have looked on me as though I were the most exalted of men.'"

See The John Newton Project notes on this sermon, https://vimeo.com/56214220.

27. Note: John and Polly were reinterred at the Church of St. Peter and Paul in Olney in 1893. Also of note, Newton's friend William Wilberforce, in correspondence to his sons, said that remorse for Newton's own early share in slavery's iniquity kept it so constantly before him that "He never spent one half hour in my company without [my] hearing some allusion to it."

28. Note: Published in 1788, the full text may be found here: https://www.biblestudytools.com/classics/newton-posthumous-works/thoughts-upon-the-african-slave-trade.html.

29. Note: On March 25, 1807, the Act to Abolish the Transatlantic Slave Trade was passed. August 1, 1838, saw the abolishment of slavery throughout the British Empire.

30. Note: Nine months later, on December 21, 1807, Newton died. William Wilberforce continued fighting against slavery. In 1833 Wilberforce saw slavery officially abolished—three days before he died.

31. John Newton, *Thoughts upon the African Slave Trade* (London: J. Buckland, 1778), p. 1.

Chapter Four—Elizabeth Fry

1. Elbert Hubbard, "Little Journeys to the Homes of Famous Women" (Roycrofters at their Shop at East Aurora, NY, 1911). Note: This statement was made in an 1830 letter, "Report on Paris Prisons," that was addressed to the king of France, Louis-Philippe d'Orléans. Elizabeth was invited by the French government to visit the prisons of Paris and report on her findings. Although this was spoken with the idea that prison should be a place of reform, not revenge, it was a truly bold statement for a woman to make to a king. As Quakers do, Fry had a habit of treating royalty and unfortunates alike, and as equals. For more information: http://www.kellscraft.com/LittleJourneysWomen/Littlejourneyswomeno2.html. N

2. Elizabeth Gurney Fry, Katharine Fry, and Rachel Elizabeth Cresswell, *Memoir of the Life of Elizabeth Fry* (Philadelphia: J. W. Moore, 1847), p. 18, paraphrased.

3. Ibid., p. 23.

4. June Rose, *Elizabeth: A Biography* (New York: St. Martin's Press, 1980), p. 20.

5. Note: Written in her sister Richenda's journal for this day.

6. Mrs. E. R. Pitman, *Elizabeth Fry* (Cambridge: Roberts Brothers, University Press, 1884), p. 10.

7. Huntsman, Bruin, and Holttum, *Twixt Candle and Lamp: The Contribution of Elizabeth Fry and the Institution of Nursing Sisters to Nursing Reform* (Cambridge Univ. Press, Medical History, 2002), https://www.ncbi.nlm.nih.gov/pmc/articles/PMC1044528/. Note: According to this research, because of her efforts to vaccinate the children (done through the cooperation of the local priest), smallpox was scarcely known in that entire area.

8. Mrs. E. R. Pitman, *Elizabeth Fry* (Cambridge: Roberts Brothers, University Press, 1884), p. 15.

9. Laura E. Richards, *Elizabeth Fry, Angel of the Prisons* (New York: D. Appleton, 1916), p. 38.

10. Elizabeth Gurney Fry, Katharine Fry, and Rachel Elizabeth Cresswell, *Memoir of the Life of Elizabeth Fry* (Philadelphia: J. W. Moore, 1847), p. 60.

11. Susanna Corder, *Life of Elizabeth Fry* (Philadelphia: Henry Longstreth, 1855), p. 48. Note: Elizabeth had six rules of life that she wrote for herself at age eighteen: "First,—Never lose any time; I do not think that lost which is spent in amusement or recreation some time every day; but always be in the habit of being employed. Second,—Never err the least in truth. Third,—Never say an ill thing of a person when I can say a good thing of him; not only speak charitably, but feel so. Fourth,—Never be irritable or unkind to anybody. Fifth,—Never indulge myself in luxuries that are not necessary. Sixth,—Do all things with consideration, and when my path to act right is most difficult, put confidence in that Power alone which is able to assist me, and exert my own powers as far as they go."

12. June Rose, *Elizabeth: A Biography* (New York: St. Martin's Press, 1980), p. 39.

13. History's Heroes Website, *Elizabeth Fry*, http://historysheroes.e2bn.org/hero/howviewed/108. Quote of the turnkey (jailer) at Newgate Prison, 1816.

14. Susanna Corder, *Life of Elizabeth Fry* (Philadelphia: Henry Longstreth, 1855), p. 199.

15. Note: Those rooms totaled about 1700 square feet. An average three-bedroom home in the U. S. today is about 1500 square feet.

16. Elizabeth Fry, letter written to three of her children, February 13, 1813, Spartacus Educational website: http://spartacus-educational.com/LONnewgate.htm.

17. Quakers in the World website: http://www.quakersintheworld.org/quakers-in -action/13/Elizabeth-Fry.

18. Note: Between 1788 and 1868, Britain sent about 164,000 convicts to Australia and 52,000 to colonial America.

19. Spartacus Educational, http://spartacus-educational.com/REfry.htm. Note: Elizabeth made these observations in 1827.

20. Spartacus Educational, http://spartacus-educational.com/REfry.htm. Note: Queen Victoria wrote in her journal of Elizabeth: She is a "very superior person." It is thought that Victoria may have modeled herself after Elizabeth.

21. Mrs. E. R. Pitman, *Elizabeth Fry* (Cambridge: Roberts Brothers, University Press, 1884), p. 38.

22. Spartacus Educational, http://spartacus-educational.com/REfry.htm.

23. Brighton Provident & District Society Report for the year 1845, with the Rules and Regulations (A Google Book), p. 13.

24. Note: By 1897 Fry was known as "the founder of nursing." The purpose of the research project noted in Endnote 7 was to find out why her contribution to nursing reform has been largely forgotten. The authors fault her two daughters, who chose to devote only 3 out of 1,061 pages in their 1847 biography to her nursing efforts. "This concentration on Elizabeth Fry's work on penal reform, at the expense of her pioneer work in nursing reform has been perpetuated by the numerous biographers that followed," they said.

25. Note: Vaccinations were not popular. In 1885 the Leicester Demonstration was one of the biggest anti-vaccination demonstrations, with 80,000–100,000 demonstrating against vaccines. Political opposition arose because mandatory vaccinations were said to violate personal liberties. Religiously, the vaccine was objected to because it came from an animal. Others objected because of health reasons—scoring the flesh on a child's arm and inserting foreign matter. Scientifically, there was a general distrust in the medical field.

26. Susanna Corder, *Life of Elizabeth Fry* (Philadelphia: Henry Longstreth, 1855), p. 662.

27. Note: Quakers do not have funerals; the thousand people attended her burial, which was in Barking, Essex.

Chapter Five—Sojourner Truth

1. Frances W. Titus, *The Narrative of Sojourner Truth, Part 2: Book of Life* (Battle Creek, MI, published by the author, 1875), p. 141. Note: Truth's visits with Abraham

Lincoln and Harriet Beecher Stowe have many versions. Titus's account of Truth's visit to Stowe is merely a reprint of Stow's April 1863 *Atlantic Monthly* article and is quite different from the account told by her friend Lucy Colman, who was there. Steve Coates provides the two narratives of the Lincoln visit in the October 29, 2010, issue of the *New York Times*, here: https://artsbeat.blogs.nytimes.com/2010/10/29/abraham -lincoln-and-sojourner-truth/. With regard to the Stowe article, written from memory many years later (https://www.theatlantic.com/magazine/archive/1863/04/sojourner -truth-the-libyan-sibyl/308775/), many consider that Stowe treated Truth as an amusing performer.

2. Note: No one knows what Sojourner really sounded like other than that she had a heavy Dutch accent—the Ulster County was settled by the Dutch. Located in the southeast corner of New York, it was part of the Netherland County settled in 1652.

3. Note: Sojourner was one of the twelve or thirteen children of James and Betsey, the property of Colonel Johannes Ardinburgh. After the death of Colonel Ardinburgh, ownership passed to his son, Charles. Charles then sold her at auction with a flock of sheep for $100 to John Nealy. She was sold twice more, eventually to John and Sally Dumont.

4. Note: The lifelong beatings were merciless. She said that Neely once whipped her with "a bundle of rods, prepared in the embers, and bound together with cords."

5. Juan Williams and Quinton Dixie, *This Far by Faith* (New York: Harper Collins, 2005), p. 78 (companion to the PBS television series).

6. Olive Gilbert, ed. 1850. *The Narrative of Sojourner Truth Dictated by Sojourner Truth*, p. 19,

7. Note: Sojourner had five children: James, Diana (1815), Peter (1821), Elizabeth (1825), and Sophia (1826). James and Diana likely were fathered by a slave named Robert who was owned by a neighboring farmer, Charles Catton Jr. James died in infancy. The other three were either fathered by Dumont or by an older slave named Thomas, whom Dumont forced her to marry.

8. Sojourner Truth, *Saginaw Daily Courier*, June 14, 1871.

9. Olive Gilbert, ed. 1850, *The Narrative of Sojourner Truth Dictated by Sojourner Truth*, p. 21.

10. Ibid., pp. 21–22.

11. Ibid., p. 22.

12. Note: Sojourner was in court or made official complaints a total of four times: once with Gedney; once to charge Benjamin Folger with slander against her; once to charge John Weeden, a conductor on the Seventh Street railroad, with assault and battery; and another time for not being allowed on the train. She won all of them.

13. Olive Gilbert, ed. 1850, *The Narrative of Sojourner Truth Dictated by Sojourner Truth*. p. 35.

14. Frances W. Titus, *The Narrative of Sojourner Truth, Part 2: Book of Life* (Battle Creek, MI: published by author, 1875), p. 66.

15. Harriet Beecher Stowe, "Sojourner Truth, The Libyan Sibyl," *The Atlantic Monthly*, April 1863. See endnote 1.

16. Note: From 1832 to 1846, Florence was run as a communal project by abolitionists who believed that the rights of all should be "equal without distinction of sex, color or condition, sect or religion." Sojourner stayed there for thirteen years.

17. Nell Irwin Painter, *Sojourner Truth: A Life, A Symbol* (New York: W. W. Norton, 1996), p. 44.

18. Carol Mason, "The Naked Truth about Sojourner Truth," *The Baltimore Sun*, February 18, 2004, http://articles.baltimoresun.com/2004-02-18/news/0402180136_1 _sojourner-truth-i-a-woman-audience.

19. Nell Irwin Painter, *Sojourner Truth: A Life, A Symbol* (New York: W. W. Norton, 1996), pp. 220, 227.

20. Ibid., p. 136, paraphrased.

21. Note: This is the text of her speech as published by Rev. Marius Robinson in the *Anti-Slavery Bugle*, 1851, shortly after she gave it. Twelve years later another version of this speech, now known as the "Ain't I a Woman?" speech, was published by a white abolitionist named Francis Gage. She changed Truth's words and gave her a Southern dialect, even though Sojourner Truth had never lived in the South. Gage thought her version more palatable and felt that it better served her women's rights movement. See here for an in-depth discussion of this speech: https://www .thesojournertruthproject.com/. Also note that she did say "I am a woman's rights," not I am for woman's rights."

22. Note: For the full article, click here: https://www.theatlantic.com/magazine/ archive/1863/04/sojourner-truth-the-libyan-sibyl/308775/.

23. Note: The Libyan Sibyl (or Phemonoe) was the prophetic priestess presiding over the Oracle of Zeus in the Libyan Desert. The word *sibyl* comes from the ancient Greek word *sibylla*, meaning prophetess. There were many sibyls in the ancient world, but the Libyan Sibyl, in classical mythology, foretold the "coming of the day when that which is hidden shall be revealed."

24. Nell Irwin Painter, *Sojourner Truth: A Life, A Symbol* (New York: W. W. Norton, 1996), p. 163. Note: Her rebuttal letter was addressed to the abolitionist Mr. Redpath in the Boston Commonwealth, July 3, 1863.

25. Ibid., p. 236.

26. Olive Gilbert, *Sojourner Truth's Narrative and Book of Life*, 1881, p. 116.

27. Ibid., p. 74.

28. Note: Sojourner Truth is buried in Oak Hill Cemetery, Michigan.

Chapter Six—Abraham Lincoln

(Except for noting the date, quoted references to Lincoln's writings are not cited as they are readily available from many sources, including his Collected Words referred to at the end of Lincoln's chapter.)

1. David Herbert Donald, *Lincoln* (New York: Simon & Schuster, 1995), p. 355. Note: Remarks made at a delegation of Progressive Quakers on June 20, 1862. Because of the

discussion, one of the Quakers said, "Perhaps he might be an instrument in God's hands of accomplishing a great work and he certainly was not unwilling to be."

2. Note: The Gettysburg Address is paraphrased in the first three paragraphs. You will note that the phrase "under God" is not included. He wrote out the address on five different occasions. This phrase doesn't appear until the third revision—the Everett copy. It is not certain whether he actually spoke it.

3. Michael Burlingame, *The Inner World of Abraham Lincoln* (University of Illinois Press, 1997). pp. 94–95.

4. National Park Service website: https://www.nps.gov/abli/planyourvisit/lincoln-pets.htm.

5. Abraham Lincoln in a letter to Fanny McCullough, dated December 23, 1862.

6. Note: All three of them (Nancy Hanks Lincoln; her sister Elizabeth; and her husband, Tom Sparrow) died from milk sickness. A horrible way to go, it is characterized by trembling, vomiting, and severe intestinal pain. It happens when milk, other dairy products, or meat from a cow that has fed on white snakeroot plant, which contains the poison tremetol, is ingested. Rare today, milk sickness claimed thousands of lives in frontier areas along the Ohio River Valley and its tributaries, where white snakeroot was prevalent. Nursing calves and lambs may have died from their mothers' milk contaminated with snakeroot, although the adult cows and sheep showed no signs of poisoning.

7. David Herbert Donald, *Lincoln* (New York: Simon & Schuster, 1995), p. 57.

8. Abraham Lincoln in a letter to John T. Stuart, dated January 23, 1841.

9. Abraham Lincoln.org., Speeches and Writings, http://www.abrahamlincolnonline.org/lincoln/speeches/1832.htm.

10. Campaign circular from Whig committee, March 4, 1843. Lincoln's reference to a house divided is taken from Matthew 12:22–28 and Mark 3:23–26.

11. Biennial Report, Nebraska, Dept. of Public Instruction, Biennial Report, Volume 1, January 1, 1903, p. 213. https://play.google.com/books/reader?id=DeAcAQAAIAAJ&hl=en&pg=GBS.PR4.

12. Note: Besides Douglas, other candidates were John Bell of the Constitutional Union Party and John Breckinridge of the Southern Democratic Party.

13. David Herbert Donald, *Lincoln* (New York: Simon & Schuster, 1995), p. 256.

14. Farewell Address at Springfield, Illinois, February 11, 1861. Note: Lincoln would indeed return to Springfield a little more than four years later, in a coffin. I don't think he would have been surprised, for he had many premonitions of his death.

15. Shaun Usher, ed., *Letters of Note, An Eclectic Collection of Correspondence Deserving of a Wider Audience* (San Francisco: Chronicle Books, 2014), pp. 205–207.

16. Note: Stephens delivered his speech, known as the Cornerstone Speech, without notes, but a local newspaper printed a transcription of it. See here for an account of that speech: http://teachingamericanhistory.org/library/document/cornerstone-speech/.

17. Letter to Albert G. Hodges. April 4, 1864, paraphrased.

18. Abraham Lincoln, *First Inaugural Address*, March 4, 1861, addressed to "Fellow Citizens of the Unites States."

19. Abraham Lincoln, *Second Inaugural Address*, March 4, 1865. Full quote: "Both parties deprecated war, but one of them would make war, rather than let the nation survive, and the other would accept war rather than let it perish. And the war came."

20. Note: Estimates of Civil War casualties have changed. By examining newly digitized census data, the death toll has been recalculated to somewhere between 650,000 and 850,000. That would greatly impact all related statistics, e.g., widows, orphans, and ratios of dead to the total population count. In the absence of more definitive research, I am using the earlier number.

21. David Herbert Donald, *Lincoln* (New York: Simon & Schuster, 1995), p. 514.

22. The first draft was written and shown to his Cabinet on July 22, 1862. A preliminary proclamation was issued September 22, 1862, and the final proclamation issued January 1, 1863.

23. Eric Foner, "The Emancipation of Abe Lincoln." *The New York Times*, Dec. 31, 2002, http://www.nytimes.com/2013/01/01/opinion/the-emancipation-of-abe-lincoln.html?_r=0\. Note: 750,000 slaves remained in bondage; 3.1 million were freed.

24. Note: The 13th Amendment was passed by the Senate on April 8, 1864, and the House on January 31, 1865. It was submitted to the states on February 1, 1865. By month's end, eighteen states had ratified it. Three-fourths of the states were required for it to become law. (Illinois was the first to ratify on February 1, 1865. Georgia was the twenty-seventh on December 6, 1865.) On December 6, 1865, the 13th amendment became part of the Constitution.

25. Ida Minerva Tarbell, *The Life of Abraham Lincoln, drawn from original sources* (1924), Vol. 4, p. 12.

26. National Park Service website: https://www.nps.gov/resources/story.htm%3Fid%3D235.

27. Letter to Eliza P. Gurney, October 26, 1862.

28. Second Inaugural Address, March 4, 1865, addressed to "Fellow Countrymen."

29. Note: This might be a legend; I could not find a source.

30. Note: Confederate soldiers, evacuating Richmond on April 3, 1865, set fire to tobacco warehouses; the fire spread throughout the commercial heart of the city, leaving most of the business district in ruins. The so-called Burned District was chronicled in dramatic images made by Union photographers eager to capture the extent of the devastation and to give a graphic representation of the punishment being endured by the defeated foe. The irony was that the fires were started by the Confederates themselves, and it was the Union soldiers who contained the blaze. Lincoln and Tad walked to the Confederate White House and also visited Libby Prison. On April 8 Lincoln headed back to Washington. There is a statute, on the grounds of the Trafalgar Iron Works, commemorating his visit: https://www.rvariverfront.com/monuments/lincoln.html.

31. David Herbert Donald, *Lincoln* (New York: Simon & Schuster, 1995), p. 576.

32. Second Inaugural Address, March 4, 1865.

33. Henry B. Rankin, *Personal Recollections of Abraham Lincoln* (New York: G. P. Putnam's Sons, 1916), p. 325. Note: Lincoln was quoting Mark 9:24, which tells of a boy's father asking Jesus to heal his son. When Jesus tells the boy's father that everything is

possible for one who believes, the father says: "Help thou my unbelief." Lincoln's old friend and law partner, William Henry Herndon, who knew him from his unbelieving days in Springfield, believed that Lincoln remained an atheist. But Lincoln's old friend Joshua Speed tells a different story. Mr. Speed, in delivering a lecture fifteen years after Lincoln's death, reported detail of a conversation he had had with Lincoln about faith. Mr. Speed expressed his own disbelief. "You are wrong, Speed," Lincoln is reported to have said. "Take all of this Bible upon reason that you can, and the balance on faith, and you will live and die a happier and better man." Lehrman Institute website: http://www.abrahamlincolnsclassroom.org/abraham-lincoln-in-depth/abraham-lincoln-and-the-bible/.

34. Note: John Nicolay, private secretary to Lincoln from 1861 until his death, wrote: "Mr. Lincoln did not, to my knowledge, in any way change his [atheistic] religious views, opinions, or beliefs, from the time he left Springfield to the day of his death." Yet Nicolay also wrote: "His nature was deeply religious, but he belonged to no denomination: he had faith in the eternal justice and boundless mercy of Providence, and made the Golden Rule of Christ his practical creed." Lincoln's Springfield law partner, William Herndon, called him an infidel, yet Herndon did not know the Lincoln of the While House.

35. Henry B. Rankin, *Personal Recollections of Abraham Lincoln* (New York: G. P. Putnam's Sons, 1916), p. 324.

36. Ruth Painter Randall, *Mary Lincoln: Biography of a Marriage* (Boston: Little, Brown and Company, 1953), p. 380. As told by Mary Lincoln to the portrait painter Francis Carpenter.

37. Steven Mansfield, *Lincoln's Battle with God* (Thomas Nelson, 2012), p. xvii. Note: Mr. Mansfield notes that some historians report this conversation to have taken place during the carriage ride. Mr. Mansfield also reports that Dr. J. Cornelius, curator of the Lincoln Collection at the Abraham Lincoln Presidential Library in Springfield, Illinois, stated, in referring to Mary's assertion that the conversation took place in the theater: "We believe these words to be substantiated" (p. xix).

38. Note: After a three-week-long funeral procession by train, passing through 444 communities, Lincoln was buried on May 4, 1865, at Oak Ridge Cemetery in Springfield, Illinois, alongside Mary and three of their four sons, Edward, William, and Thomas. (Lincoln's oldest son, Robert, is buried in Arlington National Cemetery.)

39. Allen Thorndike Rice, ed., *Reminiscences of Abraham Lincoln by Distinguished Men of His Time* (New York: North American Pub. Co., 1886), pp. 56–57.

Chapter Seven—Harriet Beecher Stowe

1. Claire Parfait, *The Publishing History of Uncle Tom's Cabin, 1852–2002* (Routledge, NY, 2016), p. 179. Note: this quote appeared in the 1879 introduction of the book.

2. Dr. Edward H. Clarke, *Sex in Education, A Fair Chance for the Girls* (Boston: James R. Osgood, 1873), p. 106 and pp. 97–98. Note: Actual quote: "When the school

makes the same steady demand for force [using the brain] from girls who are approaching puberty . . . that it does from boys, there must be failure somewhere. Generally either the reproductive or the nervous system suffers."

3. Harriet Beecher Stow Center, https://www.harrietbeecherstowecenter.org/harriet-beecher-stowe/harriet-beecher-stowe-life/. Note: Harriet had an older sister who died in infancy. She was named after her. Frederick was one when he died. These two deaths might account for the fact that some biographies report that there were eleven children, while others say twelve. However you count, it was large family.)

4. Lyman Beecher, *Autobiography, Correspondence, etc., of Lyman Beecher, D. D.*, ed. by Charles Beecher (New York: Harper & Brothers, 1866), p. 295.

5. Note: Lyman Beecher was widowed twice. He married his third wife, the widow Lydia Beals Jackson, in 1836, one year after Harriet died. Lydia died in 1869, six years after Lyman. They had no children together.

6. Note: Tapping Reeve Law School was the first law school founded in the U.S. (in 1784 by Mr. Tapping Reeve). One of his students was his brother-in-law, Aaron Burr. Reeve later became the Chief Justice of the Connecticut Supreme Court. Located in Litchfield, Connecticut, it was declared a national Historic Landmark in 1965.

7. Note: Lyman Beecher created quite a stir with his forty-page sermon, "The Remedy for Dueling." Delivered in 1806, it was in response to the Hamilton-Burr duel, in which the vice president of the United States, Aaron Burr, shot and mortally wounded Alexander Hamilton, the former Secretary of the Treasury. He called dueling a form of vigilantism and urged pastors to deny any duelist a Christian burial or to condone the practice in any way, refusing membership in the church to anyone involved in such a venture until repentance had been demonstrated. Incidentally, alcoholism was a much greater problem in the 1830s than it is today, with consumption at 3.9 gallons annually per capita—twice the level consumed in 1975, according to W. J. Rorabaugh, *The Alcoholic Republic: an American Tradition* (Oxford Univ. Press, 1981), p. 134.

8. Note: The only Beecher child who did not make any kind of public contribution was Mary Foote Beecher Perkins. Her claim to fame was, as she liked to say, being the daughter of Lyman Beecher and the sister of Harriet and Henry Ward.

9. Note: Since John Bunyan's time of the 1600s, and even before, ministers were the most influential members of any community. Church pulpits were the equivalent of today's social media platforms.

10. Note: Harriet's father, Lyman Beecher, became president of Lane Seminary in 1832; it operated from 1829 to 1932, when it merged with the McCormick Theological Seminary in Chicago. It was known for its slavery debates

11. Joan Hedrick, *Harriet Beecher Stowe: A Life* (New York and Oxford, Oxford Univ. Press, 1994), pp. 72, 115.

12. Ibid., p. 182. Note: Harriet's uncle Samuel Foote invited her and Catharine to join this club. Other members were Judge James Hall, the editor of *Western Monthly Magazine*; Salmon Chase, the future Supreme Court justice; and Elizabeth Blackwell, who would become America's first female physician.

13. Note: This play on words is much more entertaining (and sophisticated sounding) when "Semi-Colon" is pronounced in Italian.

14. Note: Calvin taught at Lane Seminary, then at Maine's Bowdoin College, and eventually in Massachusetts at Andover Theological Seminary. Like Harriet's father, Calvin fully supported the equality of the sexes. He told her she "must be a literary woman" (Joan Hedrick, *Harriet Beecher Stowe: A Life*), p. 138.

15. Joan Hedrick, *Harriet Beecher Stowe: A Life*. New York and Oxford, Oxford Univ. Press, 1994), p. 97.

16. Harriet Beecher Stowe. *Uncle Tom's Cabin* (1852), Kindle edition, p. 397.

17. Ibid., p. 371.

18. Joan Hedrick, *Harriet Beecher Stowe: A Life*. (New York and Oxford, Oxford Univ. Press, 1994), p. 109.

19. Note: Harriet and Calvin's children: twins Harriet and Eliza, Henry (drowned at nineteen), Frederick (an alcoholic who disappeared), Georgiana (addicted to morphine and died in her forties), Samuel Charles (died in infancy), and Charles.

20. Joan Hedrick, *Harriet Beecher Stowe: A Life* (New York and Oxford, Oxford Univ. Press, 1994), p. 239.

21. Ibid., p. 119

22. John R. Adams, *Harriet Beecher Stowe* (Boston: Twayne, 1989), p. 87.

23. Note: Harriet was very perplexed by the widely embraced beliefs of Perfectionism, which taught that mortals could become perfect. Perfectionism claimed that it was possible for anyone to be as perfect as God by understanding, accepting, and living according to God's rules. Millerism was also popular. The Millerites were followers of William Miller, who incorrectly predicted that the world would end with the return of Jesus Christ in 1843. This became a national movement—crops were abandoned, shops closed, and people quit work and freely gave away their possessions.

24. Joan Hedrick, *Harriet Beecher Stowe: A Life* (New York and Oxford, Oxford Univ. Press, 1994), p. 155.

25. "Only a Year," 1850. Clifton Waller Barrett Collection. Note: Harriet wrote a poem about Charlie. You can read it here: http://utc.iath.virginia.edu/sentimnt/snpohbsat.html.

26. Joan Hedrick, *Harriet Beecher Stowe: A Life*. (New York and Oxford, Oxford Univ. Press, 1994), p. 196.

27. Harriet Beecher Stowe, letter to Eliza Cabot Follen, February 16, 1853, http://www.gutenberg.org/files/6702/6702.txt.

28. Joan Hedrick, *Harriet Beecher Stowe: A Life* (New York and Oxford:, Oxford University Press, 1994). p. 205.

29. Harriet Beecher Stowe, letter to Mr. Gamaliel Bailey, March 9, 1851, transcribed from Typescript, Boston Public Library: http://utc.iath.virginia.edu/uncletom/utlthbsht.html.

30. Harriet Beecher Stowe. *Uncle Tom's Cabin*, p. 311, http://utc.iath.virginia.edu/uncletom/utfihbsa45t.html.

31. Note: Here are three sources that talk about this vision: https://www.huf

fing ton post .com/joan -d -hedrick/harriet -beecher -stowes -prophetic -engine _b _2481986.html; http://utc.iath.virginia.edu/uncletom/utcmshp.html; http://www .sandiegouniontribune.com/sdut-study-slaves-stay-inspired- uncle-toms-cabin -2013sep02-story.html#. The Harriet Beecher Stowe Slavery to Freedom Museum tells the story of Harriet's visit to the Marshall House and her subsequent witnessing of a slave auction that was the inspiration for the book; they are careful, however, to use qualifiers, as there is no written evidence of that legendary visit. https://www.facebook .com/www.stowehousecincy.org/posts/yesterday%27s-post-about-cincinnati%27s -abolitionist/797676163642475/.

32. Note: One of the stories that inspired her was the slave narrative *The Life of Josiah Henson, Formerly A Slave, Now an Inhabitant of Canada, as Narrated by Himself,* 1849, https://docsouth.unc.edu/neh/henson49/henson49.html.

33. Harriet Beecher Stowe, undated letter to "Dear Sister Kate," in Claire Parfait, *The Publishing History of Uncle Tom's Cabin, 1852–2002* (Routledge, NY, 2016), p. 15. (Retrieved from Stowe Microfilm Collection Manuscripts and Archives, Yale University Library, Sterling Memorial Library.)

34. Ibid., p. 15. Letter from Harriet Beecher Stowe to Henry Ward Beecher, February 1, 1851 (Stowe Microfilm Collection).

35. Harriet Beecher Stowe letter to Frederick Douglass, 1851, Harriet Beecher Stowe Center Library.

36. Harriet Beecher Stowe, *Uncle Tom's Cabin,* chap. 22.

37. Note: The full title is *Uncle Tom's Cabin; or Life Among the Lowly.* It began with the Shelby family deciding to sell two of their slaves, Uncle Tom and Harry, to make some money. Tom and Harry are warned by Harry's mother, Eliza, and the novel follows their journey and the characters they meet. It's long and complicated, and the outcome is positive for everyone but Tom. Tom escapes but is eventually caught and sold to the evil slave owner Simon Legree. Legree, knowing that Tom knows the whereabouts of other slaves, has him whipped unmercifully. Tom keeps silent and dies, but not before he forgives Legree and the men who have beaten him. The news gets back to Shelby, who has a change of heart and frees all his slaves, telling them to remember that they owe their freedom to the influence of Uncle Tom.

38. Note: Stowe neglected to secure the rights as a drama. At one time nineteen companies were playing it simultaneously across the country. In some places it played three performances a day, and the characters just stayed in costume all day long.

39. Note: See the home here (it's still standing): https://preservation.mhl.org/80 -bartlet-street.

40. Harriet Beecher Stowe Center Website. Note: Some say this is legend. However, Stowe and her twelve-year-old son Charley went to see her other son, Fred, stationed at Fort Ryan in Maryland, and then on to Washington D.C., to meet with the president. Charley reported this event in his biography of Stowe. It was also reported in an 1896 issue of the *Atlantic Monthly Magazine,* excerpted from an 1896 biography by Annie Fields. You can find it here, on page 148: https://books.google.com/books

?id=8FoCAAAAIAAJ&printsec=frontcover&source=gbs_ge_summary_r&cad=o#v
=onepage&q&f=false.

41. Noel B. Gerson, *Harriet Beecher Stowe* (Praeger, 1976), Kindle edition Endeavour Press Ltd., 2015, Location 1204.

42. Note: Because no English royalties were paid, a movement arose to donate a penny to Harriet and her causes for each book sold. She went home with that $20,000 and a twenty-six volume set of the petitioners' signatures, enshrined and titled *Affectionate and Christian Address from the Women of Great Britain*.

43. Note: You can see the gold "Slave" bracelet presented to Harriet Beecher Stowe by the Duchess of Sutherland at Stafford House on May 7, 1853 at the museum in Hartford, Connecticut. Nine of the bracelet's ten links are inscribed, the inscriptions having been engraved on three separate occasions. The first three inscriptions are:

(1) 562,848/March 19, 1853—The number and date of the final compilation of the twenty-six-volume petition presented to Stowe ("The Affectionate and Christian Address . . .")

(2) Aug.t 1, 1838—the date of the abolishment of Great Britain's slave trade ("Aug.t" is the abbreviation for August)

(3) March 25, 1807—the date slaves were emancipated in her colonies

Five inscriptions were added by Stowe in accordance with a charge from the Duchess of Sutherland, indicating the dates of the progress of American emancipation:

(4) Emancipation D.C. Apl. 16 '62

(5) the Emancipation Proclamation, Jan. 1 '63

(6) Maryland free, Oct. 13 '64

(7) Missouri free Jan. 11 '65

(8) Constitution amended by Congress/Jan. 31. 63 and the Constitutional amendment ratified

The last link was inscribed after Harriet's death:

(9) Harriet Beecher Stowe/June 14, 1811-July 1, 1896.

44. Note: Frederick would become Captain Stowe of a cavalry unit. Declared unfit for duty after his injury at Gettysburg, he struggled with alcoholism. Harriet sent him to medical school in Boston. Many people seemed to take delight in letting her know that they had seen her son, drunk and stumbling; they knew how much she favored temperance. When it became apparent that Fred couldn't be a doctor, she bought a plantation in Florida and installed him as the manager. When he failed in that endeavor, Harriet suggested a long voyage to San Francisco. That was in 1871, and he was never seen again. Harriet was grief stricken, and unlike the situations following the deaths of

her other children (Henry, Georgiana May, and Charles), she hardly ever talked about him again.

45. Note: Lincoln wrote those words a year later in a letter to Albert G. Hodges, April 4, 1864, https://quod.lib.umich.edu/l/lincoln/lincoln7/1:617?rgn =div1;singlegenre=All;sort=occur;subview=detail;type=boolean;view=fulltext;q1 =If+slavery+is+not+wrong.

46. Note: Oakholm was torn down in 1903. For more information: http://www .fingerpostproductions.com/nook_farm/pages/oakholm-index.html, and https:// connecticuthistory.org/where-mr-twain-and-mrs-stowe-built-their-dream-houses/.

47. Joan Hedrick, *Harriet Beecher Stowe: A Life* (New York and Oxford, Oxford Univ. Press, 1994), p. 316.

48. Note: In what came to be known as the "Bryon Scandal," Harriet had written an expose on Lord Bryon, defending her good friend Annabella Milbanke, Lady Bryon. The backlash for exposing his extramarital affair was strong, and she fell out of grace with the public for a time. Twain wrote a total of six editorials supporting Harriet.

49. Note: Harriet died on July 1, 1896, ten years after her husband. She is buried at Andover Cemetery.

Chapter Eight—Harriet Tubman

1. Kate Clifford Larson, *Bound for the Promised Land: Harriet Tubman, Portrait of an American Hero* (New York: One World Ballantine Books, 2004), Kindle Location 5188.

2. Note: The Thompson Plantation was located in the Peters Neck district south of Tobacco Stick near the Blackwater River. It's now known as Madison.

3. Benjamin Drew, *The Refugee: Or the Narratives of Fugitive Slaves in Canada* (Boston: John P. Jewett, 1856), p. 30.

4. Kate Clifford Larson, *Bound for the Promised Land: Harriet Tubman, Portrait of an American Hero* (New York: One World Ballantine Books, 2004), Kindle Location 977.

5. Catherine Clinton, *Harriet Tubman: The Road to Freedom* (New York: Little, Brown and Co., 2004), p. 38.

6. Kate Clifford Larson, *Bound for the Promised Land: Harriet Tubman, Portrait of an American Hero* (New York: One World Ballantine Books, 2004), Kindle Location 1537.

7. Note: Harriet didn't know that Brodess lay dying when she prayed that prayer.

8. "Another Amazing Historical Find: The Original Runaway Slave Advertisement for Harriet Tubman." BlackHistory.com website: http://blackhistory.com /content/175167/another-amazing-historical-find-the-original-runaway-slave -advertisement-for-harriet-tubman.

9. Philadelphia had a large population of freed people; it was easy for Tubman to blend in.

10. George Sullivan, Harriet Tubman, first published in 1927 (Scholastic, 2001), p. 44.

11. Ibid., p. 45.

12. Note: It is a widespread myth that Harriet freed more than three hundred slaves in nineteen trips. She did not, and she repeatedly said in public meetings that the total number was about seventy and that they were all family and friends. That claim was made popular by an early biographer, Sara Bradford, who exaggerated the numbers. (Sarah was a writer of children's stories.) You'll find it repeated on monuments and plaques, in documentaries, and everywhere on the internet. Her missions also did not extend throughout the South. She only went to the places she knew. Nor did she ever say she could have freed one thousand more if they only knew they were slaves. Syracuse University explains more about the myth here: https://www.maxwell.syr.edu/news.aspx?id=262.

13. Kate Clifford Larson, *Bound for the Promised Land: Harriet Tubman, Portrait of an American Hero* (New York: One World Ballantine Books, 2004), Kindle Location 1821.

14. Ibid., Location 1813.

15. Note: Vincent was tried, after a fashion, and after a ten-minute deliberation was acquitted.

16. Kate Clifford Larson, *Bound for the Promised Land: Harriet Tubman, Portrait of an American Hero* (New York: One World Ballantine Books, 2004), Kindle Location 3574.

17. Ibid., Location 2443.

18. Ibid., Location 2571.

19. Note: John Brown introducing her to Wendell Phillips, as quoted in *The Underground Railroad from Slavery to Freedom* (1898) by Wilbur Henry Siebert, p. 185.

20. Note: John Brown was hanged on December 2, 1859. In October 1859 Brown led a raid of twenty-one men (sixteen white men, three free blacks, one freed slave, and one fugitive slave.) on the federal armory at Harpers Ferry, West Virginia, to start a liberation movement among the slaves. During the raid seven people were killed and ten or more were injured. He intended to arm slaves with weapons from the arsenal, but the attack failed. Within thirty-six hours all of Brown's men had fled or been killed or captured by local pro-slavery farmers, militiamen, and U.S. Marines led by Robert E. Lee. (Five escaped the raid and its aftermath.) Tried for treason against the Commonwealth of Virginia, the murder of five men, and inciting a slave insurrection, Brown was found guilty on all counts.

21. Kate Clifford Larson, *Bound for the Promised Land: Harriet Tubman, Portrait of an American Hero* (New York: One World Ballantine Books, 2004), Kindle Location 3379.

22. Note: Harriet was the only woman to lead a raid during the Civil War.

23. *The Commonwealth Newspaper*, July 10, 1863, vol. 1, no. 45.

24. Note: The Emancipation Proclamation on January 1, 1863, freed all slaves in the Confederate States.

25. Note: The Union suffered 1,591 casualties, the Confederates 174. The 1989 movie *Glory* tells the story. It won three Academy awards.

26. Earl Conrad, *Harriet Tubman* (Associated, 1943), p. 181.

27. Kate Clifford Larson, *Bound for the Promised Land: Harriet Tubman, Portrait of an American Hero* (New York: One World Ballantine Books, 2004), Kindle Location 5132.

28. Note: The Harriet Tubman Home for Aged and Infirm Negroes was opened

in Auburn, NY, at 180–182 South St. It became a National Historic Landmark in 2017: https://www.harriettubmanhome.com/.

29. Milton C. Sernett. *Harriet Tubman: Myth, Memory, and History* (Duke University Press, 2007), p. 180. Note: As reported in the *Auburn Citizen Newspaper*, March 14, 1013, Harriet Tubman to her friend Mary Talbert on the occasion of their last visit, 1913.

30. George Sullivan, *Harriet Tubman*, first published in 1927 (New York: Scholastic, 2001), p. 111. Note Harriet is buried at Fort Hill Cemetery in Auburn, New York.

Chapter Nine—George Washington Carver

1. Gary R. Kremer, *George Washington Carver, In His Own Words* (Univ. of Missouri Press, 1987), p. 17.

2. Note: George had one brother and three sisters. His mother and one sister were never found. George was in Fort Scott years later, when he learned that his brother Jim (who was half-white) had died of smallpox. The other sisters died too, but, as Carver said, "I know them to be dead only as history tells me." Carver's father, who was owned by the next-door plantation owner Mr. Grant, was killed shortly after his birth while hauling wood to town on an ox wagon.

3. Linda O. McMurry, George Washington Carver: Scientist and Symbol (Oxford University, 1981) p. 4.

4. William J. Federer, *George Washington Carver: His Life & Faith in His Own Words* (Amerisearch, 2002), p. 72. Note: This quote is from a letter written to Hubert W. Pelt dated February 24, 1930.

5. John Perry, *George Washington Carver* (Thomas Nelson, 2011), p. 8.

6. Most of Carver's paintings were destroyed in a fire at the museum in 1947.

7. John Perry, *George Washington Carver* (Thomas Nelson, 2011), p. 59.

8. Ibid., p. 21.

9. Note: He did receive an honorary doctorate degree from Simpson College in 1928. In addition, he received many honors and awards, and many institutions were named after him.

10. John Perry, *George Washington Carver* (Thomas Nelson, 2011), p. 28.

11. Carver issued bulletins from 1898 until his death in 1943. Here's a sampling of his bulletins: "How to Grow the Peanut and 105 Ways of Preparing It for Human Consumption," "How to Make Cotton Growing Pay," "Three Delicious Meals for the Farmer," and "The Pickling and Curing of Meat in Hot Weather."

12. Note: Morris K. Jesup, a New York financier, financed this movable school. It was part of Tuskegee's extension services. It also carried agricultural exhibits to county fairs and community gatherings.

13. Gary R. Kremer, *George Washington Carver, In His Own Words* (Univ. of Missouri Press, 1987), p. 172.

14. Jean Toomer, "November Cotton Flower" from *Cane*, copyright 1923 by Boni & Liveright, renewed 1951 by Jean Toomer, reprinted with permission by W. W. Norton.

15. Note: "In 1974 the Carver Museum at Tuskegee Institute . . . credited him with 287 peanut products. One hundred twenty-three were foods and beverages, sixty-eight were paints or dyes, the rest were cosmetics, stock foods, medicinal preparations and miscellaneous uncategorized items. The catalog was inflated by much near duplication" (Mackintosh, Barry, "George Washington Carver: The Making of a Myth," *The Journal of Southern History* 42, no. 4 [1976]. p. 510). Though Mackintosh is critical of the value of Carver's scientific contributions, he said Carver's real worth was in his ability to improve race relations, to promote the value of improving soils, in his humility, and in his relationship with his Creator.

16. Note: According to Dana R. Chandler, University Archivist and Associate Professor with Tuskegee University Archives, it was always believed that Carver didn't keep detailed records. However, it was about 2014 that Chandler found long lost missing notebooks of Carver's that revealed carefully written details of his work.

17. Note: George had whooping cough as a child which damaged his vocal cords, leaving him with a permanently high-pitched voice.

18. Gary R. Kremer, *George Washington Carver: In his Own Words* (Univ. of Missouri Press, 1987), p. 65.

19. John Perry. *George Washington Carver* (Thomas Nelson, 2011), p. 77.

20. Ibid., p. 88.

21. William J. Federer, *George Washington Carver: His Life & Faith in His Own Words* (Amerisearch, 2002), p. 35.

22. Mackintosh, Barry, "George Washington Carver: The Making of a Myth," *The Journal of Southern History* 42, no. 4 (1976), p. 511.

23. Tuskegee University, *The Legacy of Dr. George Washington Carver*, https://www.tuskegee.edu/support-tu/george-washington-carver.

24. Note: This job offer from Edison may or may not be myth. Check out the details here: http://edison.rutgers.edu/myth.htm.

25. Note: Carver established the George Carver Foundation on February 10, 1940, using all of his savings, totaling $32,374.19. With his death, the remainder of his estate went to the foundation. The $60,000 he donated would be equivalent to half a million dollars today.

26. Dennis Abrams, *George Washington Carver, Scientist and Educator* (Infobase Pub., 2008), p. 109.

Chapter Ten—Amy Wilson Carmichael

1. Amy Carmichael, *Things as They Are: Mission Work in Southern India* (London: Morgan and Scott, 1905), p. 27.

2. Note: Amy Wilson Carmichael was born on December 16, 1867. She wasn't technically born in Northern Ireland because it didn't exist as an entity at the time. Northern Ireland, which was created in 1921, is one of four countries that make up the United Kingdom. The others are England, Scotland, and Wales.

3. Frank L. Houghton, *Amy Carmichael of Dohnavur* (CLC Pub., 1953), Kindle Location 293.

4. Ibid., Kindle Location 282.

5. Elisabeth Elliot, *A Chance to Die: The Life and Legacy of Amy Carmichael* (Grand Rapids, MI: Fleming H. Revell, 1987), p. 24.

6. Frank L. Houghton, *Amy Carmichael of Dohnavur* (CLC Pub., 1953), Kindle Location 519, paraphrased.

7. Ibid., Location 519. Quote written by one of Amy's brothers.

8. Warren W. Wiersbe. *50 People Every Christian Should Know* (Grand Rapids: Baker Books, 2009), p. 301, paraphrased.

9. Frank L. Houghton, *Amy Carmichael of Dohnavur* (CLC Pub.,1953), Kindle Location 593, paraphrased.

10. Note: The hall is now the Welcome Evangelical Church. You can visit the Amy Carmichael Center there: https://www.welcomechurch.co.uk/amy-carmichael/.

11. Amy Carmichael, *Mountain Breezes: The Collected Poems of Amy Carmichael* (CLC, 1999). The line is from the poem "Make Me Thy Fuel."

12. Note: The Keswick Convention is an annual gathering of evangelical Christians in Keswick, in the north of England. Its first meeting was in 1875 with 400 attendees. In 2015 there were 15,000 attendees. It is run by Keswick Ministries, and its purpose is to promote Bible teaching. It is "committed to the spiritual renewal of God's people for his mission in the world."

13. Frank L. Houghton, *Amy Carmichael of Dohnavur* (CLC Publ., 1953), Kindle Location 845, paraphrased.

14. Elisabeth Elliot, *A Chance to Die: The Life and Legacy of Amy Carmichael* (Grand Rapids: Fleming H. Revell, 1987), p. 52.

15. Frank L. Houghton, *Amy Carmichael of Dohnavur* (CLC Pub., 1953), Kindle Location 946.

16. Elisabeth Elliot, *A Chance to Die: The Life and Legacy of Amy Carmichael* (Grand Rapids: Fleming H. Revell, 1987), p. 55.

17. Note: Ceylon became Sri Lanka in 1972. It is an island country off the southern coast of India.

18. Note: For further discussion, see "Caste and Prostitution in India: Politics of Shame and of Exclusion," https://www.omicsonline.org/open-access/caste-and -prostitution-in-india-politics-of-shame-and-of-exclusion-2332-0915-1000160.php ?aid=69301.

19. Note: The Hindu practice of temple prostitution in India is called devadasi (day-vah-dah-see) and has existed for more than five thousand years. Devadasi means "god's female servants" and it is estimated that eight to ten thousand twelve-year-olds still today become "brides" to the temple each year. They are exploited until they are no longer desired and then left to fend for themselves. According to UNICEF, 33% of them are between thirteen and eighteen, 75% of them perform intercourse five to nine times per day, 66% of men choose children between the ages of ten and fourteen, and 70% of the prostitutes have the HIV virus. Once they are no longer wanted, they beg on the

streets or sell their own daughters as a way to stay alive. India banned the practice in 1988, and there are stiff penalties, but it has simply gone underground.

20. Amy Carmichael, *Mountain Breezes: The Collected Poems of Amy Carmichael* (CLC, 1999). The line is from the poem "Royal Scars."

21. Note: For a discussion of the 1986 amendments to the Immoral Traffic Prevention Act, click here: http://www.childlineindia.org.in/Immoral-Traffic-Prevention -Act-1986.htm. To learn more about the legalities against child prostitution, click here: http://www.legalserviceindia.com/legal/article-44-a-legal-framework-about-child -prostitution.html.

22. Note: Adult prostitution is legal in India. The statistics for child prostitution across the world are mind-boggling. Here are a few websites for more information: PUCL Bulletin (People's Union for Civil Liberties) http://www.pucl.org/from-archives/ Child/prostitution.htm; Free A Girl, https://www.freeagirl.nl/en/; and http://gvnet .com/humantrafficking/India.htm; https://www.unicefusa.org/mission/protect/ trafficking.

23. Elisabeth Elliot, *A Chance to Die: The Life and Legacy of Amy Carmichael* (Grand Rapids: Fleming H. Revell, 1987), p. 311.

24. Amy Carmichael, *Edges of His Ways* (CLC, 1955), p. 30.

Chapter Eleven—Mary McLeod Bethune

1. Chiazam Ugo Okoye, ed., *Mary McLeod Bethune, Words of Wisdom (Indiana: Au-thorHouse, 2008)*, Kindle Location 536.

2. Note: This is only a partial résumé. The National Park Service's website details her many and great accomplishments: https://www.nps.gov/mamc/learn/ historyculture/bethune-resume.htm.

3. Note: The National Park Service lists eleven honorary degrees. However, she was awarded a twelfth one by Bethune-Cookman University in 2011. Her grandson received it on her behalf.

4. Transcribed interview with Mary McLeod Bethune, ca. 1940 (Used by permission of Florida Memory, State Library & Archives of Florida), p. 7. Note: The transcriber did not insert a comma between the two names William and Thomas. See https://www .floridamemory.com/onlineclassroom/marybethune/lessonplans/sets/interview/?set =2. Known birth dates, according to U.S. Census figures: Samuel (father) 1830, Patsy (mother) 1833, Sallie 1849, Samuel 1854, Rebecca 1859, Beauregard 1861, Satira 1862, Julia 1863, Kizzie 1867, Kissie (different spelling) 1868, William 1870, Hattie Bell, 1881. Ancestry.com: https://www.ancestry.com/genealogy/records/samuel-mcleod _129486255.

5. Interview with Mary McLeod Bethune, ca. 1940 (Florida Memory, State Library & Archives of Florida), p. 10, https://www.floridamemory.com/onlineclassroom/ marybethune/lessonplans/sets/interview/?set=2.

6. Emma Gelders Sterne, *Mary McLeod Bethune* (New York: Knoph, 1957), p. 42.

7. Transcribed interview with Mary McLeod Bethune, ca. 1940 (Florida Memory, State Library & Archives of Florida), p. 4.

8. Ibid., p. 2, https://www.floridamemory.com/onlineclassroom/marybethune/lessonplans/sets/interview/?set=3.

9. Ibid., p. 17.

10. Ibid., p. 18.

11. Ibid.

12. Emma Gelders Sterne, *Mary McLeod Bethune* (New York: Knoph, 1957), p. 76.

13. Transcribed interview with Mary McLeod Bethune, ca. 1940 (Florida Memory, State Library & Archives of Florida), p. 19, https://www.floridamemory.com/onlineclassroom/marybethune/lessonplans/sets/interview/?set=4.

14. Note: The name Jim Crow is attributed to "Jump Jim Crow," a song-and-dance routine of blacks performed by white actor Thomas D. Rice in blackface. After the Reconstruction Period, Southern states enacted state laws, sanctioned by the federal government—some states even put the law in their constitution—mandating the segregation of public schools, public places, and public transportation. Drinking fountains, restrooms, and restaurants were segregated. The laws, which were designed to return the South to the way it was during the Civil War, stayed in place until declared unconstitutional by the United States Supreme Court in "Brown v. Board of Education" in 1954. It was not until the Civil Rights Act of 1964 and the Voting Rights Act of 1965 that all these segregation laws were overturned. Even then, it took years in the courts to get rid of all the institutional practices.

15. Beverly Johnson-Miller, Biola University database: "Christian Educators of the 20th Century," https://www.biola.edu/talbot/ce20/database/mary-mcleod-bethune.

16. Note: In 1886 there were no public schools for African Americans.

17. Interview with Mary McLeod Bethune, ca. 1940 (Florida Memory, State Library & Archives of Florida), https://www.floridamemory.com/onlineclassroom/marybethune/lessonplans/sets/interview/?set=2.

18. Mary McLeod Bethune, "Faith that Moved a Dump Heap," *Who: The Magazine about People*, June 1941.

19. Christianity.com website: http://www.christianity.com/church/church-history/church-history-for-kids/mary-mcleod-bethune-a-missionary-to-her-own-people-11635125.html.

20. Chiazam Ugo Okoye, ed., *Mary McLeod Bethune, Words of Wisdom*, (Indiana: AuthorHouse, 2008) Kindle Location 1597.

21. Rackham Holt, *Mary McLeod Bethune: a Biography*. (Garden City, New York: Doubleday, 1964), p. 110.

22. Note: As told by Johnnetta B. Cole at the 2013 Smithsonian Folklife Festival, https://www.youtube.com/watch?v=H9U3MnK2z6Q&feature=youtu.be.

23. Emma Gelders Sterne, *Mary McLeod Bethune* (New York: Knoph, 1957), p. 70.

24. Mary McLeod Bethune, "Faith that Moved a Dump Heap," *Who: The Magazine about People*, June 1941, and here: Sara Evans, *Born for Liberty* (New York: Simon & Schuster, 1997), p. 208.

25. Mary McLeod Bethune, speech: *What Does American Democracy Mean to Me?* November 23, 1939, in James Daley, ed., *Great Speeches by African Americans* (Dover Publications, 2006), p. 110.

26. Elaine Smith, editorial advisor, *Mary McLeod Bethune Papers: The Bethune-Cookman College Collection, 1922–1955*, a microfilm project (Bethesda, MD: University Pub. of America, 1995), p. v., https://www.roosevelt.nl/sites/zl-roosevelt/files/mary_mcleod _bethune_papers_part_5.pdf.

Chapter Twelve—Aimee Semple Mcpherson

1. Matthew Avery Sutton, *Aimee Semple McPherson and the Resurrection of Christian America* (Cambridge, MA: Harvard Univ. Press, 2007), Kindle Location 2300.

2. Note: Aimee was born Aimee Elizabeth Kennedy on October 9, 1890, near Ingersoll, Ontario, Canada. She was the only child of James and Minnie Kennedy.

3. Aimee Semple McPherson, *Life Story of Aimee Semple McPherson* (Los Angeles: Foursquare Pub., 1979), p. 22.

4. Ibid.

5. Ibid., p. 23.

6. Ibid., p. 24.

7. Ibid., p. 25.

8. Note: There was no prohibition against sending women out as missionaries. In fact, the majority of missionaries, especially in the eighteenth and nineteenth centuries, were women; this is still the case today.

9. Note: They were married in August 1908. That October she would turn eighteen. One of her first sermons was to a group of Mohawk Indians in New York in 1909. While in Belfast with her husband Robert, she saw a group of shipbuilders on break and asked whether she could preach to them. They were building the *Titanic*. Courtesy of Steve Zeleny, Foursquare archivist.

10. Note: Aimee began speaking in tongues and interpreting in 1909. Speaking in tongues, as well as interpretation, are spiritual gifts (1 Corinthians 12). Speaking in tongues means speaking in a language not known by the speaker; this ability is imparted by the Holy Spirit. If no one in the assembly can interpret the speaker's words, then the gift of tongues is not to be publicly exercised.

11. Aimee Semple McPherson, *Life Story of Aimee Semple McPherson* (Los Angeles: Foursquare Pub., 1979). p. 75.

12. Ibid., p. 87.

13. Note: In those days one had to provide a reason for divorce.

14. Note: It was not a Packard automobile plastered with signs, as reported elsewhere. Courtesy of Steve Zeleny, Foursquare archivist.

15. Note: The *Bridal Call* is a reference to Jesus being the bridegroom and the church his bride.

16. Aimee Semple McPherson, in *Foursquare Legacy: The Los Angeles Revival of 1918*,

April 28, 2009, https://www.foursquare.org/news/article/the_los_angeles_revival_of _1918.

17. Daniel Mark Epstein, *Sister Aimee* (Orlando, FL: Harcourt, Brace, Jovanovich, 1993), p. 129.

18. Ibid., p. 220. Note: Whenever possible, and before a healing prayer was said over someone, that person would be counseled. They needed to understand that only Jesus healed, their heart must be in the right place, and they must be willing to be held accountable. Had they, for instance, forgiven all those who needed forgiving? (How can Jesus heal someone who harbors ill will in their heart?) The healing must be an "only God" moment. In the Angelus Temple, these talks took place in the 500 Room. Special healing sessions were reserved, usually on Wednesday afternoons, and people on stretchers were particularly encouraged to come. The ambulance drivers started a tradition of each putting $2.00 in the pot, and the drivers who would return with an empty ambulance (meaning that their patient was healed and had walked out on his or her own) got the pot. Courtesy of Steve Zeleny, Foursquare archivist.

19. Note: According to a letter from her publisher in 1919, circulation of the *Bridal Call* magazine in 1918 was 10,000. Courtesy of Steve Zeleny, Foursquare archivist.

20. Note: Located at W. 5th St. and Olive St., Los Angeles, it was the historic home of the Los Angeles Philharmonic; it was demolished in 1985.

21. Aimee Semple McPherson, *This is That* (Foursquare Pub., 1923), chap. 22, p. 163.

22. Note: Most of the money for the Angelus Temple was raised outside of Los Angeles. When the building was finished, it was appraised at $1.5 million. Courtesy of Steve Zeleny, Foursquare archivist.

23. Matthew Avery Sutton, *Aimee Semple McPherson and the Resurrection of Christian America* (Cambridge, MA: Harvard Univ. Press, 2007), Kindle Location 857.

24. Note: The doctors were sent by the American Medical Association. There are hundreds of reports and eyewitness accounts that attest to the veracity of McPherson's healings. A report issued by the American Medical Association of San Francisco stated that "healing was genuine, beneficial and wonderful" (*San Jose Mercury*, August 30, 1921). The September 12, 1921, issue of the *Red Bluff Daily News* reports that the "well-known physician" Dr. J. A. Owen of Red Bluff, after he had attended the eight-day revival meetings held by McPherson in San Jose, said that "Dr. Owen said if he ever had had any doubts as to the complete healing power of God they were all dispelled now. Among the multitude of healings effected by this means, Dr. Owen declared that he had seen not less than one hundred persons cured of deafness and blindness." See https:// cdnc.ucr.edu/cgi-bin/cdnc?a=d&d=RBDN19210912.2.48&srpos=4&e=01-01-1921-05-09 -1922--en--20--1--txt-txIN-Aimee+Semple+McPherson-------1.

25. Aimee Semple McPherson, *This is That* (Happy Joliver), originally published June 1919, this edition 2012, Kindle Location 4432.

26. Matthew Avery Sutton, *Aimee Semple McPherson and the Resurrection of Christian America* (Cambridge, MA: Harvard Univ. Press, 2007), Kindle Location 188.

27. Note: In September 1921, for example, Sister McPherson was in San Francisco,

where she pledged to reach every one of the twelve thousand. Several days later she was in San Jose, and from dawn to midnight, without stopping, she and sixteen local ministers dispensed healing to the crowd of twenty thousand. (By the way, she was never called Sister Aimee. It was always Sister or Sister McPherson.) Courtesy of Steve Zeleny, Foursquare archivist.

28. Daniel Mark Epstein, *Sister Aimee* (Orlando: Harcourt, Brace, Jovanovich, 1993), p. 234, paraphrased.

29. Matthew Avery Sutton, *Aimee Semple McPherson and the Resurrection of Christian America* (Cambridge, MA: Harvard Univ. Press, , 2007), Kindle Location 372, paraphrased.

30. Note: Romans 8:31.

31. For source and background to this sermon, see page 12 of the *Bridal Call*, May 8, 1925, www.pentecostalarchives.org. Note: Some claim to have seen Aimee ride the motorcycle. She never did—and said so. The advertisement for an August 15, 1926, sermon said "See Floyd B. Johnson Operate a Police Motor Cycle and Illustrate His Sermon on Temple Platform." Courtesy of Steve Zeleny, Foursquare archivist.

32. Edith L. Blumhofer, *Aimee Semple McPherson: Everybody's Sister* (Grand Rapids, MI: Wm. B. Eerdmans, 1993). p. 153.

33. Krista Tippett, *Reviving Sister Aimee*, Podcast June 9, 2011. https://onbeing.org/programs/anthea-butler-arlene-sanchez-walsh-reviving-sister-aimee-2/.

34. Aimee Semple McPherson, *Life Story of Aimee Semple McPherson* (Los Angeles: Foursquare Pub., 1979), p. 180.

35. Note: Chief Cline of the Los Angeles Police Department reported that her shoes were not scuffed, she was not dehydrated, she was wearing a watch she hadn't had with her, and she had a scar on her hand that could have come from being burned by the kidnappers; however, he was not an eyewitness. It was later proven that the DA's office cleaned up her shoes before others saw them. Those who actually saw her said she was barely recognizable. Still others said that the seventeen-mile trek was an easy one. She offered to replicate that walk but was never taken up on it. Courtesy of Steve Zeleny, Foursquare archivist.

36. Note: All passenger services were transferred to Union Station in 1939. The Central Station was demolished on August 22, 1956.

37. Louella Parsons, "Planes Drop Rosebud Carpet along Route," *Los Angeles Examiner*, June 27, 1926. Note: Firemen loved Aimee for all the work she did helping them and those in need.

38. Aimee Semple McPherson, *Life Story of Aimee Semple McPherson* (Los Angeles: Foursquare Pub., 1979), p. 177.

39. Note: Using an annual inflation of about 2.94%, $500,000 in 1927 would have amounted to $6,963,955 in 2018 dollars.

40. Note: Ron Ormiston, KFMG's engineer, was named as McPherson's adulterous partner. Ormiston did admit to having had an affair and being at the Carmel cottage during that time period but stated before the judge that it was not with Sister McPherson.

41. Note: In April 1990 the Court of Historical Review and Appeal in San Francisco re-examined all of the evidence and found: "There was never any substantial evidence to show that her story was untrue. She may not have been a saint, but she certainly was no sinner, either." For more information, see: http://articles.latimes.com/1990-10-09/local/me-2159_1_sister-aimee.

42. Note: Joel 2:28.

43. Note: 1 Corinthians 14:3.

44. Courtesy of Steve Zeleny, Foursquare archivist. Note: In 1 Timothy 2:11 Paul prohibits women from preaching or exercising authority over a man. There is much controversy over this passage and the context in which it was said. For example, the use of the present tense suggests that this could have been a temporary ban. (Since women were not educated, would they have been able to contribute to the message?) It should also be remembered that in Paul's time Greek and Jewish culture did not allow women to teach or be witnesses in court.

45. Note: Roberta had her own room, but she said there was never a day when she wasn't sharing it with some young girl who had knocked on the parsonage door, thrown out of her parent's house because she was pregnant. She would have her baby, Aimee would reconcile the family, and another girl would show up. Courtesy of Steve Zeleny, Foursquare archivist.

46. Aimee Semple McPherson, *Aimee Semple McPherson, The Story of My Life* (Word, 1973), p. 233.

47. Note: The actor Anthony Quinn said the Hispanic population of Los Angeles would have died out had it not been for sister McPherson. Courtesy of Steve Zeleny, Foursquare archivist.

48. Note: Courtesy of Steve Zeleny, Foursquare archivist.

49. Note: The International Church of the Foursquare Gospel, a Protestant denomination, was founded by McPherson in the 1920s. She said that Hebrews 13:8, "Jesus Christ the same yesterday and today and forever," was a cornerstone of her work. McPherson also believed that the Foursquare Gospel came to her by divine inspiration. In an October 1922 sermon she expanded on her vision as it came about through the biblical book of Ezekiel, in which the prophet revealed God symbolically as a being with four different faces—those of a man, a lion, an ox, and an eagle. Her vision of Ezekiel became the four phases of the gospel of Jesus Christ: Jesus as the Savior, the Healer, the Baptizer with the Holy Spirit, and the Soon-Coming King. The word *foursquare* also means something that is marked by boldness and conviction.

50. Heritage Department of the Church of the Foursquare Gospel, *A Look Back: Aimee Semple McPherson*, VCR video, 1991.

51. Note: There is a famous photograph of the bottle of pills, spilled with pills splayed everywhere. That was a staged photo, made by the photographer on scene. It was a new bottle, and the examiner's office verified that only one pill from the bottle was missing. Courtesy of Steve Zeleny, Foursquare archivist.

52. Daniel Mark Epstein, *Sister Aimee* (Orlando: Harcourt, Brace, Jovanovich, 1993), p. 440. Note: An inquest ruled out suicide. The pathologist said: "Mrs. McPher-

son was a very sick woman, with a bad kidney condition, which seriously damaged the liver, thus increasing the effect of the drug she took."

53. Matthew Avery Sutton, *Aimee Semple McPherson and the Resurrection of Christian America* (Cambridge, MA: Harvard Univ. Press, 2007), Kindle Location 2079.

Chapter Thirteen—Corrie ten Boom

1. Corrie ten Boom interview 1974, Christian Broadcast Network (CBN), The 700 Club, paraphrased, http://www1.cbn.com/content/corrie-ten-boom-pt-1.

2. Note: The ten Booms had been praying for Jerusalem and the Jewish people since 1844.

3. Note: Corrie was the first woman in the Netherlands to be licensed as a watchmaker. The "Beje" was their house, so nicknamed because of the address: Barteljorisstraat 19, Haarlem, Holland.

4. Frank R. Jacobson, producer, *Corrie: Behind the Scenes with The Hiding Place* (World Wide Pictures, 1983), https://youtu.be/B3DPRiDXvcI.

5. Ibid.

6. Note: Nazi Germany invaded Holland in 1940. The Gestapo played a key role in the Nazi plan to exterminate the Jewish people of Europe. They were called *secret* because they had the power to imprison people without judicial proceedings. They were above the law.

7. Corrie ten Boom, *Tramp for the Lord* (CLC Pub., 1978), p. 118, paraphrased.

8. Note: Casper ten Boom and his wife, Cornelia, married in 1884, and they had five children: Betsie, Willem, Henrick (who died as an infant before Corrie was born), Nollie, and Corrie. Cornelia died in 1921, and Willem and Nollie had both married and moved away by the time the Nazis invaded. On that fateful February day, Willem and his son Peter were visiting. They were among the thirty arrested.

9. Note: The Jewish fugitives were Eusie, Mary, Martha, and Ronnie. The underground workers were Reynout Siertsema and Hans van Messel.

10. Frank R. Jacobson, producer, *Corrie: Behind the Scenes with The Hiding Place* (World Wide Pictures, 1983), https://youtu.be/B3DPRiDXvcI.

11. Corrie ten Boom with Elizabeth and John Sherrill. *The Hiding Place* (Chosen Books, 1971, 1984), p. 173

12. Corrie ten Boom, *Tramp for the Lord* (CLC Pub., 1978), p. 15, paraphrased.

13. Ibid., p. 16.

14. Note: Corrie spent six months in two prisons (one of them in solitary confinement) before being sent to Ravensbrück. She was at Ravensbrück for four months.

15. Frank R. Jacobson, producer, *Corrie: Behind the Scenes with The Hiding Place* (World Wide Pictures, 1983), https://youtu.be/B3DPRiDXvcI.

16. Note: 1 Kings 17:7–16.

17. Corrie ten Boom with Elizabeth and John Sherrill, *The Hiding Place* (Chosen Books, 1971, 1984), p. 213, paraphrased. Note: The vitamins lasted until the very day

that one of the other women in the barracks, whose name was Mien, managed to take from the hospital room some yeast compound.

18. Ibid., paraphrased.

19. Corrie ten Boom interview 1974, Christian Broadcast Network (CBN), The 700 Club, paraphrased, http://www1.cbn.com/content/corrie-ten-boom-pt-1.

20. Corrie ten Boom, *Tramp for the Lord* (CLC Pub., 1978), p. 16.

21. Ibid., pp. 10–11.

22. Ibid., p. 11.

23. Note: Corrie was not released until December 28 because she was put in a hospital in Ravensbrück due to edema.

24. Corrie ten Boom, *Tramp for the Lord* (CLC Pub., 1978), p. 30.

25. Note: When Corrie was released, for some reason she asked whether her sister could come with her. They did not know she had already died. She was told no, that Betsie would stay for the duration. Corrie then asked if she could stay with her and was again told no. She would marvel at God's providence, for how terrible it would have been for her beloved Betsie to remain in the camp without her! She praised the Lord that he had taken Betsie to himself.

26. Frank R. Jacobson, producer, *Corrie: Behind the Scenes with The Hiding Place* (World Wide Pictures, 1983), https://youtu.be/B3DPRiDXvcI.

27. Corrie ten Boom with Elizabeth and John Sherrill, *The Hiding Place* (Chosen Books, 1971, 1984), p. 230.

28. . Ibid., p. 227.

29. Corrie ten Boom, *Tramp for the Lord* (CLC Pub., 1978), p. 56, paraphrased.

30. Ibid., p. 80, paraphrased.

31. Note: "For the foolishness of God is wiser than human wisdom, and the weakness of God is stronger than human strength" (1 Corinthians 1:25).

32. Corrie ten Boom and Carole C. Carlson, *In My Father's House: The Years Before The Hiding Place* (Fleming H. Revell, 1977), p. 12.

33. Frank R. Jacobson, producer, *Jesus Is Victor: A Personal Portrait of Corrie ten Boom* (Worldwide Pictures), paraphrased, https://youtu.be/vylsn89ypWo.

34. Ibid.

35. Note: You might be interested in the movie *Return to the Hiding Place*, which is a sequel to *The Hiding Place*. It is the story of Hans Poley's encounter with Corrie and the Underground. Poley was the first person hidden from the Nazis in the ten Boom house.

36. Note: Corrie moved to Placentia in Orange County, California, in 1977, when she was eighty-five, to be close to her board of directors for Christian Incorporated, which was formed to handle her speaking engagements. She also wanted to be close to Billy Graham's Worldwide Pictures that produced her movies. She put away her passport and obtained a resident alien card, even though she had no intention of becoming a citizen—this was simply more expedient. (When she was a young Girl Scout she had signed a loyalty oath to the queen of the Netherlands.) In 1978 she suffered two strokes that left her unable to speak. Pam Moore, who became an author and speaker, was her caretaker during that time.

37. Corrie ten Boom, *The Hiding Place* (Chosen Books, 1971, 1984), p. 31.

38. Note: Dates of Corrie's imprisonment: February 28 to July 6, 1944, in the Scheveningen prison, located near the Hague; July 6 to Herzogenbusch concentration camp in Vught in the south of Holland; from September 8 until her release on December 29, 1944, Ravensbrück.

39. Frank R. Jacobson, producer, *Jesus Is Victor: A Personal Portrait of Corrie ten Boom* (Worldwide Pictures), paraphrased, https://youtu.be/vylsn89ypWo.

40. Corrie ten Boom, *Tramp for the Lord* (CLC Pub., 1978) p. 57, paraphrased.

Chapter Fourteen—C. S. Lewis

1. George Sayer, *A Life of C. S. Lewis* (Wheaton, IL: Crossway, 1988), Kindle Location 185.

2. C. S. Lewis, *The Weight of Glory and Other Addresses* (C. S. Lewis Pte. Ltd., 1949; Harper Collins e-books, 2009), p. 140.

3. Note: Clive Lewis Staples was born on November 29, 1898. His older brother, Warnie, was born in 1895.

4. George Sayer, *JACK: A Life of C. S. Lewis* (Wheaton: Crossway, 1988), p. 1. Note: Jack's father was "a practical Welsh farmer," and Jack valued that link to the soil. He said it gave him a sense of stability.

5. C. S. Lewis, *Surprised by Joy: The Shape of My Early Life* (FL: Harcourt Brace, 1955), p. 65.

6. Ibid., p. 172.

7. Ibid., p. 228.

8. Note: Partial List of his favorite authors: Chesterton, Dante, Dickens, Homer, Marlowe, Milton, Shakespeare, Spenser, Tennyson, Tolstoy, Virgil, von Goethe.

9. C. S. Lewis, *Surprised by Joy: The Shape of My Early Life* (FL: Harcourt Brace, 1955), p. 76.

10. George Sayer, *JACK, A Life of C. S. Lewis* (Wheaton: Crossway, 1988), p. 59.

11. C. S. Lewis. *Surprised by Joy: The Shape of My Early Life* (FL: Harcourt Brace, 1955), p. 32.

12. Warren Hamilton Lewis, *C. S. Lewis: A Biography,* unpublished typescripts in the Marion E. Wade Center, Wheaton College, IL, p. 151.

13. C. S. Lewis. *Surprised by Joy: The Shape of My Early Life* (FL: Harcourt Brace, 1955), p. 72.

14. Ibid., p. 181.

15. Note: There is a German word that Lewis used to describe his longing or desire: *sehnsucht.*

16. Note: You'll find a discussion of joy in his book *The Weight of Glory.*

17. George Sayer, *JACK, A Life of C. S. Lewis* (Wheaton: Crossway, 1988, 1994), p. 101.

18. C. S. Lewis, *Surprised by Joy: The Shape of My Early Life* (FL: Harcourt Brace, 1955), p. 111.

19. Ibid., p. 110.

20. Note: The honors were in Greek, Latin, philosophy, ancient history, English, and English literature.

21. C. S. Lewis, letter to Albert Lewis, in Albert Lewis, ed., *The Lewis Papers*, vol. 7 of 11 (Leeborough Press), pp. 20–21.

22. Warren Hamilton Lewis, *C. S. Lewis: A Biography*, unpublished typescripts in the Marion E. Wade Center, Wheaton College, IL, p. 231.

23. C. S. Lewis, *Surprised by Joy: The Shape of My Early Life* (FL: Harcourt Brace, 1955), p. 229.

24. Ibid., p. 237.

25. Ibid., p. 225. Note: You can also find it here: *The Question of God*, PBS Series (Boston: WBGH, 2004), transcript from Program 2, "The Four Loves," http://www.pbs.org/wgbh/questionofgod/transcript/four.html.

26. Roger White, Judith E. Wolfe, and Brendan N. Wolfe, eds., *C. S. Lewis and His Circle: Essays and Memoirs from the Oxford C. S. Lewis Society* (Oxford Univ. Press), p. 202.

27. Note: *The Lion, the Witch, and the Wardrobe* is a fantasy novel. Peter, Susan, Edmund, and Lucy Pevensie are four siblings sent to live in the country with the eccentric Professor Kirke during World War II. The children explore the house on a rainy day, and Lucy, the youngest, finds an enormous wardrobe. Lucy steps inside and finds herself in a strange, snowy wood. From there begin their many adventures. Aslan, the King of the Lions, is the main character. He is a wise guardian and savior of the land of Narnia. Lewis uses him as imagery for Christ.

28. Note: Lewis's Christian writings were often criticized, especially by his Oxford colleagues, who thought that only a theologian should be tackling such heady material. Others criticized some of his writings for not being biblically grounded, expressing doubt that he'd even make it to heaven. His response: *I can only affirm what my* Uncle Toby used to say: "They are written in the Common Prayer Book." (C. S. Lewis, *Mere Christianity*, introduction, Complete C. S. Lewis Signature Classics (New York: Harper One, New, 2002), p. 6.

29. Note: The idea was borrowed from G. K. Chesterton. Lewis greatly expanded upon it.

30. Note: To read Lewis's discussion of lunatic or LORD, see chapter three in *Mere Christianity*, titled "The Shocking Alternative."

31. Note: Lewis uses the salt analogy to help explain what happens when a person loses himself he becomes more of himself. Look for it in *Mere Christianity*, Book Four, chapter eleven, "The New Men."

32. C. S. Lewis, *The Screwtape Letters*, Complete C. S. Lewis Signature Classics (New York: Harper One, 2002), chapter 12, p. 150.

33. Note: Justice Scalia died on February 13, 2016. I imagine the two delight each other with their repartee!

34. Casey Cep, "The Devil You Know." The New Yorker, October 17, 2003. https://www.newyorker.com/books/page-turner/the-devil-you-know.

35. C. S. Lewis, *A Grief Observed*, Complete C. S. Lewis Signature Classics (New York: Harper One, 2002), chapter 1, p. 444.

36. Sheldon Vanauken, *A Severe Mercy* (New York: Harper & Row, 1977), pp. 227–28.

37. Ibid., p. 398.

38. Note: Joy died July 11, 1960.

39. C. S. Lewis, *A Grief Observed* (London: Faber and Faber, 2015), p. 7.

40. Ibid., p. 3.

41. C. S. Lewis, *Surprised by Joy: The Shape of My Early Life* (FL: Harcourt Brace, 1955), p. 238.

Chapter Fifteen—Gladys May Aylward

1. Gladys Aylward, *Gladys Aylward: The Little Woman* (Moody Publishers, 1970), Kindle Location 2238.

2. Ibid., Kindle Locations 25, 40.

3. Note: Young Life is an international organization devoted to sharing the gospel with young people. It began in the early 1930s when an elderly woman, Clara Frasher, recruited a group of friends to pray for the teenagers attending Gainesville High School in Texas. In 1939 a young seminarian, Jim Rayburn, started a chapter in Gainesville, and it grew from there. In 2016 there were 7,300 ministries, one in every state and in 102 countries.

4. Gladys Aylward, *Gladys Aylward: The Little Woman* (Moody Publishers, 1970), Kindle Location 46.

5. Ibid., Kindle Location 51.

6. Note: That would have been about $560 in 2017 dollars. Other accounts said it cost 90 pounds, which would have meant the ticket would have cost $1,127 in today's dollars. Gladys would have had a more difficult time buying that ticket were it not for the generosity of others who donated to her cause.

7. Gladys Aylward, *Gladys Aylward: The Little Woman* (Moody Publishers, 1970), Kindle Location 90.

8. Ibid., Kindle Location 111.

9. Gladys Aylward, *Gladys Aylward: The Little Woman* (Moody Publishers, 1970), Kindle Location 166.

10. Note: Gladys had a brother, Lawrence, and a sister, Violet.

11. Note: There are many variables in the accounts of Gladys's adventures, which is understandable. In the machinist vs. missionary story, there is a question as to whether the information was changed on her passport initially or to get her out of a jam later on down the road. When in doubt, I refer to the book penned by Gladys herself (in this case it was the first edition).

12. Alan Burgess, *The Inn of the Sixth Happiness*, originally published under the title *The Small Woman* [Ann Arbor, MI: Servant Books, 1957] (New York: Bantam Books / E. F. Dutton, 1971), p. 18.

13. Phyllis Thompson, *A London Sparrow* (London: Pan Books, 1971), p. 45.

14. Note: Gladys was mortified that the plot included a love interest and that she purportedly left her children to be with him, neither of which was true. She did fall deeply in love with Colonel Linnan (he was not half European, as the movie portrayed); indeed, they had talked of marriage, but it never happened. In addition, the name of her inn was The Inn of the Eight Happinesses. Hollywood thought "sixth happiness" sounded better.

15. Note: These mule caravans carried coal, raw cotton, and iron goods.

16. Gladys Aylward, *Gladys Aylward: The Little Woman* (Moody Publishers, 1970), Kindle Location 563.

17. Note: Foot binding was outlawed in 1912, and foot inspectors began levying fines in 1915. The practice began in the tenth century, continued into the early twentieth century, and was considered a status symbol and a way out of poverty, for rich men would marry only women with "lotus feet." Foot binding was very painful and usually resulted in lifelong disability. It has been estimated that in the nineteenth century forty to fifty percent of all Chinese women had bound feet, with one hundred percent of upper class women so bound.

18. Alan Burgess, *The Small Woman* (Ann Arbor, MI: Servant Books, 1957), p. 83. This was later republished as *The Inn of the Sixth Happiness* (New York: Bantam Books / E. F. Dutton, 1971).

19. Note: She officially adopted five children, though hundreds unofficially.

20. Gladys Aylward, *Gladys Aylward: The Little Woman* (Moody Publishers, 1970), Kindle Locations 849–70. Paraphrased.

21. Note: The Second Sino-Japanese War, between the Republic of China and the Empire of Japan, was fought between 1937 and 1945. (Sino-Japanese refers to that portion of the Japanese vocabulary that is of Chinese origin.) Japan surrendered in 1945. This conflict merged into World War II after the Japanese attack on Pearl Harbor. (Some assert that World War II originated with the Second Sino-Japanese War.) Statistics vary: Chinese casualties range from twenty to thirty-five million. Three million civilians were targeted in the *kill all, loot all, burn all* operation. The Japanese casualty estimates range from one to two million.

22. Note: Her bounty would be worth more than five thousand pounds in 2018. They really wanted her!

23. Note: In Chinese numerology *bei* is one hundred. She did not have exactly one hundred children under her care, but it was almost that many.

24. Gladys Aylward, *Gladys Aylward: The Little Woman* (Moody Publishers, 1970), Kindle Location 1246.

25. Ibid., Kindle Location 1303.

26. Ibid., Kindle Location 1313.

27. Gladys Aylward, *Gladys Aylward: The Little Woman* (Moody Publishers, 1970), Kindle Location 1312.

28. Note: The 28th day incorporated a train ride because the orphanage in Sian wouldn't take them and they were sent to Fu-Feng.

29. Note: There are some references suggesting that Rue Mai may have accompanied her.

30. Note: Gladys is buried in a cemetery on the campus of Christ's College in Guandu, New Taipei, Taiwan. It faces toward Yangcheng, China.

31. Obituary, *New York Times*, January 4, 1970, http://www.nytimes.com/1970/01/04/archives/gladys-aylward-missionary-dies-briton-who-prompted-inn-of-sixth.html?mcubz=1.

Chapter Sixteen—Louis Zamperini

1. Louis Zamperini and David Rensin, *Don't Give Up, Don't Give In* (Dey Street Books, 2014), p. 76.

2. Note: Louis was born in Olean, New York, on January 26, 1917. His parents moved to Torrance, California, in 1920.

3. Louis Zamperini and David Rensin, *Don't Give Up, Don't Give In* (Dey Street Books, 2014), p. 7, paraphrased.

David Rensin and Louis Zamperini, *Devil at My Heels* (HarperCollins, 2009), Kindle Edition, p. 5.

4. Ibid.

5. Note: Louis set the national high school record for the mile in 1934. His record time of 4 minutes 21.2 seconds stood for twenty years.

6. Scott Wolf, *Los Angeles Daily News*, July 3, 2014, http://www.dailynews.com/sports/20140703/louis-zamperini-was-a-usc-track-legend-before-becoming-world-war-ii-hero.

7. Louis Zamperini and David Rensin, *Don't Give Up, Don't Give In* (Dey Street Books, 2014), p. 28.

8. Note: The B-24 Liberator was a heavy bomber, designed by Consolidated Aircraft of San Diego, California. A workhorse, it was able to carry a heavy bomb load at long ranges with a high cruise speed. The wheels had no steering, and the plane jerked along by throttling back and forth between the right and left engines and working the left and right brakes independently. Dive bombing a heavy plane was a new tactic using an instrument called a Norden Sight, which was so secret that any bombardier was ordered to destroy it if it was thought to have fallen into enemy hands.

9. Note: The Green Hornet crashed roughly two hundred twenty-five miles north of the Palmyra Atoll. Palmyra is about nine hundred nautical miles south of Hawaii.

10. Martin Jacobs, *America in WWII*, http://www.americainwwii.com/articles/lucky-louie/.

11. David Rensin and Louis Zamperini, *Devil at My Heels* (HarperCollins, 2009), Kindle Edition, p. 93.

12. Note: Zamperini actually used the words *hot fudge sundae*. Hear him talk about it here: https://youtu.be/mkR4TVKKJQM.

13. Laura Hillenbrand, *Unbroken: A World War II Story of Survival, Resilience, and Redemption* (New York: Random House, 2010), p. 156.

14. Louis Zamperini and David Rensin, *Don't Give Up, Don't Give In* (Dey Street Books, 2014), Kindle Location 159.

15. David Rensin and Louis Zamperini, *Devil at My Heels* (HarperCollins, 2009), Kindle Edition, p. 120.

16. Note: Kwajalein, also known as Execution Island, is an Atoll in the Marshall Islands.

17. Note: Louie and Phil were separated in March 1944. Phil also survived.

18. Note: Congressional Medal of Honor recipient and Marine ace pilot Pappy Boyington of Baa Baa Black Sheep fame was at the same prison. He remembers Louie talking about his Italian recipes all the time.

19. Note: "What the Zamperinis were experiencing wasn't denial, and it wasn't hope. It was belief. Louise, Anthony, Pete, and Virginia still sensed Louie's presence; they could still feel him. Their distress came not from grief but from the certainty that Louie was out there, in trouble and they couldn't reach him" (Laura Hillenbrand, *Unbroken: A World War II Story of Survival, Resilience, and Redemption* [New York: Random House, 2010], p. 213).

20. Note: The prisoners gave nicknames—usually derogatory—to all the guards and camp officials. No one could think of a name offensive enough for Watanabe, so "Bird" it became. Besides, he could speak broken English and often listened outside the barracks. If he had heard his name he would have beaten whomever was near.

21. David Rensin and Louis Zamperini, *Devil at My Heels* (HarperCollins, 2009), Kindle Edition, p. 183. Paraphrased.

22. Laura Hillenbrand, *Unbroken: A World War II Story of Survival, Resilience, and Redemption* (New York: Random House, 2010), p. 303.

23. Note: Louie spent time in a hospital in San Francisco before flying home to the Long Beach airport.

24. David Rensin and Louis Zamperini, *Devil at My Heels* (HarperCollins, 2009), Kindle Edition, p. 1.

25. Note: "According to Cynthia's brother, Ric, his parents had no objection to Louie, but only to a hasty marriage" (Laura Hillenbrand, *Unbroken: A World War II Story of Survival, Resilience, and Redemption* [New York: Random House, 2010], p. 342). The "pushcarts and restaurants" remark was from Zamperini, *Devil at My Heels*, p. 220.

26. Note: Louie was just a few credits short of graduating from USC. Without a degree he was in stiff competition with all the other soldiers returning from war, and he could no longer run. Until his money ran out he invested in many get-rich quick schemes that always fell short.

27. David Rensin and Louis Zamperini, *Devil at My Heels* (HarperCollins, 2009), Kindle Edition, p. 236.

28. Ibid., p. 237.

29. Ibid., p. 240.

30. Laura Hillenbrand, *Unbroken: A World War II Story of Survival, Resilience, and Redemption* (New York: Random House, 2010), p. 374.

31. David Rensin and Louis Zamperini, *Devil at My Heels* (HarperCollins, 2009), Kindle Edition, pp. 242–43.

32. Note: Zamperini attempted to meet with Watanabe while he was at the Nagano Olympic Games, but his family refused. Then, at Sagamo Prison he was told that Watanabe had likely committed Hari-Kiri. When he discovered that this was false, Zamperini wrote him a letter forgiving him, but it is not known whether Watanabe ever read it.

33. David Rensin and Louis Zamperini, *Devil at My Heels* (HarperCollins, 2009), Kindle Edition, p. 282.

34. Note: Louie died on July 2, 2014, and was cremated in Hollywood, Los Angeles, California. His ashes were given to family or friends.

Chapter Seventeen—Johnny Cash

1. https://www .christianpost .com/news/happy -birthday -johnny -cash -the -unsung-disciple-for-christ-157083/.

2. Robert Hilburn, *Johnny Cash: The Life* (Boston: Little, Brown, 2013), p. 19. Paraphrased.

3. Ibid., p. 15. Paraphrased.

4. Visit the website of Johnny's sister Joanne: http://www.joannecash.com/jr-cash .html.

5. Note: Johnny was born on February 26, 1932, in Kingsland, Arkansas. He died on September 12, 2003, in Nashville, Tennessee.

6. Note: Johnny's boyhood home in Dyess, Arkansas, was listed on the National Register of Historic Places in 2008 (Farm No. 266). It is now owned by Arkansas State University. Johnny lived there from 1932 until he left for the Army in 1950. You can visit it here: http://dyesscash.astate.edu/.

7. "Five Feet High and Rising" words and music by Johnny Cash. Copyright ©1959 (Renewed) Chappell & Co., Inc. All Rights Reserved. Used By Permission of Alfred Music.

8. Ibid.

9. The Cash family children: Roy, Margaret Louise, Jack, J. R. (Johnny), Reba, Joanne, and Tommy.

10. Robert Hilburn, *Johnny Cash, The Life* (Boston: Little, Brown, 2013), p. 16.

11. Note: Johnny and Vivian wrote letters to each other every day from September 1951 to June 1954.

12. Note: Sun Records claims the title of the birth of Rock 'n' Roll. Founded by Sam Phillips in 1952 in Memphis, it was purchased by Shelby Singleton and moved to Nashville in 1969. Sun was the first to record Johnny, Elvis Presley, Carl Perkins, Roy Orbison, and Jerry Lee Lewis. A valid claim, I'd say.

13. Note: They became Johnny Cash and The Tennessee Three when drummer W. S. Holland joined the group in 1960.

14. Note: Boom Chicka Boom was the name given to Cash's unique rhythm sound in his early songs. Hear it here: https://youtu.be/lkpHiby391Y?list=PLGbb9KO9XC_Os -NnRe3TAVT_vvyT34nT3.

15. Dave Urbanski, *The Man Comes Around: The Spiritual Journey of Johnny Cash* (FL: Relevant Books, 2003), pp. 38, 44.

16. Ibid., p. 50.

17. Note: Johnny Cash sold more than 90 million albums. Grammy Awards: 13 wins, 35 nominations: https://www.grammy.com/grammys/artists/johnny-cash. CMA Awards: 9 wins, 13 nominations. For a list of all of his awards, click here: https://en .wikipedia.org/wiki/List_of_awards_received_by_Johnny_Cash.

18. Dave Urbanski, *The Man Comes Around: The Spiritual Journey of Johnny Cash* (FL: Relevant Books, 2003), p. xx. He sourced it here: Anthony DeCurtis, "Johnny Cash Won't Back Down," *Rolling Stone Magazine*, October 26, 2000, https://www.rollingstone .com/music/music-news/johnny-cash-wont-back-down-187543/.

19. John R. Cash with Patrick Carr, *Cash: The Autobiography* (Harper Collins, 1997), p. 48.

20. Robert Hilburn, *Johnny Cash: The Life* (Boston: Little, Brown, 2013), p. 124.

21. Note: It is a myth that Johnny spent hard time in prison. He didn't. Jail yes. Prison no.

22. Steve Turner, *The Man Called Cash: The Life, Love, and Faith of an American Legend* (W. Publishing Group, 2004), Kindle Location 57. Note: This quote was from an entry in Tara Cash's personal book *Dad, Share Your Life with Me*.

23. Note: Johnny and Vivian were married from 1954 to 1966. They had four children. Johnny married June in 1968. They were married for thirty-five years and had one child together. June already had two children.

24. "The Beast in Me" song lyrics written by Nick Lowe ©1994 New Sea Gayle Music (ASCAP). All Rights Reserved. Used by Permission. International Copyright Secured. Recorded by Johnny in 1994.

25. John R. Cash, *Cash: the Autobiography* (Harper Collins, 1997), p. 171.

26. Ibid., p. 173.

27. "The Beast in Me" song lyrics written by Nick Lowe ©1994 New Sea Gayle Music (ASCAP). All Rights Reserved. Used by Permission. International Copyright Secured. Recorded by Johnny in 1994.

28. "The Man Comes Around" words and music by John R. Cash. Copyright (c) 2002 Song Of Cash, Inc.

29. Johnny Cash performing at a Billy Graham crusade: https://www.youtube .com/watch?v=CYBlyMX1e8M&feature=youtu.be.

30. Robert Hilburn, *Johnny Cash: The Life* (Boston: Little, Brown, 2013), p. 104.

31. "I Walk The Line" words and music by John R. Cash. Copyright (c) 1956 House Of Cash, Inc.

32. Note: Before June died, she told Johnny to keep on making music. Johnny honored her wishes and recorded sixty songs after her death.

33. "The Man In Black" words and music by John R. Cash. Copyright (c) 1971 Song Of Cash, Inc.

34. Matt Diehl, "Remembering Johnny," *Rolling Stone Magazine*, October 16, 2003, http://www.rollingstone.com/music/news/remembering-johnny-20031016.

35. "Folsom Prison Blues" words and music by John R. Cash. Copyright (c) 1956 House Of Cash, Inc.

36. Steve Turner, *The Man Called Cash: The Life, Love, and Faith of an American Legend* (W. Publishing Group. 2004), Kindle Location 2983. Note: Dr. Bill Hamon, President of the Christian International School of Theology, personally presented him with his AA degree and ordained him as a minister. Hamon personally graded several of his courses and was amazed at his grasp of spiritual truth.

37. John R. Cash, *Cash, the Autobiography* (Harper Collins, 1997), p. 195.

38. Dave Urbanski, *The Man Comes Around: The Spiritual Journey of Johnny Cash* (FL: Relevant Books, 2003), p. 177. He sourced it here: Eric R. Danton, "Johnny Cash, the Man in Black: An American Legend," *Hartford Courant*, November 3, 2002. p. G1.

39. John R. Cash, *Man in White: A Novel About the Apostle Paul* (Thomas Nelson, 1986), Kindle Location 193.

40. Johnny Cash's last interview, August 20, 2003, with Kurt Loder (Rolling Stone): https://youtu.be/i1zRFnw4jOU?list=RDi1zRFnw4jOU.

41. Note: Johnny said this at Billy Graham Crusades, sometimes on his TV show, and in many other concerts.

42. Johnny's Cash Last Interview, August 20, 2003, with Kurt Loder (*Rolling Stone*): https://youtu.be/i1zRFnw4jOU?list=RDi1zRFnw4jOU.

43. Note: Johnny died on September 12, 2003. June died on May 15, 2003. Johnny and June are buried at Hendersonville Memory Gardens, Hendersonville, Tennessee.